*Mind: An Essay on
Human Feeling*

MIND: AN ESSAY ON HUMAN FEELING

VOLUME III

SUSANNE K. LANGER

THE JOHNS HOPKINS UNIVERSITY PRESS

BALTIMORE AND LONDON

The Johns Hopkins University Press, Baltimore, Maryland 21218
The Johns Hopkins Press Ltd., London

Library of Congress Cataloging in Publication Data

Langer, Susanne Katherina Knauth, 1895–
Mind : an essay on human feeling.
Includes bibliographies and indexes.
1. Mind and body.   2. Senses and sensation.
3. Aesthetics.   I. Title.
BF161.L28   150   66–26686
ISBN 0–8018–0360–8 (v. I)   AACR2
ISBN 0–8018–1150–3 (v. 1 : pbk.)
ISBN 0–8018–1428–6 (v. II)
ISBN 0–8018–1607–6 (v. 2 : pbk.)

V. 3
39,800

Acknowledgments

Volume III

AS THE last volume of this book goes to press at the end of twenty-five years, during which it has been furthered and supported by faithful friends, I want to thank all those who have seen it through to the final stage; first of all, of course, the trustees of the Edgar J. Kaufmann Charitable Trust, especially Mr. E. J. Kaufmann himself, who arranged for the grant to continue to the end of the work, even after the Trust had spent its fund and been dissolved. Even more, however, am I indebted to him for his careful, critical reading of the entire manuscript, as it was produced, chapter by chapter, from first to last.

No philosophical writer can name all the contributions made by personal friends, students, colleagues, and sometimes serious lay readers who take the trouble to offer their opinions and suggestions. The conversations of a lifetime lie wrapped up in our words, as these form the cadences of long thoughts. My own memorable conversations in the course of composing this last volume have been especially with Dr. Anna W. Perkins, a true lover of ideas with no prejudice against their difficulty and their often great abstractness; the late Dr. Karl Ernst Schaefer, who finished reading the entire text just before his sudden death; also I thank my friend Kenneth King, dancer and choreographer, who has incorporated some ideas from the book in his own work, for his enthusiastic moral support which even an ardent solitary thinker needs to sustain a long intellectual undertaking. Lately, but invaluably for me, my research assistant, Mrs. Linda M. D. Legassie, has given me not only constant editorial help but also the benefit of her quick understanding and stimulating responses. Mrs. Marjorie T. Dunbar has again assumed the arduous task of reading the galley proofs (Mrs. Legassie, being closest to the work, is standing in for the author who cannot read them).

Again I must express my gratitude to the director and staff of The Johns Hopkins University Press for their cooperation and courtesy throughout the whole venture.

[v]

Contents

PART FIVE:
THE MORAL STRUCTURE

Primitive men commonly supposed to be purely materialistic; ritual arising from emotional rather than practical needs; change from savage to
civilized mind with new development of symbols; human perception
governed by conception; Malinowski on two attitudes of savages; magic
activity and causal sequence; no alternation between them; "afterworlds"
without moral connotations; extravagance of savage imagination; assertion as affirmation of mind; past and future; origins of myth; ceremonial
forms natural properties, not means; ancestor worship and social organization; ritual reflecting moral order; ethical Asian thought contemplative, European scientific

Ubiquity of belief in magic in precivilized life; extravagant claims of
some magicians; generally accepted anthropological theory of magic;
meeting with Freud's theory of symbolism; non-human beings in a spirit
world; projection of sense of bodily balance into visually presented upright forms a uniquely human talent; tools used by animals like extensions of own body; apes' apparent system to maintain bodily balance;
human ability to project feeling into visual object makes the latter a
symbol; nature of intuition; intellectuality of human sensory organs;
magic and feeling of mental activity; idea of transformation; "ritual ignorance" of "facts of life"; "sympathetic magic" really empathetic; magic
not imitation but initiation of an act; may go back to shift from animal to
human estate; mimetic ritual as conceptual aid; magic a transference of
human impulses to more powerful agents; mimetic ritual a drama with
appropriate stage techniques; white man's natural misinterpretation; sa-

cred actions treated as secular in rehearsal; magical healing a sacred drama; alterations of consciousness easily achieved in mystical minds; shamans' claims to miraculous powers; savage and civilized uses of hypnosis; difference between witchcraft and sorcery; "taboos" as personal possessions; power of names and sacred words; price of power; recognition of death a natural crisis in history of mind

Contents

CONTENTS

tion of visual ambient by dancer's movements; number series from finger counting; intellectual potential of hands; transfer of number sense from feet to hands by drum

List of Illustrations

*Mind: An Essay on
Human Feeling*

The Moral Structure

19

The Spirit-World

MANY evolutionists who try to derive human mentality from what they know or suppose animal mentality to be assume, naturally enough, that the most primitive creatures which could be fairly called men still had entirely material interests, centering on food, safety (especially by defense), comfort, sexual gratification, and dominance over competitors.[1] Consequently they tend to speculate on what might have been the survival value, with regard to those practical interests, of the peculiarly human talents and tendencies in their earliest stages, which would have allowed processes like imagination, myth-making, ritual, divining, and magic to persist and become elaborated to the high forms in which we know them. Such advantages, however, are hard to establish. A squirrel that tried to open nuts by beating a hollow tree with its tail instead of by gnawing holes into the nuts would not seem to exhibit much intelligence. Yet its evident fantasy would probably be much closer to human mentality than that of a normal rodent, which turns the nut between its paws while its teeth feel for a spot to penetrate the shell.

The survival value of man's mental achievements is undeniable, but it may have been a long time in coming to the fore. Speech was certainly a huge advantage from the beginning of its communicative use; before that, its protoforms of spontaneous, semi-articulate utterance may have had many other important functions—the formation of auditory rhythms which, in turn, rhythmicized motions and shaped terminating postures, the sense of communion in the mingling of voices, and (perhaps above all) the concentration of subjective feeling in formalized self-expression, which each individual found in choric chant, yell, or articulate utterance

---

[1]Such was the assumption categorically declared the only reasonable one by Arnold Hauser. See above, Vol. I, p. 131. The same belief was held by the authors mentioned in Vol. II, p. 315n. Raymond Dart, in his Smithsonian Report, "Cultural Status of the South African Man-Apes" (1955), p. 335, wrote in the same vein: "Just as the language of agriculture was based upon the nomenclature of farming actions and the tools with which those farming actions were performed, so man's earliest babblings must have been intimately concerned with, nay erected upon, his 'nomenclature' of hunting actions and the tools with which those actions were performed."

without verbal value. Yet few, if any, of these effects were practical assets that could give direct aid in the struggle for life of the stock; and furthermore, not all human specialties which arose, like the gift of language, from the symbolic substitute consummations of impulses in the overtaxed hominid cortex show even such indirect, ultimate values. The world built up by primitive minds was not what fully humanized minds would build; and present-day people, savage or civilized, have inherited that world of their remotest forebears with varying degrees of modern improvement.

The differences in those degrees are great enough to make the world views of persons in widely separated cultural ambients incomprehensible each to the other's holders. They do grade into one another, yet it is in comparing the present-day extremes—the view of civilized "common sense" with the "common-sense view" of tribal societies in mainly unmodified natural surroundings—that one may see the traces of early forms of thought, still freely mixed with dream elements and instinctual impulses, as they shaped the primitive world.

The first true human beings recognizable as such were not necessarily the cleverest primates (though, in view of their active forebrains, they may have been), but the first symbol-mongers. The erect bipedal South African "man-apes," with their human legs and simian skulls, may or may not have been among those earliest men and women,[2] isolating visual forms by their physiognomic appearances more than by contours, textures, or colors, seeing unreal shapes, eyes, and potential movement everywhere in the bush. Whoever the "dawn men" were, the world their minds created was apparently not modeled on crudely conceived laws of matter and motion, nor on any forerunner of a primitive physics; quite contrary to the widely accepted theory that they must have been pure materialists, they seem to have had no idea of inert matter and what could be done with it. Although they handled it and even did some remarkable things with it, their use of material was still largely instinctive, their knowledge of it implicit, their thinking concentrated on what was coming of their manipulations; a "thing" was a product of an act, not the stuff that had gone into the new entity.[3]

[2]Cf. above, Vol. II, p. 304, n. 80.

[3]The idea of creation of the material itself *ex nihilo* defeats most naive minds to this day. There are few exceptions to this general limitation, notably, of course, the creation myth of Genesis, which opens with the statement: "In the beginning God created the heaven and the earth. And the earth was without form and void; and darkness was upon the face of the deep." This certainly was creation of matter itself, as the next act was creation of light out of nothing that implemented the making. Of course, the Jews of the

The Spirit-World

It is this emphasis on making, giving form, giving life, and initiating growth and change that today marks spontaneous, untutored thinking. And untutored, spontaneous, the primitive modes of thought must have been. Perception of external happenings falls into the mold of the percipient's imagination; we perceive as we are able to conceive.[4] The natural way to imagine an event is in the form of an act; not really as a true act, perhaps, but in that most familiar form of subjectively known progression from one situation to another, the act form of impulse, rise, consummation, and cadence, with the likelihood of entrainment, deflection, or blocking anywhere along the way. There may be no idea at all of an agent behind the passage of an external change; only the passage itself resembles a doing. Several anthropological field workers remarked that the people they were observing had no notion of ordinary causality.[5] Bronislaw Malinowski, however, maintained that savage tribesmen had two different attitudes toward external facts, the "magical" and the "scientific," and switched from one to the other, thinking "magically" when they were engaged in ritual action (religious or conjuring) and "scientifically" in practical contexts, where they obviously knew the relation of cause and

---

time when they could write down their sacred lore were not savages, despite their tribal organization. A second instance of such relative sophistication is recorded in Roland Dixon's *Oceanic Mythology* (1916), to the effect that in the Marquesas various abstractions—firmness, space, light, etc.—are said to have arisen out of a cosmic void and finally produced Rangi (Heaven) and Papa (Earth). On this the author remarks: "We have here more of a philosophic system: in New Zealand, the briefer developmental series led only to the personified Sky Father; here it is the origin of all substance and of solid matter itself which is sought" (p. 111).

[4]See, for example, J. J. Gibson, *The Perception of the Visual World* (1950), p. 206: "The traditions and culture of an uncivilized tribe consist not merely in strange ways of behaving . . . but also in strange ways of perceiving and apprehending things. . . . The Trobrianders, it has been reported, recognize that a child resembles its father but never its mother. The former kind of resemblance is proper and to be expected; the latter is inadmissible. . . . Klineberg suggests that the effect is a failure to note any resemblance rather than an actual interference with the sensory perception, but this is hard to be certain about. In any event it is a perceptual custom which is foreign to our ways of seeing people."

[5]This was, in the main, the impression received by the early anthropologists, to whom the differences of savage cultures from their own were inexplicable because their context was still unknown, and ignorance of the white man's factual knowledge seemed the only explanation of the strange beliefs held by "backward" peoples. So Andrew Lang wrote in *Myth, Ritual and Religion* (1887), Vol. I, p. 88: "The 'actual experience,' properly so-called, of the savage is so limited and so coloured by misconception and superstition, that his knowledge of the world varies very much from the conceptions of civilized races. . . . his knowledge of physical causes and natural laws is exceedingly scanty, and he is driven to fall back upon what we may call metaphysical, or in many cases supernatural explanations. . . . These supernatural causes themselves the savage believes to be matters of experience."

effect. So he wrote, some fifty-odd years ago: "There are no peoples however primitive without religion and magic. Nor are there any savage races lacking either in the scientific attitude or in science, though this lack has been frequently attributed to them. In every primitive community, studied by trustworthy and competent observers, there have been found two clearly distinguishable domains, the Sacred and the Profane; in other words, the domain of Magic and Religion and the domain of Science."[6]

I do believe that in supposing savages, when engaged in ordinary pursuits of daily life, to be taking the "scientific attitude," Malinowski was mistaken. The undisturbed savage mind, uninfluenced by any contact with civilized thought and expression, probably never assumes the "scientific attitude." Practical as well as imaginative activity can be carried on in the natural frame, i.e., in terms of motivation, and the two sorts of context require no switch from sacred to secular; that switch, which seems to occur in many cultures, though not in all, can be made within the typical primitive mode so smoothly that a slight emotional lift or drop may be its only sign, ordinarily not even noticed. The anthropologist who remarked the true difference between savage and civilized thought was one who had originally subscribed to the doctrine that uncivilized tribesmen did not know causal relations, and who after years of experience saw her error, and recognized the possible alternative to the "scientific attitude" even for practical conception: that was Dorothea Demetracopoulou Lee. In one of her later writings, she spoke for others as well as herself when she declared: "Anthropologists have realized in recent years that people of other cultures than our own not only act differently, but that they have a different basis for their behavior. They act upon different premises; they perceive reality differently, and codify it differently."[7] In then defining that difference, she says more specifically: "To the Trobriander, events do not fall of themselves into a pattern of causal relationships, as they do for us," and adds in a note: "This absence of causal concepts, as well as of a comparative standard, seemed at first so striking to me that I wrote a paper describing Trobriand thought in terms of what it was not, as non-causal and non-comparative. It now seems to me that I was viewing the Trobrianders then through the eyes of my own culture, relationally, seeing them according to what they were unlike, and so stressing the absence of concepts which have no relevance to their thought.

[6]"Magic, Science and Religion," in *Magic, Science and Religion and Other Essays* (1948; orig. pub., 1926), p. 17.
[7]"Being and Value in a Primitive Culture" (1949), p. 401.

"We ask here, how is influence or motivation or effect phrased among the Trobrianders? How is magical action understood, for example? The answer is, it is understood in exactly these terms, as action, not cause. The magician does not *cause* certain things to be; he *does* them. As the gardener with his material implements burns the brush, breaks the clods, etc., so the garden magician with his various formulas 'awakens the sprout,' 'drives up the shoots overground,' . . . 'pushes the taytu tubers into the soil,' according to Trobriand account. This is not influence, nor the force of magic; rather it is 'to magic.'[8]

"The Trobrianders have their own equivalent for cause, in terms of their concept of pattern. For this they use the term 'u'ula.' . . . It stands for the trunk of a tree below the branches; for the base of a pole, or the bottom of a structure; it means the organizer of an expedition or the initiator of an undertaking; it refers to the first part of a magical formula. The u'ula is sometimes contemporaneous with the rest of the object or pattern, sometimes not. . . . Realized or not, the pattern is always there; the pole has a bottom, the spell a beginning; and this pattern is known as a whole, not as a temporal process. Once made evident through the u'ula, the total must be realized. To this extent, and in our terms only, can we understand u'ula to be the equivalent of *cause*; the u'ula is dynamic but only in reference to pattern, not toward the next event.

"Once the pattern has been initiated, has been given evidence, . . . the whole is inevitably there."[9]

It is fairly obvious that the "pattern," which is self-contained yet dynamic, is the act form, as presented above in Chapter 8 of this essay: an act is a special sort of natural event arising from a matrix of similarly patterned events, and so organically involved in that matrix that all influences which can affect a particular act must do so by affecting the matrix, or organism, as a whole. That complex relation—causal, but so deeply rooted as to be highly indirect—is the phenomenon I have designated as "motivation." If the "pattern" is the form of the act in question, then it is comprehensible that "realized or not, the pattern is always there." We do not usually think, in our terms, of a causal sequence, such as a cloudburst followed by a local flood, as a "realization"; but in the vital contexts in which the South Sea Islanders think, the "u'ula" of any object, event, undertaking, or what not "is known as a whole, not as a temporal process. Once made evident through the u'ula, the total must be realized."[10]

---

[8]*Ibid.*, pp. 406–7. The German language has a verb, "zaubern," which means precisely, "to magic." "Zauber" is the noun, "magic," and "zaubern" the cognate verb.
[9]*Ibid.*, pp. 411–12.
[10]Those modern scientists who have recently studied neurological activity in animals

As the present-day person of European culture ordinarily conceives causality, it is a relation between two terms, known as "the cause" and "the effect," both equally objective and impersonal and typically mechanical. The ambition of the scientific thinker is to break down his materials into inanimate units with known physical properties, and into no others that might be ultimately irreducible to cause-and-effect statement. That such scientific statements may be of staggering complexity is evident; yet by rigorous operational principles and far-sighted logical imagination in the choice of elementary terms and functions, one can build highly abstract mathematical systems which promise to express all occurrences in our known universe as causally related changes, thereby making them not only comprehensible but predictable to astounding degrees. To the laity, such scientific achievements have to be presented in a simpler language as concatenated imaginable events; and that is the language and imagery in which we are habituated to think, perceive, and believe.

The world picture created by the "scientific attitude" is, thus, radically different from the "natural" view of events based on the feeling of organic processes, i.e., in the pattern of impulse, effort, and realization. Impingements and behavioral effects are objective aspects of acts, while impulse and effort and many other elements, gross or subtle, are subjective. The two aspects intersect, alternate, or fuse in experience; one cannot truly say that seeing ambient events in act-like form is "personification" of lifeless objects, though in a somewhat special sense one might call it "animation." Living and non-living things are not conceptually distinguished. People whose thought still runs freely and naturally in the mythic mode do not change to the scientific mode when they employ practical techniques. Even as they cook, build, plant, or shape their hunting gear, they handle the material as something active, not passive. An excellent illustration of such thinking is given by three unusually perceptive and sympathetic white observers of Eskimo life on Southampton Island, one of whom watched an ivory carver shaping the figure of a seal (all Eskimos, he remarks, carve as habitually as we write): "As the carver holds the unworked ivory lightly in his hand, turning it this way and that, he whispers, 'Who are you? Who hides here?' and then: 'Ah, Seal!' He rarely sets out, at least consciously, to carve, say, a seal, but picks up the ivory, examines it to find its hidden form and, if

---

have attested the significance of this conception, as they find the minimal act to be prefigured in the complex pattern of its impulse before it leaves the initiating neuron and is passed along the axon. Cf. Vol. I, pp. 299–306.

that's not immediately apparent, carves aimlessly until he sees it, humming or chanting as he works. Then he brings it out: seal, hidden, emerges. It was always there: he didn't create it, he helped it step forth.

"The carver never attempts to force the ivory into uncharacteristic forms, but responds to the material as it tries to be itself, and thus the carving is continually modified as the ivory has its say." The man, for his part, constantly adjures it—"You who are the big seal! You who are the brown seal!" Or chanting, as the report quotes him:

> Ringed seal, one carves it
> Hiding now,
> Ringed seal, one carves it
> Moving now
> Ringed seal comes to me. [11]

The constant ritual actions attending the everyday, sober practices of people living in the wild, generally viewed by the civilized spectator as religious or magical and said by the performers themselves (if a white visitor raises such an outlandish question) to insure success in the work or future luck with the product, have a more direct, unavowed purpose of making the procedure comprehensible as it is carried on. An American farmer, similarly, might say to himself, "If this rain-wet hay be put in the loft it might ferment, and the fermentation might produce enough heat to cause spontaneous combustion which might cause a fire and burn down the barn," as he spreads the hay to dry more thoroughly. He thus takes stock of the situation in causal terms; the tribesman does the same thing in motivational terms as he enlists the material, the tool, even the hand, calling them into action.

The motivational conception of events expresses, by its formulation of them, the act of conceiving them; the product of thinking reflects the basic pattern of the thinking process itself, much as the living body, the product of growth, expresses the dynamics of the physiological acts of growing. [12] That is why the act form is the natural form for primitive conception of events to take, and as such it governs the immediate perceptions as well as the imagination of people who have not originated or received the causal perspective. It is, in fact, the development of that causal perspective, and with it the "scientific attitude," that really pre-

---

[11] Edmund Carpenter, Frederick Varley, and Robert Flaherty, *Eskimo* (1959), unpaged. The writing was done by Varley.
[12] Cf. above, Vol. I, Chapter 9, especially pp. 331 ff.

sents an anthropological problem, and accordingly will be discussed when it arises.

The act-form of experience is so fundamental a condition that it creates a different universe from that in which civilized, scientific-minded societies exist (and it is in them that people alternate between the causal pattern of their common sense and the motivational pattern of their religious thought). To understand the mythical beliefs of savage tribesmen—their ritual defenses against hosts of supernatural beings, their magic practices, comprising witchcraft, sorcery, divination, exorcism, and mysterious personal powers such as flying or climbing a rope that stands on end[13]—one has to realize, above all, that a fundamental attitude of mind entrains and encourages particular mental acts which are in harmony with it. At the time when conceptual thought began and language arose, imagination, even if fragmentary and brief, was still free from all rational constraints, and perception presented material for its work rather than revealing the limits of its excursions. The basic elements of all supernatural beliefs, from the earliest we know to the ones we hold seriously today, were probably created in that pristine, hyperactive phase of untrammeled fantasy, when wholly subjective consummation of mental acts was new. A new ability, even a newly discovered voluntary muscle, invites a creature to exercise it for pure enjoyment.[14] First dream, asleep or awake, then intentional envisionment and its objectification in speech made the teeming spirit-world into which our earliest human ancestors were born. When one looks at the assortment of spooks held in honor by people living today, some in remote corners of our world, some in the midst of advanced societies, it seems very likely that many of those phantasms go back through history and prehistory to really primitive imagination, to what one French psychologist, Émile Cailliet, called the "vegetative" period of symbol-making,[15] when any unusual sounds,

---

[13]Mircea Eliade, in a short essay, "Remarques sur le 'Rope Trick'" (1960, pp. 542–43), states that the famous delusion created by fakirs was found in ancient and modern times in India, China, Mexico, and, oddly enough, in Ireland. Outside of India the fakir's role was taken by jugglers or prestidigitators or, in Australia, by "clever men" ("men of medicine").

[14]William James noted that voluntary muscles were discovered by feeling their unintended, random earliest movements, whereupon the feeling could be induced in those muscles again; see *The Principles of Psychology*, Vol. II (1899), p. 487. Although his theory of volition, like most analysis of "faculties" in his time, requires much modification today, the guiding function of muscular sensation in voluntary movement certainly exists. As for the enthusiasm with which such newly found controls are exercised simply "for fun," see the instance of Kavanau's mice cited above, Vol. I, pp. 151–52.

[15]In *Symbolisme et âmes primitives* (1936). Cf. *Phil. N.K.*, pp. 148–49.

shapes, or lights and all distinct phenomena of nature received some exciting interpretation.

However and whenever this great rise of imagination took place—slowly or explosively, repeatedly or only once—it added a whole new dimension to man's world, the supernatural dimension. With that evolutionary breakthrough transcending the confines of animal realism came the host of imagined beings that fill his world: deities and demons, ghosts, ghouls, and goblins, mythical heroes and legendary ancestors. Where every event appears in the guise of an act instead of an instance of simpler, non-biological mechanics, some agency seems to be implicated even where none is apparent; and a prodigal imagination finds scope for marvelous inventions. It has created a spirit multitude, so great that the earth could not contain it but was expanded to possess higher and lower realms holding a limitless number of beings—gods and goddesses, demiurges, also devils, and especially souls of the dead, sometimes visible as stars,[16] sometimes living a dim life under the earth or suffering there in a fiery furnace for their sins. The belief of most Christians, Moslems, and Jews in heaven above and hell below, making a three-story edifice of the world—perfect, imperfect, and utterly horrible—is a restrained version of the widely held notion that there are many levels, many *Lebensräume*, piled one above another. These are not necessarily distinguished by relative values, and even if they are, those values are not always what we would consider moral values; for instance, according to Knut Rasmussen, the Inuit who dwell in the central regions of arctic America, around the north magnetic pole, believe that the dead go either to a land above the sky, a real heaven of pleasure and ease, or to one of two nether worlds, an upper one just below the surface of the earth and a very deep one, far below. Who goes to the sky and who under ground seems to be unpredictable. The lowest realm is like the heavenly one, and life there is much as on earth, but without hardships and dangers. The only place that is linked with the previous behavior of its denizens is the region just under the surface, a dim, dreary place where there is little to eat (butterflies, scarce and elusive, being the only food) and nothing to do; and that mezzanine level is not reserved for wicked people but for those who were lazy, apathetic, and indifferent in life and for women who would not stand the pain of being tattooed "to make them pretty." They sit below their former homeland, with drooping heads and idle hands; their

---

[16]See Émile Durkheim and Marcel Mauss, "De quelques formes primitives de classification" (1901–2), p. 23, writing about the aborigines of Australia: "Presque partout les noirs disent que tel astre est tel ancêtre determiné."

Hereafter is the fitting counterpart of themselves, as the happier realms are of the normal, energetic, playful folk.[17]

Four worlds, however, are a very modest total. Clyde Kluckhohn tells of Navaho legends "dealing with the emergences of the Navaho from the eleven lower worlds";[18] a German anthropologist, Christian von Fürer-Haimendorf, who studied the rather little-known peoples in the mountainous hinterlands of northeastern India, reports that one of their tribes, the Lhota, believe in a great horde of spirits (*Potso*) dwelling in the heaven above our earth, which in turn has a heaven occupied by supernatural beings, and so on, so that worlds are stacked on worlds to an indefinite height and number. The human sphere is but a small center of the imagined space, the spirit-world, which surrounds and also pervades the realm of man's experience.[19]

Stranger than the many heavens, hells, dreamlands,[20] and limbos of ancient creative fantasy are their supernatural possessors. There seems to be really no limit to the macabre forms that these will take, especially for people living in the wild. Our own conception of ghosts as diaphanous white human figures embodying spirits of dead or absent persons, and generally doing nothing more violent than to warn, accuse, or prophesy, is a very tame sort of bugaboo beside the uncanny spooks that are popularly known to savages and may be encountered by them at any time in darkness or daylight, in jungle or veldt, while hunting, working, love-making, or by night in dreams. Two anthropologists[21] who had fairly long, friendly contact with the Yir Yoront, an Australian tribe of very simple material culture, in the course of collecting dream protocols[22] made acquaintance with some popular ghosts; one woman reported: "I dreamed a great many *min marle* (ghost shadows) came flying at me,

[17]*The Netsilik Eskimos* (1931), pp. 315–18.

[18]"Navaho Categories" (1960), p. 77. To this statement Kluckhohn added parenthetically: "a very widely distributed plot among Indians of Western North America but with variations and elaborations more or less special to each tribe or group of tribes."

[19]"Zur Religion einiger hinterindischer Bergvölker" (1936), p. 277: "Sie glauben an eine grosse Anzahl von Himmelsgeistern (*Potso*), welche in einer Welt über der unseren leben. Diese Welt hat wieder einen Himmel, über dem noch eine andere Geisterwelt liegt und in derselben Weise sind eine unbekannte Zahl von Welten übereinander geschichtet."

[20]The idea that in dream the soul goes to "dreamland" is not a product of fairytale, but is seriously held in some societies as an article of belief.

[21]D. M. Schneider and Lauriston Sharp, *The Dream Life of a Primitive People* (1969).

[22]An easy task, as the informants talked without any ethical or other restraints; dreams of breaking taboos caused no embarrassment; dreams of sexual intercourse—the dominant content, with death as a close second—were reported with all clinical detail. In fact, the authors remarked that dreams were a "safe" subject of conversation, since no one would ever take them seriously.

alighted on my back, and wrestled with me. . . . *Min marle* are the shadows of dead men; they look like flying foxes and fly like them" (p. 105). Another dreamer, a man, dreamed of a very different ghost, but also, apparently, an accepted species: "I was up on hard dry ground [watching a shark in a river]. I sat down there. A bad ghost sat face to face opposite me. It was a bush ghost. Many ghosts appeared and sat opposite me. Then the ghosts went away. . . . The ghosts had a kind of grass growing on their backs, arms, chests, and rest of body, like hair. But their head hair and beard were real. They had small mouths, long finger nails, ugly faces. They were colored like grass. They had no ornaments or dress. They hide in the bushes" (p. 112).

We do not know, of course, how much of the vision was peculiar to the dream and how much was true to traditional imagery, but the narrator did name his first *vis-à-vis* as a bush ghost, *wangar kar'alin*, and his statement "they hide in the bushes" seems to be a comment on a generally known "they" for the benefit of the interlocutor, who also had to be informed what "they" look like. The general idea of bush ghosts seems, indeed, to be widespread; Hans Fischer, who made a study of the Watut in northeast New Guinea, far from the Yir Yoront in northwest Queensland, reported: "Bush ghosts live in the woods, on mountains, in caves or rivers. . . . They have long fingernails and toenails, short legs and long heels. Female ghosts especially are supposed to have extremely crippled legs and be hardly able to walk. Ordinarily they are invisible, but one can always see their shadow. They have the power of transforming themselves into people (even specific persons), also into dogs and other animals, and they may suddenly disappear before one's eyes. Some of them can fly."[23]

Far northward of these savage tribes, another imaginative people, the Ainu, aboriginal denizens of Japan, established their own peculiar spirit-world, teeming with supernatural beings that are mainly deities and demons. Ainu culture, which persisted for centuries on Hokkaido and southern Sakhalin after the Japanese conquest of the islands, is rapidly disappearing, since its chief home, Sakhalin, has fallen to Russia and the Ainu population has fled to the more crowded confines of Hokkaido; but fortunately an anthropologist, Emiko Ohnuki-Tierney, versed in Japanese, English, and Ainu, with the aid of "a gifted Sakhalin Ainu woman named Husko," has gathered treasures of the oral tradition in a

---

[23]*Watut. Notizen zur Kultur eines Melanesier-Stammes in Nordost-Neuguinea* (1963), pp. 97–98. In one of the fifty-seven stories collected in that book, a changeling found by human beings in their child's place had crippled legs, by which they knew it to be the child of a bush ghost (p. 148). Fischer, by the way, states that bush ghosts are not souls of dead persons but spirits of older, unknown origin.

monograph, *Sakhalin Ainu Folklore* (1969). Husko's deities are bears and
sea mammals to ordinary eyes, and the demons have numberless forms—
such as the rat demon, that has its hole in the riverbank like a perfectly
respectable rat, but sends a hairy arm clear across the river to rob a
storehouse on the opposite shore.[24]

Another uncomfortable spirit-thing reported from the same source is
the crying and rolling Orok skull, which one may encounter anywhere on
shore or upland. The Orok are a tribe traditionally hostile to the Ainu,
living on the eastern shore of Sakhalin. They are said to find no rest in
death, even after all funeral rites have been duly performed, because they
cannot give up their grudges. Husko, the faithful informant, thus explained what happens: "The Oroks put their dead in a coffin and place it
on a raised wooden structure. Therefore, the coffin will eventually rot
away and will fall to the ground. Then the skull . . . will fall out and start
rolling around the field, while crying, 'ha:ray, ha:ray.' . . .

"If an Ainu happens to be fishing on a river when an Orok skull goes
by, and he jokingly tells the skull to sing, it will sing '*Ha:ray, ha:ray.*' If
someone strikes the skull with a stick or something else, it would break
into pieces, and yet each of the broken pieces would jump up onto the
boat. They will then stick on the edge of the boat and keep crying,
'Ha:ray, ha:ray.'

"When one encounters situations involving the Orok skulls, one
should perform . . . the Ainu informal rite of offering whatever is avail-

[24]The transcriber, who quotes the literal form, in Ainu and English, of the strictly
worded recitations, also gives us a synopsis of this story, according to which "there were
three adjacent settlements along a river. The chiefs of these settlements were brothers.
The oldest resided at the upper reaches of the river, the middle brother at the middle
reaches, and the youngest one at the river mouth. One day the oldest brother [who alone
had the "super-Ainu power" to see demons] heard rumors that at the settlements of his
two younger brothers the food was disappearing. Thus the people in these settlements
were dying of hunger, and yet nobody knew the cause. Therefore, one morning he went
down the mountain to investigate the situation at the middle brother's settlement. As he
sat down to smoke . . . he saw a big hairy arm coming from the river bank on which he
was sitting. The arm reached the opposite side, and then went into a storage house in the
settlement. Pulling out a huge bundle of dried trout, the arm went back into the river
bank on which the elder brother was sitting. The arm repeated this action. . . . As the
arm . . . came out of the river bank for the fourth time, he shot at it. The arm shook and
withdrew into the river bank." [He shouted across the river and was fetched by boat; his
brother's people were largely dead or very weak, but he took those who could still work
along to the rat demon's den.]

"As they dug out the dirt around the den, they could hear the groaning of the rat
demon. They stabbed and sliced the demon into pieces to distribute its flesh to all the
grass and trees in the universe [which prevents demons from coming to life again]. They
also carried out the food which the rat had stolen . . . and brought it back to their
settlement across the river" (pp. 138–39).

able, e.g., tobacco which one always carries. Then the Orok skulls will leave."[25]

There are many other fantastic beings in that populous and probably very ancient world which Husko referred to as "super-Ainu," i.e., super-human ("Ainu" meaning "mankind"), such as bear deities, fox-men, and the *femmes fatales* with teeth in their vaginas.[26] These women are said to be made pregnant by the wind[27] and to bear only female children. But the weirdest trait of many Ainu spooks is their origin, for they may be ghosts not of men or even animals, but of household objects, implements, or other possessions that have been left behind and not fittingly disposed of when their owners moved away from the house. Any abandoned object should be broken up and distributed to the trees, bushes, and grass of the universe, or it will become a demon. So Husko recited a tale of a chief who came upon a house in which an old woman was hopping around a fire in the center of the room, crying "Koh, koh," while she roasted human heads. The chief went back to his settlement and got his men; after they shot the demonic creature, which returned her to her true form, she proved to have been the ghost of a loom rod, an implement used in the Ainu method of mat-weaving. It had been carelessly left in the house. They found the rod with an arrow stuck in its middle.[28]

Another story—a more sacred one, for it deals with the culture hero Yayresupo, who is considered a semi-deity—hinges on the identity of two demons, who are unmasked as ghosts of two musical instruments, to which they are thereby magically retransformed.[29]

Even further from the European fancy of wraithlike ghosts of dead persons are some Eskimo conceptions. A number of these are presented by Asen Balikci in a short essay, "Shamanistic Behavior among the Netsilik Eskimos" (1967), where ghosts appear among other strange embodiments of mystic power. Here we find, for instance, an inventory of one shaman's magical helpers and the author's explanatory comment: "The Eskimo universe was peopled by a vast number of supernatural beings with diverse characteristics, mostly malevolent. Shamans had con-

[25]Pp. 138–39.
[26]The author-reporter remarks (p. 152) that such stories, however odd, tend to be widespread, and says: "Even the restricted theme of *vagina dentata* seems to have a wide distribution, including Siberian tribes, groups south of Japan, including groups in India, and both North and South American Indians."
[27]Like the mother of Hiawatha, in the legend collected by Schoolcraft and versified by Longfellow.
[28]*Sakalin Ainu Folklore*, pp. 130–31.
[29]*Ibid.*, pp. 54–55.

trol of only one class of spirits, the *tunraqs*. They continued to acquire *tunraqs* throughout their lives, usually as gifts from other shamans or following the spirits' own volition. Thus Iksivalitaq, the last Netsilik shaman of importance, at the end of his life around 1940 had the following seven *tunraqs*:

(1) Kingarjuaq (Big Mountain), about 3" long and 1" high, with black and red spots. The shaman could remove this *tunraq* from his mouth, where it was in the habit of staying, and make it run on his hand.

(2) Kanayuq (Sea Scorpion), residing also in Iksivalitaq's mouth, whence it showed its ugly head.

(3) Kaiutinuaq, the ghost of a dead man.

(4) Kringarsarut, the ghost of a dead man, big as a needle, with a crooked mouth and one very small ear.

(5) Arlu, the killer whale, white, very big.

(6) Kunnararjuq, a black dog with no ears.

(7) Iksivalitaq, the ghost of Iksivalitaq's grandfather.

"Other collections of supernatural helpers revealed a similar composition: animals, monstrous creatures with little semblance to anything living, occasionally plants, and many ghosts." Somewhat later we are told: "*Tupiliqs* were another important kind of evil spirits. Round in shape and filled with blood under considerable pressure, they caused sickness."[30]

Even high gods may take astonishing forms. John Middleton, in his book on the Lugbara,[31] a tribally organized people in northwestern Uganda and eastern Zaire, makes quite evident that they have a relatively high concept of a Supreme Being. This Being, whose name, Adroa, he translates as "God,"[32] is creator of the world and of man; he is also the only giver and taker of life. Since the Lugbara are truly monotheists, admitting no supernatural rival or antagonist to God, i.e., no devil, both good and evil must derive from the sole deity. Consequently, the author says, "they conceive him as having two aspects, one transcendent and the other immanent [in Nature]. The transcendent aspect is usually named

[30] Pp. 194–95.
[31] *Lugbara Religion* (1960).
[32] Pp. 252–53: "I translate Adro and Adroa as 'God,' although the correspondence of meaning is not exact. Adro, the basic form of the term, refers to a personified force, outside the control and beyond the understanding of the living men who are his creatures. There is no way of distinguishing gender in Lugbara. God is referred to as *eri*, which can mean 'he,' 'she,' or 'it.'" The difficulty of any translation is evident when, not far below this passage, we find: "unlike our term 'God,' Adro is used also to refer to a category of objects which are manifestations of divinity and beyond the control and understanding of men. Many apparently miraculous things are called *adro*, such as what I have called the guardian spirit of a man, or even matches; the word is sometimes used for testicles and for the power of procreation."

Adroa or *Adronga*, forms which are diminutives of *Adro*, which is used for the immanent aspect. The diminutive is used because God in the sky is more remote, both spatially and in intensity of contact, than God on the earth. Offerings are made to him in his immanent aspect and not to him in his transcendent aspect" (p. 252).

It is Adro, God in his immanent aspect, that presents a fearful appearance to people who are unfortunate enough to meet him in his twilight haunts (he makes his home in rivers, but also may appear, especially around sunset, in thickets, on crags, and in groves): "He is said to be formed like a man, and very tall and white; but his body is cut down the centre and he has only one eye, one ear, one arm and one leg, on which he jumps about. He is very terrible to see."[33]

If the Supernaturals are strange to behold and their provenience sometimes surprising, the origins of mankind, and in some cases its early forms, are certainly no less so. The Yạnomamö of the deep jungle round the headwaters of the Amazon, for instance, believe that before there were men there were miraculous "first beings," an assortment of spirits (Periboriwä, spirit of the moon) and animals (Haya, deer; Öra, jaguar; Iwä, alligator) and many characters that seem to have been mythic personages from various forgotten sources.[34] Periboriwä, the moon spirit, "had a habit of coming down to earth to eat the soul parts of children. On his first descent, he ate one child, placing his soul between two pieces of cassava bread and eating it. He returned a second time to eat another child, also with cassava bread. Finally, on his third trip, . . . Suhiriva [one of the anomalous "first beings"] took one bamboo-tipped arrow . . . and shot at Periboriwä when he was directly overhead, hitting him in the abdomen. The tip of the arrow barely penetrated Periboriwä's flesh, but the wound bled profusely. Blood spilled to earth. . . . The blood changed into men as it hit the earth, causing a large population to be born. All of them were males. The blood of Periboriwä did not change into females. Most of the Yạnomamö who are alive today are descended from the blood of Periboriwä. *Because they have their origin in blood, they are fierce and continuously making war on each other.*

"Where his blood was thickest, in the areas directly underneath the spot where Periboriwä was shot, the wars were so intense that the Yạnomamö in that area exterminated themselves. Where the blood had

---

[33]P. 254. In an article, "The Concept of 'Bewitching' in Lugbara" (1967), p. 62, Middleton describes this same apparition as "white or transparent."

[34]Napoleon Chagnon, *Yạnomamö: The Fierce People* (1968), p. 45: "The first beings cannot be accounted for. The Yạnomamö simply assume that the cosmos originated with these people."

an opportunity to thin out, the Yąnomamö were less fierce and therefore did not become extinct. . . .

"After this, there were only men. One of the men, a descendant of the blood of Periboriwä, was called Kanaboroma. . . . One day his legs became pregnant. Women came out of the left leg, and men out of the right. . . . They rapidly multiplied and also contributed to the present population of Yąnomamö. . . . The original beings all changed into *yai*: spirits."[35]

Hans Fischer, in his aforementioned study of the Watut, records a myth in which a brood of tadpoles arises from the body of a boy killed by a ghost; the tadpoles come ashore and change into boys and girls who play on the beach, grow up, and take possession of the earth.[36] But tadpoles are not the most improbable predecessors of humanity; they are, after all, living creatures, and are larvae destined to change into something that seems very different; children instead of frogs could be imagined. It might even recur in our own fairytales. A much more bizarre myth of human origins is reported from Borneo by Roland Dixon, according to which a sword handle, long ago, mated with a spindle, giving rise to offspring without arms or legs, which produced more and more human forms until they engendered not only mankind, but finally all the gods.[37]

At this point one may well wonder how human beings who are intelligent enough to carry on the practical affairs of life can possibly imagine such absurdities and assert them as facts, and even more how anyone besides their inventors can give credence to them. The answers to those two questions prove to be indicative of a whole psychological dimension involved in the motivational view of the external world. The primitive outlook raises its own problems of psychology and even epistemology, i.e., not only of the sources of belief, but of its grounds, the standards of reality and knowledge. They are different from the scientific or at least factual standards of our own common sense. The gap between the savage mind and the civilized is greater than the European-based administrators of uncivilized conquered peoples realize, so great that the rulers and their subjects view each other as inane, if not insane.[38] One consequence of

---

[35]*Ibid.*, pp. 47–48.

[36]Fischer, *Watut*, pp. 145–47. Note that the boy antedates the beginning of human history. To think of the earth without mankind seems to be impossible for savages.

[37]*Oceanic Mythology*, p. 159. This is the only myth I have heard of which places the origin of man before that of the gods.

[38]By way of example, Leonhard Adam, in an article, "Recht im Werden" (1936), p. 231, evaluated savage thinking as vastly inferior to his own, even as he remarked the radical difference of standpoint between them: "Der primitive Mensch sieht, vermöge

this basic mutual repellence is the abuse, often unintended, of persons or whole populations in the colonial holdings of European powers, which will come under discussion in a later chapter; another is the fantastic character attributed by many tribal societies to the white invaders, who are said to walk on their heads at home in their own domains, to be able to disappear in the earth and move under its surface with tremendous speed, and to be cannibals.[39] Several quite unrelated peoples believe that individuals of other races are only half-human, that in most cases at least one of their "first ancestors" was a dog—not a deity, like the "Great Hares," the divine ancestors claimed by some American Indians, but an ordinary domestic dog, which, despite its low birth, had been able to take on human guise.[40]

---

seiner magischen Einstellung, . . . Menschen und Sachen, Natur und Menschenwerk . . . wesentlich anders an als der Europäer, dessen Kultur der primitiven um ideelle Jahrtausende voraus ist." The same utter lack of rapport is evinced by the words of E. Best in reference to the Maori, quoted by Leo Simmons in *The Role of the Aged in Primitive Society* (1945), p. 101: "How many times has the writer, over a space of five decades, listened to these puerile folk tales . . . told in rough huts, in the darkening solitude of the old, old forests. . . . Fancy a tattered old bush fighter . . . relating the myths of Uenuka the Rainbow God and the Mist Maid, or such puerile folk tales as that of the woman who ate her child's heart."

From the opposite angle, a Frenchwoman, Alexandra David-Neel, who lived for years in the snow country of Tibet in order to study Lamaism and finally became a Lama herself, has written: "The British expedition penetrating into the forbidden territory and parading his capital . . . had probably led the Dalai Lama to understand that foreign barbarians were masters in a material sense, by right of force. The inventions that he noticed during his trip through India must also have convinced him of their ability to enslave and mould the material elements of nature. But his conviction that the white race is mentally inferior remained unshaken. And, in this, he only shared the opinion of all Asiatics—from Ceylon to the northern confines of Mongolia" (*Magic and Mystery in Tibet* [1937], pp. 3–4).

[39]Middleton, in *Lugbara Religion*, p. 234, says of the Europeans who have administered or visited Lugbara: "Those who first entered Lugbara are called by various names, but they are all given similar attributes. They were cannibals (as all Europeans even today are thought to be, except those well known to Lugbara as individuals), they would disappear underground, and they walked on their heads and could cover vast distances in a day by this means. As soon as they were noticed they began to walk on their legs, and if attacked they would vanish into the ground and come up some distance away; they would then walk away on their heads. I have heard it said that this is still the way in which Europeans behave in their own country 'on the other side of Lake Albert.'"

[40]See A. E. Jensen, "Beziehungen zwischen dem alten Testament und der nilotischen Kultur in Africa" (1960), p. 463: "Bei den Sidamo und Darassa gibt es eine Mythe wonach die verachteten Töpfer von einer Hündin abstammen, die sich in einen Menschen verwandelt hat." [The potters were a despised caste that seems to have represented an ancient, conquered population.] Rasmussen, in *The Netsilik Eskimos*, pp. 227–28, relates a myth of a woman who married a dog that assumed human form, whereupon she bore "a litter of young" (we are not told whether puppies or babies) who grew up into Indians and white men.

The difference between the two modes of interpretation, which I have called the motivational and the causal, respectively, rather than the religious and the scientific (since either may, ideally, cover the whole realm of thought), is not enough to meet all the problems which the beliefs and practices of wilderness dwellers pose for the anthropologist. Each of these ideas or actions has its own etiology in the general context of act-oriented thought and language, and has to be traced to its own evolutionary conditions. In the course of such speculation and reflection (for that is really all our theorizing on prehistoric human mentality amounts to) some interesting psychological principles come into play. Most of these have been discovered by psychologists, anthropologists, or other scholars in special connections, but in the biological frame of the present study they come together from all quarters to form the rational basis of thought even in its most primitive stages. For, although it is fairly certain that no human stock on earth is older than another and none living today is truly "aboriginal," those people who have not developed the causal view of nature still reveal connections between cerebral activities and more general patterns of vital function which scientific civilization has obscured. Some of their mental productions may be very old indeed, for they strongly suggest processes that are likely to have played a vital role in the formation of mind itself, drawing on all the brain's potentialities, laying the foundations for the later specializations—the arts and sciences, moral and legislative controls—as we know them in historic times. Once we recognize a truly primitive trait of human experience in a naive form, we usually end up by finding it still operative in our own subjective experience.

So we may question, first of all, how perfectly sober people with pressing social and economic interests could ever invent such nonsense as the mating of a sword handle with a spindle, and regard it as the historic source of themselves and of their gods. One important step toward the answer, I think, may have been given almost half a century ago by Daniel Essertier, who pointed out that assertion is one of the primary acts of mind, both in phylogeny and in ontogeny. Of its phylogenetic role he said: "This is not a simple matter of linking concepts, but of a double and indivisible affirmation: in affirming anything, the mind[41] affirms itself. And even further: it is for the sake of thus affirming itself that it makes any affirmation at all. Similarly, when the hand of a little child closes as

[41]Literally, "consciousness," "la conscience"; at the time when this was written, "consciousness" was still largely considered (especially in Europe) to be synonymous with "mind," and both with "reason."

tightly as it does on an object it grasps, that is less from the fear of losing the object than in order to feel its own strength.

"Thus the horror of doubt is natural to consciousness. Doubt is its supreme menace, for it threatens the keystone of the whole mental structure: the affirmation of the self. Dogmatism and lazy-mindedness are usually, above all, primitive means whereby somewhat weak and vaccilating personalities parry that threat.

"Consequently the assertions of primitive minds are first and foremost immediate, arbitrary, and unconcerned about their objective content."[42] In the asserter's own thinking there was probably never any question of the truth or falsity of his allegations; anything he could imagine served for a statement. Essertier's text goes on to say just that. The double function of assertion—affirmation of an idea and of the mind itself—may have been what carried the human activity of propositional thought from its earliest, sporadic beginnings a long way toward easy and complete articulation, before any question of plausibility ever arose.[43]

But what would lead other people than the author of a fantasy to believe his words? Another facet of the same condition; in the earliest stages of human mental evolution, when thinking and verbalizing were new and therefore exceedingly active functions, not yet reduced to the servosystem attending on practical life that they are, for the most part, today, people may have been ready to accept not only their own but also any other notion born of any flash of imagination, any suggestion no matter how it was made, much as some gregarious animals like geese or schooling fish fall in with a suggested act at the first move of the first companion to give overt expression to an impulse befitting the momentary situation. Similarly, in the irresponsible thinking of truly primitive human beings, the production or reception of a thought may have involved no judgment whatever of truth-value; it probably was more like a direct sparking-over from the impulse generating the subjective act of ideation to the feeling of reality pervading the figment even as it took shape; that is to say: the character of reality, which for us today requires some credentials such as objective perception or trusted information, may originally have belonged to all ideas and may only have acquired a distinctive value with experiences of disillusionment and the gradual discovery of fictitiousness.

[42]*Les formes inférieures de l'explication* (1927), pp. 57–58.
[43]*Ibid.*, p. 59: "Les images sont si vives qu'elles emportent d'emblée l'assentiment: elles se lient entre elles avec une telle force et une telle soudaineté qu'il n'y a aucune fissure par où le doute pourrait pénétrer."

It is a curious fact, often undiscovered and unappreciated, that the most primitive humanizing requirements seldom—if ever—are entirely transcended. They may be met in such new ways that they do not seem the same demands as before. I think this is true of the need to make assertions in order to assure ourselves of our own mental power. We are no longer in the world-building stage of rampant imagination, when every person could indulge in the most extravagant fantasies and every invention passed for a reality; most civilized people today limit their categorical religious assertions to the affirmation of formally stated tenets shared by a number of other persons. That number may be small—the membership of a deviant sect or even a secret cult—or immense, like that of the Roman Catholic Church, Islam, or Hinduism, each uniting millions. The passionate feeling with which we tend to profess our faith shows that even in modern society the average person has a deep need of asserting the nature of his world, in order that he may constantly realize and confirm his own being. The content of such assertions is, of course, no longer individual in the framework of a great religion. With the passing of the pre-rational, boundlessly creative ages of symbolic thinking, other growing functions such as logical judgment, evaluation, and negation made the plethora of rival ideas a battle scene that discouraged and frustrated the average thinker's personal production of assertible beliefs.[44] Then there had to be tenets the unimaginative, intimidated, or confused could borrow; and as such conceptions had not emerged spontaneously from the mind that employed them, there had to be supports to its self-affirmation. This may explain the emotional value of conservatism and dogmatism, which is often expressed in a defensive, merciless intolerance.

The degrees to which the loss of spontaneous fantasy and personal assertion has extended in various populations differ widely. Anthropologists who base general conclusions about "the savage mind" on their observations of extreme conservatism in two or three tribal societies, or on the opposite attitude found in one or more, may not have noted the exact circumstances that determine the degree of freedom or conformism in the cultural pattern of those tribes. For example: the Yąnomamö in the jungle of the Amazon sources, described in detail by Chagnon, seem to have great liberty to exercise their own poetic talents and to elaborate

44Cf. George Santayana, *Skepticism and Animal Faith* (1923), p. 8: "What kills spontaneous fictions, what recalls the impassioned fancy from its improvisations, is the angry voice of some contrary fancy. Nature, silently making fools of us all our lives, would never bring us to our senses; the maddest assertions of the mind may do so, when they challenge one another. Criticism arises out of the conflict of dogmas."

religious ideas, especially the physical structure of heavens and underworlds, concepts of the soul, *noreshi* animals (indwelling animal familiars identified with their human host's soul and duplicated in the outer world), infernal punishment and how to evade it, and a wealth of mythical invention. The material culture of these Indians is extremely poor, but they vie with each other in story-telling and set a high premium on forceful and fluent use of language.[45] Their springs of imagination have certainly not run dry.

The reason is that they have not let them. The Yąnomamö are confirmed drug addicts, taking huge doses of hallucinogenic drugs derived from the bark of the *ebene* tree or the seeds of the *hisioma*, despite highly unpleasant side-effects;[46] consequently their brains are constantly stimulated to produce visions and wild ideas in a dreamlike state. This may well have held back other cultural advances. It is interesting to speculate on the possibility that such popular indulgence in drugs which have obvious

[45]See Chagnon, *Yąnomamö,* p. 44: "The comparative poverty of Yąnomamö material culture is more than compensated for by the richness and complexity of their theological concepts, myths, and legends.

"One of the distinctive features of Yąnomamö cosmology and theology is the opportunity it provides for inventiveness. Individuals can and do modify concepts, embellish them and, in general, use their imaginations when trafficking in myths or concepts of the soul and afterlife. In short, there is room for thinkers in Yąnomamö culture.

"The result of this is that many variants of the same basic myth can be found over a relatively small area. Indeed, each village will contain people who tell the myth a slightly different way; the basic elements remain the same each time, but personal views are interjected and reflect the idiosyncrasies of the narrator. The Yąnomamö appear to enjoy these intellectual exercises, for in myth and cosmology they are able to demonstrate their personal abilities as users of their language, the true language of man."

Such freedom is rare in the wild, yet A. R. Radcliffe-Brown makes a very similar report on the Negritoes in *The Andaman Islanders* (1948). The motivation in the case of those little hunters, who had very little governmental or religious constraint, seems to have been mainly the absence of any standard form. The same personal ambition, however, seems to have inspired the Pygmies as it did the fierce Indians, for the author says: "The desire on the part of each *oko-jumo* [authority on legends] to be original and so to enhance his own reputation is a fertile source of variation in the legends" (p. 187).

[46]Chagnon, *Yąnomamö,* p. 24: "A small quantity of the powder is introduced into the end of a hollow cane tube some three feet long. . . . One end of the tube is put into the nostril of the man taking the drug, and his helper then blows a strong blast of air through the other end, emitting his breath in such a fashion that he climaxes the delivery with a hard burst of air. . . . The man who had the drug blown into his nostrils grimaces, groans, chokes, coughs, holds his head from the pain of the air blast, and duck-waddles off to some leaning post. He usually receives two doses of the drug, one in each nostril. The recipient usually vomits, gets watery eyes, and develops a runny nose. Much of the drug comes back out in the nasal mucus that begins to run freely after the drug has been administered. . . . The drug allegedly produces colored visions . . . and permits the user to enter into contact with his particular *hekura*, miniature demons that dwell under rocks and on mountains."

[23]

toxic properties has, in the course of generations, affected the emotional character of their lineage, producing their strange ideal of ferocity. It may be that the helplessness attendant on so many transient yet rather protracted periods of alienation from actuality has established a deep feeling of insecurity in these men, which makes them seek compensation in flaunting their readiness to hurt and kill not only their enemies but their females and weaker fellows. Their poetic freedom and unabated myth-making may themselves be partially atavistic traits—influenced, of course, by the evolutionary progress of the whole human race to which their stock belongs, yet a relic of a phase that other societies have long left behind.

Most people, "primitive" or sophisticated, today concentrate their religious fervor on a received dogma. Their spirit world is not built on original experiences, but on tradition; and because they do not feel as if their own creative genius could replace any lost deity, ancestry, or mythic history, yet have still the psychological need of testifying to the structure of their world for the sake of self-affirmation, the content of their traditional belief tends to be conservative, even to a point of fanatical defense against the smallest threat of heresy.

But if the contents of assertions which were made first of all for the sake of self-affirmation are, as Essertier maintained, unimportant and arbitrary, why do those contents not consist of trivial, everyday items concerning familiar objects and routine affairs? Why do they deal with cosmic events, the origins of the world and of man? In pursuing such questions one discovers that Essertier's statement, important though it is, is only a first step in the understanding of the entire complex of motivations underlying the impulse to declare opinions about ambient conditions, past, present and future. That strong and constantly recurrent impulse is not a simple "drive" to deliver a judgment, but a highly articulated one whose many forms are closely related as so many aspects of a basic activity. The double function which Essertier attributed to mythological assertions—to say something about the world, and to affirm the power of the mind to say it—runs through all our assertions to this day, though certainly without awareness, let alone intention. But trivial statements make no affirmation of their maker's whole mind; they give implicit assurance of detailed mental functions, of this or that potentiality of discrimination, concatenation, response, recollection, the covert, subjective counterpart of the overt expression,[47] to which the motives con-

---

[47]Recognition of this action lends some support to John Locke's "axiomatic" belief that the mind is intuitively aware of its own activities. But intuition is a conscious, cognitive

trolling the latter are irrelevant. The function of self-affirmation in such current, chiefly communicative acts is, after all, only one element in their motivation, so ubiquitous and familiar that only the affront of contradiction brings it to our notice in a surge of emotional feeling, which may be of any degree from scarcely discernible to uncontrollable.

It is in making assertions about the world as a whole that the mind affirms itself as a whole; hence the sacredness and inviolability of the cosmic myths that are incorporated in religions. These are the tenets to which Essertier's remarks about the "horror of doubt" fully apply. Yet this horror is probably a fairly late cultural phenomenon; as long as all allegations about unknown realms, the distant past or the future (that is, anything beyond personal experience), were uncritically received as true, there could be no concept of untruth except with respect to empirical, still current facts, no acknowledged fictions except lies. Myths of world creation, human origins, destiny, and life after death (whether as a ghost in familiar haunts or as a denizen of some other world) are products of unhampered imagination, and the wildest tales often prove to be acceptable. So are the myths about deities or demons belonging to particular places or having made or destroyed particular things: Cerberus stationed at the gate of Hades, the Indian "culture hero" Manabozho, also known as Hiawatha, whose beaver dams are our Great Lakes,[48] the serpents or dragons that periodically swallow the sun,[49] the demons of darkness ever threatening to devour mankind.[50] Such myths tend to disappear as the higher divinities are developed and exalted in religious conception; but the more universal themes—the origins of the world and of man—however fantastic, are more tenacious and prone to accommodate new symbolic imagery which arises with expansions, reverses, or other changes befalling the community; new visions and rites may push out decadent ones, but if the sacred tradition is to live the new sacra must be as mystical as those which they displaced.

act, and the self-asserting process of which Essertier spoke takes place far below the conscious level of thought.

[48]D. Brinton, *The Myths of the New World* (1896), p. 194 f.

[49]See, for example, W. W. Skeat's *Malay Magic* (1966; 1st ed., 1900), pp. 11–12: "Eclipses of the sun or moon are considered to be the outward and visible sign of the devouring of those bodies by a sort of gigantic dragon or dog. Hence the tumult made during an eclipse by the Malays, who imagine that if they make a sufficient din they will frighten the monster away."

[50]K. T. Preuss, in an essay, "Die religiöse Bedeutung der Paradiesmythen" (1936), tells of a defensive rite (*Abwehrritus*) described in the Mexican Codex Borbonicus, practiced every fifty-two years at the drilling of a new fire to assure the continued rising of the sun: "Man fürchtete dann, . . . dass die Dämonen der Finsternis, die sterngeister Tzitsimime, vom Himmel herabkommen und die Menschen fressen könnten" (p. 122).

Myths of creation and long-past events, of impending dangers or conquests, and of life continued in other realms after death have been as important to man's orientation in his mind-made world as his belief in the snake or stony rim that encircled the ocean to hold it in place, the heavens above his head and hells beneath his feet, for as such fabled geography first gave the world spatial dimensions, so the myths of origins and superhuman adventure have given it the character of duration, or time.

In the context of motivational thinking, however, time is not the one-dimensional structure that it is in civilized thought, arbitrarily divisible into temporal segments—years and days, hours, minutes, seconds, and for scientific purposes milliseconds—into which historical fact and observable events are fitted to present the causal order of nature. For intuitive perception, time is a stream of acts; and acts, like mixing and branching currents in a river, and unlike metrical units, have forms, proportions, interrelations, so the time they define has a complicated flow: it eats into the future and builds up a past, and those two components meet in an ever-changing, yet ever-present "Now." From that center they both appear in perspective, but each in its own, for acts record themselves primarily in feeling, nameable or nameless and not necessarily emotional, and the respective appearances of past and future are made, if not out of very different conceptual elements, at least by radically different involvements with the "specious present"[51] "Now," giving the two orders quite distinct qualities. The past is a structure in the mode of memory; not composed of memories, though a person's own past may embody a great many, but composed of events (for motivational thinking, of acts) which have entered ineradicably into the subsequent world situation. They may never come to awareness, or, if they do, may be quickly forgotten, but their traces are left upon the progressive "Now." This is as true of imaginary historical elements as of realistic ones. It is the basic, unsystematic "time past" which naive as well as ingenious minds may embroider as they will, covering few or many ages (usually reckoned by lifetimes) and weaving great or small figments to fill in that universal background.

The "sense of pastness" that belongs to normal recollection is produced by several psychological effects, chiefly upon our attitudes, of acts that appear finished but are still providing motivations of present overt and, particularly, covert acts. The most striking characteristic of such acts (which need not be one's own) is that no matter what behavior or thought

---

[51]For the meaning and source of this term see above, Vol. II, p. 333.

they motivate, their own occurrence can no longer be eluded. They contain no potentialities, offer no choices; nothing can block or deflect them. A. N. Whitehead once remarked that it takes a strong spirit to contemplate history because of its unalterable reality. Events which have occurred are given in the situation of every individual matrix of activities forever after; that is "the Past."[52]

The Future is built up of cumulative conceptions containing many of the same elements as the Past, but these play a different role: they constitute the situation of emergent acts which are all, as yet, at least partly potential, though many (for some people, most) are rooted in the near past and are, in fact, in process of realization. So-called "projects" may be entirely unrealized, their only connection with the Past being the continuity of their motivating mental acts of imagination, perhaps felt as desire, possibly even as intention; if they have reached the stage of impulse and orientation toward a goal, they also involve expectancy. But if they are purely acts of imagination, they have a present rather than future character.

In any case, precisely those attributes which past events possess—finality, definiteness of the smallest details, permanent existence, however infinitesimal, as elements in the world for all subsequent acts—are lacking in the natural conception of future time, which is filled with options, potentialities, rational and irrational hopes, well-founded fears, and nightmarish dreads. Hopes and fears are directly related to human wishes, and wishes are strong motivating conditions which may lead to overt action or, in case such action is obviously unfeasible, to alternative, intracerebral consummation, i.e., dream or daydream or other symbolic substitute.[53] The Past, being in the mode of memory, is closed, inaliena-

---

[52]In *Symbolism, Its Meaning and Effect* (1927), he says of this finality of the past: "Time is known to us as the succession of our acts of experience, and thence derivatively as the succession of events objectively perceived in those acts. But this succession is not pure succession: it is the derivation of state from state, with the later state exhibiting conformity to the antecedent. Time in the concrete is the conformation of state to state, the later to the earlier; and the pure succession is an abstraction from the irreversible relationship of settled past to derivative present. . . . The past consists of the community of settled acts which, through their objectifications in the present act, establish the conditions to which that act must conform" (pp. 35–36).

[53]The tendency of blocked conative impulses to terminate in production of an image capable of symbolizing the object of desire (which may be performance of an overt act, possession of an object, or a changed condition) has a parallel on a purely somatic level in the perceptual illusion (also a neural product) which is apt to occur where an oculomotor act is blocked, namely, the sudden shift of the fixated image in space, such as a printed passage appearing to jump to the opposite page in an open book. See Erich von Holst, "Relations between the Central Nervous System and the Peripheral Organs" (1954), pp.

ble, and irreparable; if its "data" undergo any change, that is a change in our knowledge, and the present subjective act of correction adds itself to the judging individual's history as a complication of his Past from that moment onward. The Future, on the other hand, is an open-ended progression, and our most amazing, precise predictions are a play of emergent realizations with intellectually engendered expectancies. The whole structure of time apprehended in motivational terms is an immensely complex web, with a large "specious present" dividing two very different extensions of that central ["Now,"] which changes as they change in a direction marked by progressive realization ever making the Past, and newly emerging situations creating the vista of potentialities, the Future.

In such a framework events can have no specific dates.[54] One may be known to have come before another because it enters into the motivating situation of the latter, but apart from such interrelationships the Past is a perspective of lifetimes, ranged in grades of vividness from actual memory contents, through historical tradition, to utterly unrealistic, supernatural myth where time has no measure any more, not even by generations. Mythical beings and acts are contemplated with a "sense of pastness," i.e., are conceived in the literary mode of memory, but their occurrence was "in the beginning," "very long ago," before mankind as it is known today existed.[55]

That remote prehistory is the principal domain of free, irresponsible assertion of the most arbitrary fantasies, which seems still to inspire belief simply upon suggestion. The visibly approaching future contains too many real expectations, anxieties, intentions, hopes, and prognostications to permit sheer imagination to possess it. If it is to harbor dream images, these must be removed from actuality by being projected beyond the dreamer's life, into his "hereafter." Even at that distance, they and their setting still resemble earthly life far more than the miracles of origin;[56] they are made much more directly out of wishes than the ele-

---

92–93; also, especially, Heinz Werner, "Motion and Motion Perception: A Study in Vicarious Functioning" (1945), and references there.

[54]Cf. Lee, "Being and Value in a Primitive Culture" p. 402: "Trobriand verbs are timeless, making no temporal distinctions. A Trobriander can, if he chooses, refer to an act as completed, but that, it seems to me, is an aspect of the act, not a temporal reference."

[55]Reo F. Fortune, in *Sorcerers of Dobu: The Social Anthropology of the Dobu Islanders of the Western Pacific* (1932), pp. 30–31, reported: "The village consists of several *susu*, several women with their children and their brothers. Many cannot show a genealogical relationship, for a *susu* only knows its own genealogy back four or five generations at the most. Back of the fourth generation there is an ancestress common to all the *susu* of the village. This common ancestress is not a human being, but a bird."

[56]Rasmussen (*The Netsilik Eskimos*, p. 315) recorded the following description of heaven: "It is a land of pleasure, where all think of nothing but playing and merry jests.

ments of the imaginary Past, the real myths, on which the ethos of tribal society is based. In short, any imaginary Future (just like the expected actual future) is conceived in the mode of potentiality.

In filling the vanished ages before anyone's memory with fantastic acts of gods and goddesses, demons, animals, supermen, and beings compounded of any or all of these, what motivates such irrational inventions? And as countless minds contribute to the multitude of "supernaturals" and their stories, what is the basis of choice among them, so that at least they shall not contradict each other when a firm mythic tradition is finally created?

The motivation is essentially the same as that of dreams: the spontaneous production of "natural symbols" for ideas that are intellectually too advanced, too great with implications, or emotionally too disturbing for conscious formulation and expression in words.[57] The production of such symbols, and their conglomeration due to the dense fusion of their meanings below the level of rational conception, is what Freud, in the bold, speculative sixth chapter of his first revolutionary book, *The Interpretation of Dreams*, called the "dream work."[58] But dreams are not its only products, nor are they, in the evolution of mind, its most important. Dreams are, perhaps, all-important safety valves in personal lives, taking care of emotional strains which frustrate normal thoughts and actions and threaten the mental balance of the individual; in the long run, however, in the life of the human race, the paramount contribution of the dream work is myth.

Those same symbols which serve our subjective needs in dreams and personal daydreams, and which may take the form of delusions in mental derangement, also furnish the substance of myth. Mental products, like all organic specialties, tend to take on further functions as soon as the ones they originally grew up with do not preempt them completely. Freud himself discovered that the meanings of "natural symbols" may be

---

The houses stand in long rows and round about the houses the snow is trampled hard with the many footprints of happy, ball-playing people."

From a very different part of the world, southeastern Asia, Radcliffe-Brown, in *The Andaman Islanders*, gathered the various ideas held in the scattered communities throughout the islands concerning afterlife in the sky, under the earth, in the sea, or in the depth of the jungle; a fairly representative view (if any can be so called), he says, "is that when a man dies the spirit (*Lau*) . . . goes to another world that lies under this one and is called *Maramiku*. This world of spirits is said to be just like the actual world, with forest and sea, and all the familiar animal and vegetable species. The inhabitants spend their time just as the Andamanese do on earth, hunting, fishing and dancing" (p. 168).

[57]On the occurrence and function of such symbols in all religious thought, see Mary Douglas, *Natural Symbols: Explorations in Cosmology* (1970).

[58]English translation from the third edition, 1928.

multifarious, and called such a plethora of simultaneous meanings "over-determination" of the symbolic figments. What he did not consider—because it was not relevant to his research—was that those figments might have still other possible functions in a different, concomitant system of significance.[59] With the beginning of speech, symbolism entered a new era, the fully human era of hominid life; the primitive need in that evolutionary stage was to make assertions, trivial ones or sweeping cosmic ones, for the sake of self-affirmation and orientation in the world. That instinctive activity, which automatically created time, universe, and society, required material to fashion assertible propositions; and dream ideas were the readiest contents for eager, perhaps vehement assertions, particularly as dream images and events usually carry a somewhat disproportionate cargo of emotional feeling. Since savage listeners even today seem to sense no difference between fact and fiction, but treat all stories as real reports, the earliest speech-gifted men, whoever they were, presumably did the same, so a jumble of spontaneous fantasies was common property in each of the many small and scattered human hordes. Most of their dreamlike yarns, made up on the spur of the moment out of old and new, own and borrowed ideas, were probably told and forgotten; but some would be likely to appeal to the audience as well as to the inventor, and would be told over and over again. Presently the scene of such a story would be identified with some known place; that gave the beings in it a home.[60]

[59]In an article, "The Logic of Language," published almost fifty years ago (1932–33), N. Isaacs remarked the great range of the possible meanings that may accrue to a single word in the course of one user's life. "The different meanings," he wrote, "or at any rate a majority among them, are usually developed by different lines of derivation from some common centre, and can be ranged again round this centre. A given symbol, for which in any case only a vague typical meaning is at first formed, is applied by analogy to different kinds of things which resemble the original one in different respects; it is also extended from species to genus by dilution of its connotation; and it is transferred . . . from a process to its product, from whole to part, from an attitude to its object, etc. etc. At the same time, together with the new applications and the new meaning-formations arising out of them, the old ones are also carried along. Thus we get . . . the most extraordinary medley of relations between meanings of the most different fundamental types." Except in cases where a precise selection has been made, "all the meanings will be activated, but none fully, and a sort of composite resonance will be obtained."
[60]According to the Trobriand Islanders studied by Malinowski, mankind originally lived underground, in villages, and socially organized as it is on the surface of the earth today; it emerged from a hole in the ground near the village of Laba'i. The hole is there for anyone to see (title essay, *Magic, Science and Religion*, pp. 111–12). Similarly, the place to which the dead go is a known island, Tuma, only about ten miles from the Trobriands. "This island is inhabited by living men as well, who dwell in one large village, also called Tuma; and it is often visited by natives of the main island" ("Baloma: The Spirits of the Dead in the Trobriand Islands," *ibid.*, p. 150).

The favored fantasies are likely to have been richly overdetermined ones, which, while they gave many people some emotional catharsis, gave a few of them a mythical formulation of precocious insights which were not remotely ready, as yet, for literal statement: conceptions of life, with little distinction between human and animal or even plant life, and all the circumambient forces of nature, winds, waters, earthquake, and fire; beginnings, growth and its metamorphoses; and the intolerable, unbelievable breakdown of every personal life in death. Gradually, by dint of much repetition, connection with the fixed features of place and tribal activity, and the intrinsic emotional value of dream symbols, the tales that expressed an apprehension of such realities became traditional; and tradition, the greatest phyletic product of communication and assertion, is essentially sacred. At the same time those venerable stories were acted out in dance, while their personages were acknowledged in sacrificial rites; and as human mentality developed, even the thoughtless average person felt (rather than perceived) their import, so the myths were established without any decree, and became the basis of life and religion.

But what of the inconsistencies and even flat contradictions that would surely result from such a casual composition of ghost stories and animal fables into a body of serious beliefs, the basic beliefs of the tribe? The answer is that in tribal societies there frequently is no real body of myth, no coherent dogma at all, and contradiction does not trouble people.[61]

M. J. Meggitt, in his excellent book *Desert People: A Study of the Walbiri Aborigines of Central Australia* (1962), speaking of the totems by which that large tribe is organized and which in the native tongue are called "dreamings," as their mythical prehistory is called "the dreamtime," says: "All totems have originated in the dreamtime, and each has a local reference of some kind. . . . The local reference of a Walbiri dreaming may be a track . . . or a country. . . . Where a track is involved, dreaming-heroes or members of a dreaming species either entered Walbiri territory . . . or emerged from the earth at definite places within Walbiri bounds. They travelled about. . . . Their journeys may have covered 500 miles or more, but every place at which they halted is named and can be found today" (pp. 59–60).

[61] Thus Radcliffe-Brown, in *The Andaman Islanders*, p. 170, concludes from his many separate records: "In every tribe there are alternative and inconsistent beliefs as to the place where spirits go, which by different accounts is in the sky, beneath the earth, out to the east where the sun and moon take their rise, or in the jungle and sea of their own country. . . . There is no fixity or unanimity of belief amongst them." Malinowski, too, in "Baloma: The Spirits of the Dead in the Trobriand Islands," noted this lack of consistency in savage eschatology; see p. 150.

Middleton, in *Lugbara Religion*, p. 25, remarks: "Lugbara have no set of interconsistent beliefs as to the nature of man and the world. Their beliefs are significant in given situations." In an earlier passage concerning the Christian missions, he wrote: "Most Christians, evangelists and others, practise both some form of Christianity and their traditional rites, and find little difficulty in reconciling the beliefs belonging to each, as

[31]

They seem to think of a single narrative at a time, as one does with a fictitious story, but while they tell it or contemplate it thus in isolation they believe it.[62] Perhaps it were better to say that they "believe in" it; for they are excited by its meaning, which is not literally expressed, and affirm the ostensible facts without any "scientific attitude," i.e., without conceiving them factually and fitting them into a larger historical frame. Mythical incidents accrue to superhuman beings, representatives of man, whose adventures symbolize uncontrollable processes—birth, growth, passion, age, and in the world the changes of seasons, the coming and going of fish, birds, game, insect swarms—opportunities and threats, daily and nightly challenges to human power. Because the "culture heroes," deities, and spooks of primitive imagination are natural symbols, they are generally overdetermined, and the development of their implicit (and profoundly unconscious) interpretations in several directions makes different cycles of myth which are related only by being centered in one personage, not through story elements cohering with each other. Consequently, on the face of it, they look irrational, yet the contradictions do not trouble the believers.

The deep, unconscious, evolutionary motivation of myth, the early but driving effort to conceive world and man in terms of symbolic imagery and dreamlike action, is even more apparent in ritual than in story. Ritual is almost certainly older than narrative, because its materials are given in an entirely prehuman state of animal existence, with the rise of emotional, self-expressive movement. Such movement is unintentional, instinctive, perhaps even unconsciously performed. But it has two biological properties which destine it to become the stuff of symbolic rather than directly symptomatic expression: the tendency of habitual animal acts to become formalized, which supplies strict repetitious patterns of movement apart from immediate, close-fitted stimulations, and the fact

---

they are significant in different situations. All but a very small minority of Lugbara still accept their indigenous religious beliefs and teach them to their children; and they still practise the rites associated with them" (p. 3).

[62]Cf. Radcliffe-Brown, *The Andaman Islanders*, p. 188: "The Andamanese, to all appearance, regard each little story as independent, and do not consciously compare one with another."

In view of these well-established findings, it is surprising to meet Clyde Kluckhohn's statement in "Navaho Categories," p. 78: "Navaho beliefs and practices relating to the supernatural certainly constitute a ramified system. From the Navaho viewpoint everything is related to everything else. . . . Every ceremonial has a color, directional, sex, number, and sound symbolism. The intricacies remind one of the contrived systematic symbolism of Joyce's *Ulysses*." It is only upon reading his article that the unusual logicality of the beliefs of these Indians becomes self-explanatory.

that the expressive acts are visible to the performer and his fellows so that they, and he himself, experience the influence of a powerful suggestion. Both of these conditions have been discussed at some length in previous chapters,[63] and need only to be recalled here. Add to this the proneness of any specialized element of behavior, such as a purely self-expressive act without practical aim, to take on new functions,[64] and the invitation is given to develop symbolic gestures.

Such gestures, furthermore, may be overtly and also mentally addressed by their agent to another being, human or superhuman, real or visionary. Because the rite is an actual performance, the sacred objective, even if invisible, is given a convincing reality by the enactment of the attitude people bear toward it. This in turn fixes the attitude and articulates more detailed symbolic elements in the ritual, exploiting the expressive possibilities of gesture, posture, utterance, and sometimes the look and feeling of manipulated objects, in which some mysterious import is seen as an inherent quality, "holiness," until the addressed being takes shape for contemplation as deity, ancestral spirit, or totem.

The various beliefs in supernatural agents, enchanted places, staggered planes of existence, and the mythic past where everything began are not formed in succession, but grow up all together to produce the spirit-world. Malinowski maintained that savages made a clear distinction between "holy" and "profane." This may be true of the culture he observed and described,[65] but in general, the work of later anthropologists does not bear it out. Ritual runs through all the practical affairs of uncivilized peoples.[66] They do not need to think about creation, heaven, or the Ancestors to assume a religious attitude; they may be quite engrossed in carving up a wallaby or driving a hard bargain for a pearl shell or figuring

[63]For formalization see esp. Vol. II, p. 79; the subject is developed throughout Chapter 13. For suggestion, see Chapter 14, esp. pp. 129–30.

[64]Cf. Vol. I, Chapter 10, *passim*, esp. pp. 404 ff.

[65]Title essay, *Magic, Science and Religion*, *passim*.

[66]Natalie Curtis, in *The Indians' Book* (1907), one of the early collections of first-hand reports from Indian narrators of myths and legends, wrote: "In winter the Cheyennes often meet in little companies to play the 'hand-game.' . . . The game opens with a prayer, delivered by the one who may be, for the night, the leader of the game. In some tribes the hand-game is itself a religious ceremony, but this is not the case among the Cheyennes. With the Cheyennes, the details of the game may change with each night of the playing, so there is always a leader to direct the game. This leader has usually beheld in a dream the arrangement of the game . . . or he has been taught by some spirit how the game is to be played on the night of his leadership, for, with the Indian, even sports are divinely directed. Said an educated half-breed: 'I have been to school, and I have lived among white men, but I never saw any people so religious as my own. My people begin all things, even their games, with prayer'" (p. 161).

out the best use of their garden land for planting yams. But the division of meat is performed ceremoniously, the shell carries luck or may bring illness, and the planting of yams, in most tribal communities where they are an important staple, is accompanied by elaborate blessings and invocations by priests, shamans ("medicine-men," "clever-men"), or elders.

It is natural for a person reared in the atmosphere of European common sense to assume that the use of ritual in connection with ordinary, daily chores—gardening, hunting, fishing, handiwork—must have a practical aim, and to ask a native of forest or veldt how his work would be affected if the sacred forms were omitted. The native informant can only attempt to answer the question, which is meaningless to him, by saying that something would surely go wrong, the effort would not succeed. Perhaps he would be stimulated to improvise on the theme, and invent thinkable disasters, and tell them all as if they were generally expected results of such breaches, when in fact he had never thought of the proposed impiety in terms of an effect on the particular work in hand. The natural consequence that might occur to him would be "ghost sickness"—sent by angry dead progenitors—that might befall him or the whole society, for the omission would not be a technical error or folly, but a sacrilegious act, incurring personal punishment or general retaliation according to the feelings of the offended spirits.

The true need of weaving ritual actions into such quotidian occupations as planting, fishing, harvesting, and household chores is to give them a stamp of ancestral sanction, submitting them for approval to the assumed watchers and constant critics of the tribal life as it continues in its wonted way. There is no formal code for social customs except the round of rites that makes the patterns of sentiment on which anthropologists have often commented.[67] But such sentiments are supported by the belief, held in most tribal societies, that some "first beings" or one divine progenitor set the example for the daily, seasonal, or yearly activities of men, and the ancestors of the present generation continued them, so that the current ritual enactments express a sacred tradition.

In Europe, the advance of civilization, led more and more unmistakably by scientific thought, has steadily tended to break such traditions and relegate their expressions to private, elected styles of life or to religious institutions rarely binding, at the present day, on entire populations. The ascendancy of causal thinking has transformed the spirit-world into a

[67]Among these are Malinowski, Radcliffe-Brown, and V. W. Turner. The idea is old; Grace De Laguna stated it explicitly fifty years ago, and it has not been superseded by a stronger rival as yet.

mechanical world of impersonal progressive events, requiring other principles of explanation and expectation than concepts of impulse and agency. So it is a common belief among us that public ritual belongs to primitive cultures where, on a basis of false notions of cause, it is used as a means of controlling nature, but that of course it is out of place in the business of modern life. Yet there have been high civilizations which never abandoned their motivational conception of the world and never gave up their ritualized behavior in its frame. The civilization of ancient China rose to great heights, even to the creation of a recognized single empire, internally organized by feudal states or, at other times, by districts each with its hierarchy of crown officials that constituted a graded aristocracy. What made the formation of an empire possible at all under these early conditions was a ritual practice that was natural and acceptable to very lowly village communities and to the godlike emperor himself: the worship of one's own progenitors. This practice needed no studied organization, it fell of itself into a pattern of successive generations, a family seen in retrospect with the line of the worshipper's "fathers" running clearly through the web of agnatic parallels and affinic entrances. Ancestor worship is a familiar phenomenon to anthropologists the world over. It is known in Africa, in Australia, to some of the most naive savages, and to the sophisticated literati of China and Japan. It can take various forms, from real worship of totemic ancestral animal gods to the veneration of progenitors whose spirits, instead of being deified, are treated as continuing members of the living society.[68] The same essential rites can serve superstitious peasants to express their beliefs, and sages to attest their sense of social obligation and their loyalty to the emperor. The basic idea was understood everywhere.[69] The work of the great philosophers

[68]Jomo Kenyatta, president of the young republic of Kenya, in his anthropologically oriented *Facing Mount Kenya: The Tribal Life of the Gikuyu* (1956), explains the status of his people's departed forebears as follows: "The Gikuyu people have a clear idea and understanding of two supernatural elements. On the one hand is the relationship with the one High God, Ngai, which may accurately be termed one of worship. . . . when a sacrifice is made to the High God on an occasion of national (tribal) importance, the ancestors must join in making the sacrifice" (pp. 232–33). Ancestors, he makes clear, are revered, not worshipped. Thus, in a case of grave illness, when medical arts fail and the ancestors do not seem to have been offended, "the father of the family must organise the next appeal—to Ngai himself. He leads his kin in the approach to the almighty through a sacrifice. But the mortals do not go thus alone to Ngai. The living and the dead of the family now together approach the highest Power" (pp. 239–40).

[69]Hsün-tsu, in the sacred book that bears his name, remarked on the wide scope of meanings that might underlie the same symbolic expression when he wrote: "as to the height of loyalty, faithfulness, love and reverence, the richness of propriety and refinement—all these cannot be fully understood except by the sage. Sacrifice is something that

rested on the principle of self-education for public leadership by moral example and precept. Confucius had set up the idea of *jen*, or "humanity,"[70] which is the nearest an individual can come to the *tao*, or "perfect virtue"; Mencius expounded the idea of *yi*, the way to *jen*; it was Hsüntsu who saw that the method which implemented that approach was the regular enactment of rites, known as *li*, expressing emotional feeling, and by constant formal expression holding such feeling steady throughout life. *Li* is the dominant theme of his book, which teaches that the aim of a *chün-tsu*'s (cultivated man's) education is the refinement of feeling, from which superior behavior naturally follows. In the concept of ritual Hsün-tsu presents there is no element of efficacy, of safeguarding newborn children, soliciting luck, seeking aid from the dead, or forestalling their visitations. The rites are for the living, designed to clarify every moral situation as it arises and to offer an appropriate response largely preformed in phrase and gesture. The social demands are simple, though often, perhaps, onerous: perfect obedience to one's parents not only during one's childhood but as long as they live; reverent service to their souls when they die; lifelong homage, by periodic sacrifice, to the entire lineage of the family which the sacrificer now represents; and specific forms of respect in dealing with one's brothers according to one's own and their relative ages.

Filial duty and fraternal relations organized the Chinese family of the ancient empire, and were held sacred by men of high character. Their extensions made the pattern of moral values that underlay the social structure of the realm. In the words of Hsün-tsu, "*Li* rests on three bases: Heaven and earth, which are the source of life; forefathers and ancestors, who are the source of the human race; sovereigns and teachers, who are the source of government. . . . Therefore, *li* is to serve Heaven above and earth below, to honor forefathers and ancestors, and to exalt sovereigns and teachers." And further: "The *li* used on the occasion of birth is to adorn joy; the *li* used on the occasion of death is to adorn sorrow; the *li* used at sacrifice is to adorn reverence; the *li* used on military occasions is to adorn dignity. In this respect the rites of all the kings are alike, the ancient times and the present age agree; and no one knows whence they

---

the sage clearly understands, the scholar and *chün-tsu* [cultivated man] accordingly perform, officials consider as a duty, and the common people regard as established custom. Among *chün-tsu* it is considered to be the *Tao* [highest virtue] of a man; among the common people it is considered as having to do with spirits and ghosts" (C. Chai and W. Chai, eds. and trans., *The Sacred Books of Confucius and Other Confucian Classics* [1965], p. 253).

70I.e., human as against animal existence, dignified by both humanistic and humanitarian values.

came. Hence the grave and its tumulus are shaped like a house; the coffin is like a carriage screen and its cover. . . . Therefore the function of funeral rites is to make clear the meaning of death and life. . . . To serve the living is to adorn the beginning [of their life]; to send off the dead is to adorn their end. . . . The pattern of *li* and *yi* serves to send off the dead with as much respect as they enjoyed when they were alive, so as to cause both death and life, the end and the beginning, to be properly treated, and to be in accord with goodness."[71]

A society largely regulated by traditional rites—"no one knows whence they came"—seeping down through its illiterate populace from the highest seat of culture, the imperial court, and having vaguer and vaguer meaning until they become a magic instrument for banning ghosts, luring fish, and encouraging rice, is inevitably conservative, especially where the rituals of filial piety are combined with personal duties of absolute and indefinitely long obedience of children to their parents. To our age and outlook it seems that such an ideal must spell hopeless stagnation for the society that abides by it. Yet in its own day (Confucius lived in the sixth century B.C.) it may well be that no other organizing device could have held a vast domain of feudal fiefdoms and tribal territories together under a supreme ruler. Just because the rituals concerned universal human relations and expressed the attitudes appropriate to them, their basic meanings could be conceived on many levels, from the peasantry's primitive ancestor worship to the sage's contemplation of the cumulative values of life underlying the successive waves of death-bound generations; and the same pattern had a fitting high place for the emperor of sublime descent. So it was possible to make them binding on the whole population as a unifying form of behavior and belief.[72]

[71]Chai and Chai, *The Sacred Books of Confucius*, p. 242.

[72]Bernhard Karlgren, in *Sound and Symbol in Chinese* (2d ed., 1946; orig. publ. in Swedish, 1918), observed the same advantage in the use of the Chinese written language, which does not use letters representing sounds of a spoken language but symbols standing directly for the concepts meant by words: "Not only are the Chinese able, thanks to this excellent medium, to keep in contact with each other in spite of all the various dialects—so that, for instance, a paper printed in Peking is just as easily read in Canton—they are also capable of communicating intimately with the Chinese of past ages in a way that we can hardly realize. The literary language . . . has been essentially the same throughout the ages.

". . . The characters do not indicate the pronunciation of the words, and the Chinese of today have not the faintest idea how they were pronounced in ancient times. The consequence is that every Chinese reads the words of a literary text just as he pronounces them in his own modern dialect. Thus an edict issued in Peking can be read and understood everywhere in this vast country, but the Cantonese read it aloud in a way that sounds utter nonsense to a Pekinese" (pp. 37–38).

The classical Chinese ideal of morality was the cultivation of feeling, giving it form, rather than repressing it or letting it break loose in an uncontrolled flood. Hsün-tsu, especially, treated the rites or "proprieties" imposed on emotional behavior as receptacles to hold and convey and thereby articulate and modify one's feelings. So he wrote of the rites for the dead: "Why are there three years of mourning? . . . A bad wound remains for a long time; a severe hurt heals slowly; the three years' mourning arises because its rites and ceremonies are instituted in accordance with emotion. . . . Mourning garments, a rush staff, living in a hovel, eating rice gruel, using firewood for a mat and clods for a pillow— these practices are the expression of deepest sorrow. The three years' mourning is finished, and longings are not yet forgotten. This is what has been regulated by *li*. Does it not require that the funeral be terminated and ordinary life be returned at that time? . . . For this reason the early kings and sages established the mean and regulated the period of mourning to make it long enough to perform a series of appropriate and refined actions; only then is it to be laid aside."[73]

How completely free this ancient philosopher was from savage superstition appears in a subsequent passage, which attests the symbolic nature of ritual and certainly rejects any notion of bodily presence or participation in it by the dead: "to spread out tables and mats, to offer animals and grains, to pray for blessings as if the deceased enjoyed the sacrifice, to select and offer sacrifices as if the deceased would taste them, . . . to have a wine-flask ready as if the deceased would drink from the goblet . . . —all these are to express sorrow and reverence by serving the dead as if serving the living, serving the departed as if serving those who were present. What is served has neither substance nor shadow, yet this is the completion of propriety and refinement."[74]

So much, then, for pure ritual, "adorning" (Arthur Waley, in his translation, says "beautifying") expressive acts and formulating them to fit into the system of motives, impulses, and realizations that "natural symbols" present. The great Chinese moralists have developed that system as a basis for personal and public life, quite beyond what any modern Western philosopher has been able to construct in his own accepted terms of material causality. This fact corroborates the observation of the French philosopher Ignace Meyerson that the Asian civilizations, built on conceptions of impulse and act, motivation and realization, were not likely to yield a science of physics but might well produce advanced

[73]Chai and Chai, *The Sacred Books of Confucius*, p. 251.
[74]*Ibid.*, p. 254.

ethical theories; whereas the Western system of thought leads readily to scientific concepts and their amazing applications but not to any great understanding of human values.[75]

Yet, however far beyond popular mentality the thought of Chinese and Indian sages might go, it is certainly true that the vast majority of men all over the earth did and do meet their surrounding world of spirits— celestial, infernal, or intimately mundane—with magic, and that, in all but the most civilized societies or even small parts of these, ritual is used mainly for magical purposes. Psychologists have evinced surprisingly little theoretical interest in this universal human foible, apart from attempts by those who share various popular superstitions to "prove" their hypotheses concerning such processes, known as "mental telepathy," "extrasensory perception," and "thought control," by statistical demonstrations that the phenomena they would thus interpret do occur. The names given to the alleged abnormal events, of course, attach the theoretical interpretation to the very mention of them, so any skewed-looking table of statistics "proves" the fancied spiritual, electrical, magnetic, or frankly

[75]Discontinuités et cheminements autonomes dans l'histoire de l'esprit" (1948). The passages which explicitly or implicitly contain this general judgment are too scattered in Meyerson's text to be quoted here except for a few telling statements near the conclusion of his essay, e.g.: "La linguistique, l'ethnologie, l'histoire des religions, l'histoire de l'art comparées nous ont appris des longtemps que les suites des oeuvres de la Chine et de l'Inde par exemple étaient différentes de celles de la civilization européenne. Nous commençons à decouvrir que les fonctions psychologiques elles-mêmes, engagées dans ces oeuvres, sont dissemblables. Il ne s'agit pas là seulement d'une différence de rythme d'évolution, de régime de transformations, mais quelquefois de différences de nature profonde.

"Il y a une histoire européenne de l'objectivation et de l'objet. Elle est assez variée, mais c'est peut-être l'histoire de l'objet de la physique qui frappe le plus. Elle a été d'abord substantification. Longtemps l'objet de la physique a participé des propriétés de l'objet du sens commun. . . . Il y a encore une vingtaine d'années, de très emminents épistemologistes consideraient que la physique resterait toujours substantialiste. Mais quelques années plus tard, Cassirer a pu écrire que le substantialisme a été l'entrave dont la physique devait se débarrasser. . . . Mais ni Cassirer, ni aucun autre philosophe des sciences n'a écrit: la physique aurait pu suivre une autre voie que celle de son histoire réelle. Le passage par la substance a été necessaire.

"La pensée indienne, tournée plus vers les actes que vers les choses, semble avoir été dès l'origine une objectivation sans substance. . . . Specialement le bouddhisme a marqué l'importance du procès, de la tension, de la série à coté desquels les états apparaissent comme fugitifs et evanescents. Concurrement, la pensée indienne n'a pas conduit à une physique; n'est-ce pas précisément parce qu'elle était peu substantialiste? . . . dans les Brähamanes et dans les Upaniṣads, dans le Yoga, dans le Samkhya: interêt tourne vers le microcosme, analyse du sujet connaissant, autonomie de l'être intérieur, discipline des techniques du corps. . . . La critique bouddhiste même de l'âme et du moi, dont on sait l'âpreté, montre que la notion avait une force et une forme à cette époque" (pp. 285–87).

magical nature of mysterious happenings.[76] Anthropologists, too, have been content to record the practices of magicians and the effects on their clients, apparently without seeing any significance for the theoretical aspect of their science in the intriguing problem of such a fundamental tendency to unrealism in the most intelligent animal.

The fact is that the answer, which I think is not unattainable, is none the less rather difficult and elusive because it involves many coincident conditions, some of them reaching back to animal mentality, others of purely human character impinging on them to produce peculiar developments of imaginative expectancy and dreamlike, often nightmarish belief. The paramount importance of magic in savage life is certainly not easily accounted for along Darwinian lines of reasoning, though retrospectively it may fit into them well enough. But it is so central to man's life in a spirit-world that the serious discussion of it must be deferred to the next chapter.

---

[76]See, for example, Ronald Rose's *Living Magic* (1957), p. 217, where one finds: "But aboriginal [Australian] magic has its reality, for E.S.P. is real, the powers of suggestion and hypnotism are real, and the results achieved by a wide variety of tricks and devices are real.

"Aboriginal magic is . . . not to be despised; for in it we find practitioners achieving results in mental phenomena that have puzzled us for some time, exercising a subtle art, . . . in many ways a model for our future investigation into some of man's strangest powers."

A. P. Elkin, in *Aboriginal Men of High Degree* (n.d. [ca. 1945]), p. 53, writes: "Psychical research is now suggesting that the holding of an article which has been in the possession of, or in contact with, an absent person, puts the 'sensitive' *en rapport* with such subject, and then she (or he) can read the latter's mind." All very fantastic claims of medicine-men, such as Duke University would hardly dare to check, he attributes to suggestion, hypnotism, or otherwise induced trance.

In a foreword to Arthur E. Waite's scholarly and informative work *The Book of Ceremonial Magic: The Secret Tradition in Goetia* (1961), p. viii, John C. Wilson says: "Waite himself . . . is a Kabbalist. He struggled throughout his creative life with the problem of the connection between the Kabbalah that he espoused and the magic indelibly associated with it throughout its history."

20

The Dream of Power

TO SAY that psychologists and other investigators have spent relatively little theoretical thought on the etiology of the world-wide,
persistent belief in magic is, of course, not to say that no one has attempted to construct a theory to account for that seemingly ùn-zoological
behavior pattern. But the psychological explanations which so far have
been proposed are frail scaffoldings for so ubiquitous and central a phenomenon, which is really the most perplexing practice in precivilized
life, where all serious undertakings are accompanied, if not dominated,
by supposedly efficacious ritual: curing sickness, or, on the contrary,
inflicting sickness, killing people; making rain (in many regions of earth,
the prime concern of the "medicine man" or "medicine woman"); controlling the movements of game, fish, and fowl; calling plants up out of
the soil to bear fruit; and diagnosing the nature of diseases according to
their magical or supernatural origins. In some societies all sickness is
attributed to witchcraft, sorcery, or spiritual influences.[1] These are only
the ordinary uses of magic. More extravagant examples are the alleged
achievements of magicians flying through the air, often to remote places
and back in the twinkling of an eye, perhaps to heaven,[2] or climbing a

[1]This was one of the first incredible findings of anthropologists in Australia. At the turn
of the century, Emile Durkheim and Marcel Mauss, in "De quelques formes primitives
de classification" (1901–2), noted the general entertainment of that belief, saying: "On
sait que, dans toutes ces sortes de sociétés, la mort n'est jamais considérée comme un
événement naturel, dû à l'action des causes purement physiques; elle est presque toujours
attribuée à l'influence magique de quelque sorcier, et la détermination du coupable fait
partie intégrante des rites funéraires" (p. 12). L. Frobenius, at the same time, called the
medicine-man's interrogation of the corpse as to who committed the murder "a clownish
farce" (Aus den Flegeljahren der Menschheit [1901]). Later anthropologists have, of
course, viewed the peculiar phenomena with more respectful wonder, as, for instance,
Barrie Reynolds, A. P. Elkin, M. J. Meggitt, and Margaret Mead, whose work has been
or will be discussed here.
[2]Natalie Curtis, in The Indians' Book, p. 323, quotes a noted warrior and "man of
medicine" who sang one of his songs for her: "This is a holy song (medicine song), and
great is its power. The song tells how, as I sing, I go through the air to a holy place where
Yusun will give me power to do wonderful things. I am surrounded by little clouds, and as
I go through the air I change, becoming spirit only."

rope which is made to issue from the magician himself and stand on end, or cutting up a person, sometimes his own body, and subsequently restoring it to wholeness and life.[3] The hypotheses which anthropologists and psychologists have proposed to account for so unlikely a method to attain practical results as the recitation of words, especially names, in long formulas[4] and the manipulation of "medicines"—leaves, bits of clay, or less aesthetic substances, birds' down, human blood, plus all the potent ingredients that went into the cauldron of Macbeth's weird sisters—have been mainly in terms of emotion, need, intense desire, and "wishful thinking." Again, as one might expect, it was that great pioneer Malinowski who remarked (in a passage previously cited[5]) on the ubiquity of magic among "primitive" people, and offered his own rational explanation of it,[6] which seems to have satisfied most of his successors: "Man, engaged in a series of practical activities, comes to a gap; the hunter is disappointed by his quarry, the sailor misses propitious winds . . . [etc.]. Forsaken by his knowledge, baffled by his past experience . . . he feels his impotence. Yet his desire grips him only the more strongly; his anxiety, his fears and hopes, induce a tension in his organism which drives him to some substitute activity. Obsessed by the idea of the desired end, he sees it and feels it. His organism reproduces the acts suggested by the anticipations of hope, dictated by the emotion so strongly felt. . . .

"These reactions to overwhelming emotion or obsessive desire . . . engender what could be called extended expressions of emotion in act and word. . . .

" . . . First there surges a clear image of the desired end, of the hated person, of the feared danger or ghost. . . . When passion reaches its breaking point at which man loses control over himself, the words which

---

[3]Mircea Eliade, in the article already referred to (above, p. 10, n. 13), "Remarques sur le 'rope trick,'" describing the fakir's ascent of the rope, also gives an account of dismembering and then restoring an apprentice. The "trick" seems to have been less successful in Europe than further east, as he writes, "Voici comment le magicien Johann Philadelphia se produisit à Göttingen, en 1777: il fut coupé en morceaux et mis dans un tonneau. Mais, celui-ci ayant été ouvert trop tôt, on y trouva un embryon, et comme celui-ci n'avait pas pu évoluer, le magicien ne revint plus à la vie."

[4]The extreme instance of this kind of invocation was found by E. Shortland in New Zealand and other Pacific islands inhabited by the Maori, who rehearsed the names of all their known or supposed ancestors in prayers called *karakia*, in due order of age. Of these worshippers he wrote, "The cause of the preservation of their Genealogies becomes intelligible when we consider that they often formed the groundwork of their religious formulas, and that to make an error or even hesitation in repeating a *karakia* was deemed fatal to its efficacy" (*Maori Religion and Mythology* [1882], p. 11).

[5]See above, p. 6, n. 6.

[6]A. R. Radcliffe-Brown cites a predecessor, Alfred F. Loisy, who proposed a similar explanation in 1920. See below, pp. 63–64.

he utters, his blind behavior, allow the pent-up physiological tension to flow over. But over all this outburst presides the image of the end. It . . . directs words and acts towards a definite purpose. The substitute action in which the passion finds its vent . . . has subjectively all the value of a real action, to which emotion would, if not impeded, naturally have led.

"As the tension spends itself in these words and gestures and the obsessing visions fade away, the desired end seems nearer satisfaction, we regain our balance, once more at harmony with life. And we remain with a conviction that the words of malediction and the gestures of fury have traveled towards the hated person and hit their target. . . . In brief, a strong emotional experience, which spends itself in a purely subjective flow of images, words, and acts of behavior, leaves a very deep conviction of its reality, as if of some practical and positive achievement, as if of something done by a power revealed to man."[7]

Psychologically, the gestures which usually constitute a magical performance might well be regarded as substitute acts where no physically effective action is possible. Yet in view of the popularity of magic despite its causally inappropriate techniques, its unfailing, ubiquitous presence and especially its long persistence make such an explanation seem inadequate; they point to some deeper roots. I find it hard to believe that an accepted type of conduct which pervades all but a small fraction of human social life and forms a basis, in large measure, of individual status and even tribal power[8] should be essentially a by-product of despair or fury. In our own society a person in utter desperation or driven by hate might resort to occult practices, but it is unlikely that his fellow men, young and old, would expect to see a miracle take place in response to his behavior.

The reason why the emotive theory found such ready acceptance was probably the recent impact, at the time when it was proposed, of Freud's psychoanalytic doctrine, with its powerful concepts of symbolic sub-

---

[7]*Magic, Science and Religion*, pp. 79–81 *passim*.
[8]See, e.g., R. F. Fortune, *Sorcerers of Dobu*, p. 171, where it is said, in connection with possession of magic power, "It must be remembered that magic is an element of social prestige." The same evaluation is assumed by A. P. Elkin in *Aboriginal Men of High Degree*, when he says: "It is common in primitive and civilized societies for a father to desire that his son should succeed him in his social and professional position, and to help him to do so. The sphere of magic and religion is no exception to this tendency" (p. 26). As for magic as a political asset, M. J. Meggitt observed in *Desert People*, p. 41: "Walbiri relations with Pintubi are in many respects less happy than with the other Pidjandjara. Their attitude toward these people is tinged, if not with fear, at least with respect for their magical powers."

stitutes for repressed or frustrated action and of the unconscious and irrational origin of symbols, which had thrown a veritable bombshell into the psychological field. Freud's dream analyses, revealing the systematic substructure of dream thoughts progressively generating the phantasmagoria of the manifest dream content, his application of the same principles to the experience of normal, waking people in *The Psychopathology of Everyday Life*,[9] and especially his venture into anthropology in *Totem and Taboo*[10] made a deep impression on several ethnologists, as Malinowski's *Sex and Repression in Savage Society* (1927) bears convincing witness.[11]

Deep, unconscious desires and fantasies are undoubtedly expressed in the symbolic gestures and words of magicians. So are they in the fabrication of myth, where they probably have furnished the dreamlike stuff of the assertions that have come casually and uncritically together to make some strange articles of belief. But magic, even more than superstition, legend, or cosmogony, is only incidentally a vehicle for symbolic expression of desires. It may be used where the magician has no personal concern, but is hired to implement someone else's aims. Magic may be practiced by amateurs or professionals, and among the latter it has its specialists in different lines.[12] It is always mystical and fascinating, with some touch of the supernatural, but does not seem unnatural;[13] for in magic-practicing societies the distinction between earthly and unearthly powers is not sharp.

To understand the ubiquitous, everyday acceptance of magic one has to realize what it means to live in a spirit-world: far more than to live in

[9]Originally published in a German edition in 1901.

[10]Originally published in *Imago* in 1912–13 as "Über einige Übereinstimmungen im Seelenleben der Wilden und der Neurotiker."

[11]Among others, Geza Roheim, Victor W. Turner, and C. G. Seligman.

[12]Clyde Kluckhohn, in "Navaho Categories," p. 74, wrote that "'diagnosticians' seldom carry out other ceremonials. Divination is a specialty, and Navahos rather generally assume implicitly it is an exclusive one. In fact, some evidence . . . indicates that strong temperamental and selective factors operate to distinguish between 'diagnosticians' and other ceremonialists. All other ceremonies are learned; one becomes a diagnostician by a sudden gift."

Elkin, too, in *Aboriginal Men of High Degree*, says of "doctors" of the Anula tribe in Australia that "their powers consist of giving 'bones,' and not of withdrawing evil magic. This sole evil function distinguishes them from the medicine-men of other tribes. In serious cases, the natives have to call in the assistance of a medicine-man from some friendly tribe" (p. 127).

[13]". . . while the medicine-man is considered to possess great power and faculties especially developed, none of his power is regarded as *extra-ordinary*, or abnormal. It is possessed and exercised against an accepted background of belief, and in some degree, though usually in a very slight degree, it is possessed by all" (Elkin, *Aboriginal Men of High Degree*, p. 23).

the ambient which to modern men—especially those with a European heritage—is "reality," only with a large cargo of spooks and fanciful beliefs thrown in. It means to live not among things, which may be used, ignored, or destroyed, and which may have been produced by skillful handling of materials according to physical laws, but to live among hosts of agents largely non-human, whose ways of action are inscrutable, their means often invisible, their wills autonomous. Things, however produced or originated, need not be anthropomorphized to seem capable of hearing, responding, or refusing their part in human actions.[14] Clouds need not be thought of as persons in order to be called to assemble and bring their gifts of water. No one sees how they carry it or how they pour it out in drops; and it is perfectly natural for such beings then to make themselves invisible again. In a similar way, fire dwells unseen in slivers of bamboo and, by passing the sliver, saw-fashion, through a larger piece of its own wood, can be enticed to appear as flame, slowly born in a brightening, smoke-breathing red glow.

The making of the spirit-world surely belongs to a very early era of human history—in fact, to the beginning of any history. It probably goes back as far as the rise of language, and like that greatest of man's assets rests on deeply buried, species-specific organic conditions. One of these came to light, in the teen-years of the present century, through a surprising observation made by Wolfgang Köhler on the chimpanzees in his ape colony, which showed a striking difference between simian and human perceptual acts. It impressed everybody with the curious shortcoming of the ape's mentality, but no one seems to have seen its implication for the human departure, the overdevelopment and progressive specialization of the brain that has set the track of our evolution inestimably far apart from that of any other primate.

The talent in question is so familiar, so common to all people on earth that we are simply unconscious of it as a special possession: our ability to project our own bodily feelings of balance or imbalance into other physical objects, real or even only apparent, that is given to us solely through vision. To a human being every laterally symmetrical, upright form expresses the feeling of balance he maintains in his own body when he stands erect; every asymmetry suggests falling, being pushed out of the vertical. It is perfectly possible for us to "see" a center of gravity, sometimes in a purely visual presentation such as a picture, where no mechan-

[14]See Curtis, *The Indians' Book*, p. 298: "'Everything has its song,' say the Kwakiutls; 'Every person, every animal, and every thing has its song and its story.' Even objects have songs either connected directly with the object itself or through the association of song and object in ceremonial. So there is a song belonging to each totem-pole."

ical supports and no fulcral points actually exist. We know by sight how far the foot of a ladder must be from a wall against which the top of it leans to keep the ladder from falling away from the wall. This is not an instinctive judgment; young babies cannot make it. But the ability to learn it is one of our special powers. In a very short time after a child begins to build with blocks it recognizes the gravitational relationships between uprights and lintels, leaning blocks and their supports. Its eye replaces the experimenting hand, and projects the feelings of balance or imbalance into its visual image of the little structures. In viewing objects much too large for a weighing hand—rocks, buildings, statues—a human being, even a child beyond babyhood, can "see" poise and counterpoise, weight distribution, security or "top-heaviness." Köhler aptly referred to this insight as our system of "naive statics."

Other primates, monkeys and even the great apes, seem incapable of projecting bodily feeling into forms presented to the eye. Köhler made systematic observations on his chimpanzees as the animals piled up boxes to reach a lure hung from the ceiling and attempted to use a ladder to the same end. Apes are extremely visual-minded, at least as much so as men; their bodily experience of balance is highly developed; yet they seem to make no spontaneous transfer of situational response from one sensory mode to another, i.e., from their body sense to their visual sense. So, in *The Mentality of Apes* (1931) Köhler wrote: "the total impression of all observations made repeatedly on the animals leads to the conclusion that *there is practically no statics to be noted in the chimpanzee.* . . . One may observe very similar facts in the first years of childhood. . . . But while human children, when about three years old, begin to develop the elements of this naive physics of equilibrium, the chimpanzee does not seem to make any essential progress in this direction, even when he has plenty of opportunity to practise. . . . Structures grow under his hand, and often enough he can climb them, but they are structures which, according to the rules of statics, seem to us almost impossible" (pp. 149–51).

The same lack of mechanical insight appeared with regard to objects too long and thin, such as sticks, planks, or ladders, to stand up on end. Köhler said of his brightest ape: "When Sultan first made use of the ladder . . . his handling of it looked very strange. Instead of leaning it against the wall near which the fruit was hanging from the roof, he set it up in the open space directly under the objective in a vertical position, and tried to climb up it. . . . As this method meets with no result, it is altered. Sultan leans the ladder against the wall. . . , but quite differently from the way we do, so that one of the uprights rests against the wall, the

plane of the ladder extending into the room." Several other apes did the
same thing; from which the observer concluded: "The placing of the
ladder has certainly been decided by the urge to bring about visual con-
tiguity between ladder and wall. . . . The ladder which is in contact with
the wall by the length of one upright, or by the whole face of the rungs
[i.e., flat against the wall, another occasional placement] is *optically in
closer contact* than if it were supported at four points—the two extremities
of each upright—as in our human fashion. It is then statically rightly
placed, but probably appears to the chimpanzee to be "not firm," just as
his favourite position does to *us*" (p. 162).

I doubt that it seems "not firm" to the ape; it does not reach quite as
high when it is leaned, nor does it point so directly at the ceiling as when
it is held flat against the wall. Firmness only comes into consideration
when he begins to climb, and the structure wobbles.[15] Visually, the
ladder or the piled boxes look neither firm nor infirm to his eyes; and that
is the interesting point. Any object an animal uses instrumentally is an
extension of its body, more like a prosthesis than a tool. Köhler remarked
on this fact, but few other observers have realized it, since they themselves, when using even casual sticks and stones to implement an
intended act, regard those things as tools and can hardly conceive of a
ladder or a construction of boxes in any other way. To the ape, however,
a stick is an elongation of his own limbs, and piling up boxes is no more
"making an instrument" than to us the leveling of a bed to lie down and
sleep; their building is modifying the terrain for a jump or a long reach,
and is part of the jumping or reaching act, which thereby is already in
progress.

Another of Köhler's observations supports the idea that external objects
enter an animal's awareness only as elements in its own acts, and in doing
so are assimilated to its behavior and treated as parts of itself. "The
animals," he said, "partly replace the missing (everyday) statics of human
beings by . . . that of their own bodies, which is taken care of automatically by a special neuro-muscular machinery. In this respect, the chimpanzee, it seems to me, is even superior to man. . . . When he is standing on a structure, the balance of which would fill an onlooker with fear,
the first suspicious wobbling of the structure is counteracted in the most
masterly fashion by an instantaneous altering of the balance of the body,
by lifting his arms, bending his trunk, etc., so that the boxes, under the
animal, to a certain extent, share the statics of his labyrinth and cere-
bellum. It can be said that in a great number of these constructions the

[15]See *The Mentality of Apes*, p. 151.

animal itself, with the delicately-balanced distribution of its weight, con-
tributes a certain element, without which the structure would collapse"
(p. 152).

Evidently the ape's static sensations are in no way "projected" into the
visual aspect of objects in his surroundings. They are kept strictly at home
in his kinesthetic and equilibrant mechanisms, which may be the reason
why his bodily balance, unconfused by suggestive virtual presentations, is
generally superior to man's. We have sacrificed some of our athletic
ability in developing our peculiar talent for seeing, as well as physically
feeling, gravitational relationships. But the new talent, small though it
may seem as a step in evolution, was far from small, and indeed was well
worth the sacrifice; for the mental act of "projecting" a subjective element
into a percept given to a distance receptor such as the eye is an act of
objectification. It lets the subjective element come back as an impingement and be perceived as an external datum, i.e., as a quality belonging
to an independently existing object; and that object, which thus presents
our own sensory feeling to us, is a primitive symbol, conveying the first
retainable idea of an all-important sensation and, at first perhaps solely,
the possibility of its loss. Body feelings may be the first thing man projected and thus, all unwittingly, imputed to everything he objectified as
material bodies in his world. The very existence of "things" is modeled
on his own inward expectation of strains, directions, and limitations of
his felt actions; the wholeness and simplicity of molar objects is that of his
own soma. To this day we speak of "heavenly bodies," meaning in-
organic masses of minerals and gases, and near the other end of the
magnitude scale we term the tiniest mote in a person's eye a "foreign
body." By comparison with our own frame, we refer to the parts of our
earthly environment as the "foot" of a mountain, an "arm" of the sea,
etc., and, in a humbler context, the "neck" of a bottle and the "legs" of a
chair. This kind of analogizing has been remarked so often that it requires
no further comment; but its origin in the projection of subjective feeling
into the external world is not generally recognized, nor is the biological
novelty of that process appreciated as the crucial evolutionary event it
seems to have been.

The reflection of our own bodily sensations in outward things, animate
and inanimate, gives those things a symbolic function, but on so low a
level that one can hardly call them symbols; their conceptual value is
entirely embedded in the presenting form; there is no hint of an abstract
thought inspired by their appearance of balance or imbalance, danger or
security. Even today those elements impinge most directly on our faculties as qualities of the things perceived, and in the case of primitive men

could at best have appeared in that way. Yet they are the basis of that conceptual seeing which S. T. Coleridge called "primary imagination,"[16] and which appears to be a hominid specialty. It is for this reason that mind is a purely human phenomenon, evolved from a unique mental proclivity, and that a treatise on mind is an essay on human feeling.

The objectification of the subjective sense of balance—and, perhaps, of physical tensions generally—has a natural counterpart, the subjectification of the protosymbolic object as an image. The feeling projected into the well- or badly balanced external object comes back to its producer as an image of equilibrium, secure or precarious as it may be; the object looks centered or off-center. On the same principle all other kinesthetic, thermal, tactual, in short: corporeal feelings are "seen" in the shapes that meet our eyes, and give such shapes the meaning of spatial entities, potential opportunities for action if not actual ones at the moment; they confront us as possible implements, obstacles, more or less permanent carriers of their own qualities. The recognition of characteristics like form, relation, and every sort of meaning is the lowest denominator of intellect, the function of intuition.

The development of that faculty must be very ancient in man, and may have gone through many apparently useless steps before the dawn of voluntary imagination and of symbolic thought beyond the production of dream. Today, when that first dawn is fairly far behind us, man's entire way of perceiving is shot through and through with intuition. In all our seeing there is the dialectical interchange of objectification and subjectification, external dictate and autogenic creation—"*La recréation du réel,*" Philippe Fauré-Fremiet called it.[17] This dialectic, so highly developed in contemporary man, savage or civilized, that it functions automatically below the level of consciousness, is "experience" in the distinctively human sense. Our sole contact with the world around us is through our sense organs, yet they are also the gate-keepers, the electors and composers of what the mind accepts; they formulate, even in the swiftest transmission, the images it retains, the sensory impingements it will imbue with feeling and find significant; that constant dialectic of projection and symbolically transformed "feedback" is the dynamism of experience.[18]

To see our ambient as a homogeneous and permanent space furnished

[16]*Biographia Literaria*, chap. 13, esp. the last section.
[17]In *La re-création du réel et l'équivoque* (1940). Cf. above, Vol. I, pp. 100–103.
[18]This is an interesting parallel to the observation made by William Montagna on the human skin, the dividing surface that both sets apart and connects each organism with its ambient. See above, Vol. I, pp. 419 ff. and, for Montagna, the notes.

with other bodies besides our own is the modulus of intuitive perception; as we project our muscular and gravitational sense into those external things we also, just as involuntarily, see our other feelings reflected in their shapes, which consequently seem to present attitudes—threatening or peaceable, tense or free or somnolent. And with expressive attitudes they objectify emotional feelings, which seem to be in them, even when they do not happen to be ours at the moment.

Weeping willows drop no tears and heave no sobs, yet look mournful; swift little brooks laugh, robins sound happy, the wood thrush's note has a yearning quality that belongs to the tone rather than the pattern of its call. Above all, the skies may look benign or angry, breakers may howl and tower, trees loom and shake their branches, and all the individuated forms of nature appear as so many potential agents which "have" the attitudes and impulses they display symbolically. Heinz Werner gave this stage of symbolic intuition the name "physiognomic seeing," a perception of expressiveness which may not only accompany, but, in naive minds, even precede any clear comprehension of the physical shape and properties of a confronting object. Before the full development of language people's conception of "things" may frequently have gone no further than that.[19]

These earliest forms of symbolic response probably did not arise in due succession, one upon the other, but in confusion, each unfolding aspect furthering some related or quite unrelated advance, gathering force in the intellectual dimension (here, the imaginative), while cutting off forever some of the pristine potentialities of the lineage. In this way the growing functions of the overstimulated, differentiating human brain carved out the channels that were to carry the flood of myths and dream figments. At the same time there must have been a beginning of realistic concern for the future, a dawning awareness of the constant threat of disasters, attacks by disease or violence, starvation, the scourge of fire, flood, or lightning. But such possibilities could hardly be conceived apart from any actual occurrence, without a symbol in the prevailing mode of spontaneous, concrete envisagement, which is the dream mode; so whatever sounds in nature were heard as voices and whatever objects, shadows, or creatures showed a fearful aspect became nightmare figures to embody the menacing powers. Only then could names be given to them, which served equally as common and proper nouns, i.e., designated both the idea and its mythical incarnation.[20]

[19]Cf. Vol. II, pp. 294 ff.
[20]The gradual emergence of the concept from its original "personified" symbol is clearly exhibited in the depersonification of mythical characters in Greek literature, where

By this process the human race has surrounded itself with countless superhuman wills and powers, all the forces of nature converging on it with intent to devour or extinguish its members upon the slightest occasion or even without any motivation except to exercise their caprice. There is no defense against such agents in fisticuffs or showers of arrows. But, as those enemies were creations of the over-excitable, over-growing hominid brain, the only opposition they could encounter was a contrary action of that same great mental organ, which strove to control them even while it constantly and profusely engendered them. The creative function, of course, is always far below the psychical limen; the defensive activity is equally spontaneous, but consciously directed against the symbols already formed, which in dream are the manifest content and in waking life the gods, ghosts, and demons of the spirit-world.

The mainspring of magical thinking is as deeply buried as that of symbol-making. The edifice of mind is so complex that the evolution of magic is as polyphyletic as that first un-animalian function, symbolization. All of the chance conditions and concomitant developments that have entered into magical practices—ardent desire, frustration, concentration of thought to the point of self-hypnotism—have been looked upon as its source; but its phylogenetic origin lies below them all, on the physiological level where even the highest cerebral impulses work and are felt before they take any distinct psychical form. It is the feeling of mental activity—of an invisible doing—that underlies the notion of exerting a non-mechanical influence on the course of events, without physical contact, without push or pull on the external objects and persons involved.

The magic-monger's apparent ignorance of causal relations, which has been the most puzzling aspect of savage mentality to anthropologists and missionaries alike (traders seldom worried their heads about it), is not simply ignorance at all, but a matter of evaluation. Causal relations are known well enough, but they are taken for granted;[21] the primary purpose

---

the custom of referring to abstractions by the names of minor divinities embodying them persisted as a traditional form far beyond the metaphorical phase of conception. H. J. Rose, in *A Handbook of Greek Mythology* (1959, orig. ed. 1928), p. 23, says: "Hesiod gives . . . a whole list of abstractions mostly unconnected with myth and cult alike and their relations to one another." As children of Night he names Fate, Doom, Death, Sleep, Dream, Grumbling, Old Age, Pain, and Strife (Eris); the last of these bore Forgetfulness, Famine, Woes, Strifes, Battles, Slaughters, Manslayings, Quarrels, False Words, Disputes, and a few other *personae non gratae*.

[21] Dr. Fortune, in *Sorcerers of Dobu*, p. 98, says of these Pacific islanders: "Technology and mundane measures are by no means despised, for they are often essential and are recognized as such; but it is most firmly believed that agricultural technology alone and gift-giving and serenading alone . . . will never grow yams or induce love."

of techniques is to implement magical processes. Those processes are essentially symbolic and their important functions conceptual; that is why imaginary results are so easily satisfactory.[22] The counter-force to the spirit-world is the human mind at its center.

The conception of an activity, such as thought, without any physical phenomenon to show for it was surely quite impossible for the earliest thinking beings, as it is for some people, not only savages, even now. But the symbolific tendency in those dawning intellects took care of that. Every stirring conception would activate some fantasy to illustrate it, and every illustration become at once the symbol and embodiment of the thought it conveyed; and somewhere among all the shapes in surrounding nature this imagined form would be suggested and emerge as a reality, the product of the clearly felt act of thinking, the invisible work of the conjurer. A monstrous figure seen in the trunk of a twisted tree would make that concrete object as convincingly a ghost tiger or a bush devil as the tree which it also was.

The basis of such creations is a very common trait of human beings (perhaps not strictly limited to them) which certainly has long been known, though not seriously studied until about a century ago: the principle of perceptual interpretation, or "gestalt." Percepts, as everyone recognizes today, are not the pure sense data that naive empiricism assumed; they are, quite literally, what we make out of the sensations that impinge on our receptors. Especially visual gestalten are heavily dependent on the organization given to them by the percipient's way of looking at things: the focus of his eyes and of his attention, his choice (usually unconscious) of perspective, and the spontaneous action of the visual organ that causes any strong line closing on itself to become, as with a jump, the contour of

[22]Any little physical help the magic requires is easily discounted. W. W. Skeat, in his serious and rich study *Malay Magic*, describes the nature and potency of "Bezoar stones," concretions sometimes found in animal bodies, and his experience with them, as follows: "The Bezoar stones known to the Peninsular Malays are usually obtained either from monkeys or porcupines. Extraordinary magical virtues are attached to these stones, the gratings of which are mixed with water and administered to the sick.

"I was once asked $200 for a small stone which its owner kept in cotton-wool in a small tin box, where it lay surrounded by grains of rice, upon which he declared it fed. I asked him how it could be proved that it was a true Bezoar stone (which it undoubtedly was not), and he declared that if it were placed upon an inverted tumbler and touched with the point of a *k'ris* (dagger) or a lime-fruit it would commence to move about. Both tests were therefore applied in my presence, but the motion of the Bezoar stone in each case proved to be due to the most overt trickery on the part of the owner, who by pressing on one side of the stone (which was spherical in shape) naturally caused it to move; in fact I was easily able to produce the same effect in the same way, as I presently showed him, though of course he could not be brought to admit the deception."

an area.[23] Most people have had the experience of looking at a honeycomb pattern, for instance in a spread of hexagonal tiles, and seeing the hexagons organized in different groupings according to whichever tile is chosen as the center (Fig. 20–1). Such patterns generally convey no meaning except for the organization of space which they help to effect. Yet there is a modicum of interest, even for sober, civilized adults, in playing at changing their arrangement simply by a shift of attention from one central form, briefly held steady, to another that brings a different pattern into prominence. All the designs are there all the time; but when one is selected the others disappear. They cannot be combined, only alternated. At the same time the display itself of perfectly similar forms is difficult to see as such because it falls so readily into figurations on a precarious, tentative background that threatens at every moment to swamp the virtual array and alter the focus-created image.

A similar phenomenon may be produced in a more complex visual experience, where a further potentiality of the form-perceptive primate eye comes into play, i.e., the rapid diminution of object size with dis-

[23]See Norbert Wiener, *Cybernetics; or Control and Communication in the Animals and the Machine* (1948), p. 156: "We can use and interpret line-drawings because somewhere in the visual process, outlines are emphasized and some other aspects of an image are minimized in importance. The beginning of the process is in the eye itself." And further: because of a different rate of fluctuation of focus induced by homogeneous and by heterogeneous areas of stimulation, "the eye receives its most intense impression at boundaries, and . . . every visual image in fact has something of the nature of a line drawing" (p. 159).
The mechanism of such outline emphasis was carefully and beautifully analyzed by W. H. Marshall and S. A. Talbot in a long article, "Recent Evidence for Neural Mechanisms in Vision Leading to a General Theory of Sensory Acuity" (1942), but the analysis is too complicated to be summarized in a footnote, so the interested reader can only be directed to the source.
There is also an interesting article by Floyd Ratliff ("Inhibitory Interaction and the Detection and Enhancement of Contours" [1961]), who found a simplified exhibition of the same principle in the compound eye of the horseshoe crab, Limulus, where the ommatidia affect each other to produce a similar enhancement of outlines, though their mutual influences are only inhibitory. In summary, he says: "These interactions accentuate contrast at sharp spatial and temporal gradients and discontinuities in the retinal image: borders and contours become 'crisp' in their neural representation. Thus, the pattern of optic-nerve activity that results is by no means a direct copy of the pattern of stimulation on the receptor mosaic; certain information of special significance to the organism is accentuated at the expense of less significant information." To these scientific findings he adds the comment: "Inhibitory interaction is undoubtedly the basis of a number of well-known visual phenomena such as brightness contrast and color contrast. . . . For hundreds of years artists have utilized these effects to brighten or subdue colors, or to alter their apparent hue, and—especially—to emphasize lines and contours. Indeed, it seems almost instinctive for the artist to accentuate the contours of an object he is representing; and he does this—as the eye does—at the expense of accuracy of representation of less significant features" (pp. 200–201).

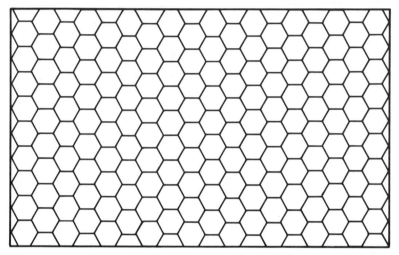

Figure 20–1. Changes in Groupings with Shifts of Attention and Focus
*a spread of hexagonal tiles . . . organized in different groupings according to
whichever tile is chosen as the center*

tance, and with it another interpretational factor, the judgment of given
forms in three dimensions. The principle of perspective adds a new
element of ambiguity which is not based on a simple displacement of
focus; it takes a subjective reorientation of vision to change one's perspective judgment of three-dimensional form. Such reorientation may occur
by chance or may be induced by tricks of viewing. A picture of a pile of
blocks or of a flight of steps will suddenly and quite irresistibly reverse its
perspective values if it is held upside down, as Figure 20–2 shows.[24]

As any line that meets itself is normally seen as the contour of an area
(the honeycomb pattern, really marking, in nature, the openings of empty cells seen end-on, in a diagram suggests flat surfaces like tiles), a three-
dimensional form is seen as a solid. A line drawing will do the same thing
if it is sufficiently analogous to the outline of a familiar or readily imaginable object. Consider, for instance, the intriguing puzzle-picture in
Titchener's venerable *Textbook of Psychology* (1911)—at first glance certainly a brain, but upon closer inspection a cluster of infants!

The examples here adduced are all artificial constructions, but the
same challenge to imaginative selection of contours met the eyes of men
in primitive stages of mental evolution. Forms seen in clouds furnish one

[24]The example is taken from the dust jacket of Volume II of the present essay.

The Dream of Power

Figure 20–2. Reversal of Perspective Values with Change in Angle of View
*the principle of perspective adds a new element of ambiguity which is not
based on a simple displacement of focus*

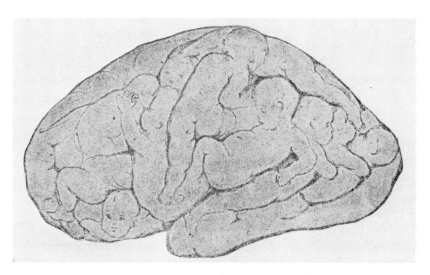

Figure 20–3. Ambiguity of Representational Forms
at first glance certainly a brain, but upon closer inspection a cluster of infants
(Drawing by R. Gudden. From Edward Bradford Titchener, A *Textbook of Psychology* [New
York: Macmillan, 1911].)

[55]

of the commonest illusions; flying human shapes, huge birds, angels, witches riding the winds have all been seen in the sky. An occasional spectacular meteor, ball of St. Elmo's fire, or parhelion lends support to the expectation of celestial wonders, and the more familiar displays of sunrises, sunsets, auroras, and rainbows make the heavens appear as a storehouse of light, multicolored, occasionally dealt out in close measures, with bolts of lightning as a reminder of its immense reserves. The shapes seen in clouds, usually shifting to other shapes that invite interpretation, are obvious forms for supernatural beings in control of the earth. Meanwhile, earth itself provides its virtual images in the trunks of distorted trees and serpentine branches, or more elusive ones in their wrinkled bark and in rock surfaces and jutting profiles. A person stealing through lonely jungle tracks can see his spooks almost anywhere.

A pure succession of different apparitions, even in one fixed place, might not be enough to beget the idea of transformation in a very simple and naive mind; but the fact that the illusory forms seen in natural conformations may change back and forth, and that while the beholder lets them alternate there is always a convincingly physical object held in abeyance but vouching for their reality and, despite the incompatibility of their appearances, for their identity, helps to negotiate that somewhat precocious conception. The change in itself seems, of course, to be objectively given rather than brought about by the subject; but with it there is always a deeply felt sense of his own mental activity as he himself shifts his centered attention and therewith changes the thing that meets his eyes. Perhaps the momentary resistance of the previous form to the radical transformation, as he alternates his fixations, makes him feel the impulse as his own; the thing before him obeys him; and there we have the magical act. Once that experience is his, the idea expands, and magic is man's mental power, not only to transmute the characters of external things but, by dint of his imagination thus excited, to influence their doings and destinies.

The power of magic has no known limits. A person knows, in a fair way, his own physical capacities, the weight of the blows he can deal, the furthest range of his arrows, the strength of his voice, the speed and endurance of his running; but the reaches of his mind are indefinite and, to his feeling, infinite. His physique may always have been inferior to that of most other animals of his size (though not, perhaps, as puny and pathetic as Arnold Gehlen imagined it), but magic holds a different sort of sway over his possible antagonists, which include real beasts as the least terrible.[25]

[25]Cf. D. Essertier, *Les formes inférieures de l'explication*, pp. 80–81: "si le sauvage a

The Dream of Power

The subjective sense of power, however, has some sobering consequences that tend to balance the odds of man against nature again: the process of transformation is quickly abstracted from the circumstance that probably engendered the idea—the ambiguity of sensory impressions[26]—and conceived apart from his action, as a capability of all living things; all sorts of beings, then, may make their own magic changes and transform themselves into animals, monsters, clouds, persons, or whatnot. They may even ensorcel him. As the magician gains new potentialities, so does the spirit-world he faces.

The result of this spread of imputed magic to the whole living world—which, for primitive men, may take in not only animals and plants but stones, stars, rainbows, and man-made things like tools and traps[27]—is that the earth is peopled with a host of uncertain characters which may be anything or anyone other than themselves, by temporary self-transformation. Some strange metamorphoses indeed are reported by the jungle tribes in Malaya (who are officially Mohammedans[28]), such as the making of a species of squirrel from caterpillars, or a sort of fish, by a similar transmutation, from a cat, and a mollusk out of a mouse. Much more uncomfortable is the assertion: "Some men, especially certain Korinchi Malays from Sumatra, are thought to have the power to change into a

peuplé son univers d'esprits invisibles, . . . c'est que les représentations qu'il a des choses vivent des émotions mêmes qui s'y rattachent. Le portrait d'un homme ou d'un animal est, en un sens, plus vivant pour eux, dans sa ménaçante immobilité, que l'homme ou l'animal lui-même. 'Nous n'avons pas peur des tigres réels, disait les Abipones à Dobrizhoffer, mais les tigres artificiels, oui, nous les craignons.'" See also Vol. II, pp. 215–17.

[26]This is, of course, a purely hypothetical reconstruction, which I would be ready to abandon at once for a more illuminating theory. We do not—and perhaps shall never—know how the notion of magical transformation arose.

[27]According to Dr. Fortune's *Manus Religion* (1935), p. 57, "*Molua* is used for the 'soul' of inanimate things that by convention are endowed with 'souls,' as generally as '*mwelolo*' is used for soul stuff of persons. . . . *mwelolo* is not allowed for inanimate things. The inanimate soul is practically confined to fishing gear of all types, fish baskets, nets, traps and the like." In a later connection, we find: "Manus religion is aimed at curing, not only sick persons, however, but also 'sick' fishing gear" (p. 103).

[28]Skeat wrote, in the Introduction to his *Malay Magic*: "it is necessary to state that the Malays of the Peninsula are Sunni Muhammadans of the school of Shafi'i, and that nothing, theoretically speaking, could be more correct and orthodox (from the point of view of Islām) than the belief which they profess.

"But the beliefs which they actually hold are another matter altogether, and it must be admitted that the Muhammadan veneer which covers their ancient superstitions is very often of the thinnest description. . . . Beginning their invocations with the orthodox preface: '*In the name of God, the merciful, the compassionate,*' ending them with an appeal to the Creed: '*There is no god but God, and Muhammad is the Apostle of God,*' they are conscious of no impropriety in addressing the intervening matter to a string of Hindu Divinities, Demons, Ghosts, and Nature Spirits, with a few Angels and Prophets thrown in, as the occasion may seem to require" (pp. xiii–xiv).

tiger and back again at will."[29] But even more confusing than the possibility of such man-beasts haunting the jungle is their potentiality for further transformation, reported by Skeat, who said: "according to a Malay at Langat, the 'were-tiger' (*rimau jadijadian*) occasionally appears in the shape of a wild boar escaping from a grave, in the centre of which may be afterwards seen the hole by which the animal has escaped."[30]

Savage mentality, which has lagged, or perhaps, in some cases, relapsed into earlier phases of intellectual life,[31] baffles the European intruder on several counts. Not only the presence of many weird beliefs but the absence of some which he holds as matters of elementary, common-sense knowledge frustrate any immediate meeting of minds. The early anthropologists—our only witnesses to the conditions of intact uncivilized life—could find no basis for understanding the tribesman's benightedness. How could people, especially women, living in a close-knit, familially organized society, fail to know that sexual intercourse leads to pregnancy?[32] The time interval between the sex act and parturition is long, but pregnancy is felt soon; and in a purely instinctive way the

[29]K. M. Endicott, *An Analysis of Malay Magic* (1970), pp. 32, 29. Though the "analysis" is in terms to horrify a logician, Mr. Endicott's thesis brings together many facts which are well authenticated.

[30]*Malay Magic*, p. 189.

[31]This possibility presents a constant threat to human culture. H. J. Rose, in a little essay, "The Wiro Sky-God" (1936), p. 52, remarked to that effect: "It is perfectly possible that in any given area, at any given time, that institution which seems to us the more savage or repugnant to civilized principles, that is, to our prejudices, has come into being after, not before, the one which we should prefer to have replaced it as men grew wiser. Degeneration and simplification are phenomena as real as advance to the higher and more complex."

M. K. Martin, in "South American Foragers: A Case Study in Social Devolution" (1969), provided some examples from the experience of the Indians whose culture was violated by white invaders, for, he observed in a prefatory abstract, "these hunters and gatherers have undergone a process of simplification from early contact to modern times. Contemporary band societies appear to represent degenerated structures formerly characterized by larger population concentrations, corporate unilineal descent groups, and heterogeneous political communities" (p. 243).

[32]There are many statements in the literature imputing such unawareness to those aborigines of Australia who were known to the first serious observers, Spencer and Gillen, Durkheim, Strehlow, and others. See the later judgment on their reports in Alf Sommer-felt's *La langue et la société; caractères sociaux d'une langue de type archaïque* (1938), pp. 140–41: "L'indigène semble ignorer le rapport de causalité qui existe entre l'acte sexuel et la conception. C'est ce que Spencer et Gillen affirment expressement. On s'est souvent montré sceptique vis-à-vis de cette affirmation, aussi bien dans le cas des Aranta que dans celui d'autres peuples de civilisation inférieure sur lesquels on possede des renseignements analogues. Toutefois, les observations de Spencer et Gillen semblent irréfutables. Les idées que les Aranta se font de la naissance seraient incompréhensibles s'ils connaissaient les conditions physiologiques de la conception. . . . Au contraire, si l'on admet leur ignorance à cet égard, leurs représentations forment un système cohérent et logique."

expectation of it would be likely to forerun even its first physical evidence, as it does with many subtle changes of condition. Dorothea Lee, who followed up Malinowski's studies of the Trobriand Islanders, spoke of "the Trobriander's ritual ignorance of physiological paternity";[33] and "ritual ignorance" is probably the exact right phrase. The causal relation between copulation and pregnancy is not unknown, but ignored; it is not important in the frame of spirit influence and magical counteraction in which the Islanders assert and maintain themselves. Their thinking is in magical, not causal, terms.[34] Their ritual, however telescoped or reduced—like a Christian's quick crossing himself in a highly realistic moment of danger—furnishes their most natural expression of ordinary as well as high and serious thought.

What, then, is the real nature of magic? If it is not—as Andrew Lang and many other early investigators maintained—simple ignorance of causal relations and incredibly stupid and mistaken theory, what is its motivation, that it should hold such a central place in social as well as individual life? The theory of overflowing emotion might account for its occasional personal uses, but surely not for the work of professional healers, rainmakers, and miracle-working priests.

Magic is intense, awesome, but not an emotional outburst. It is in essence an expression of ideas, and as such is symbolic. Its ubiquity in the life of man stems from his specialization, the overactivity of his forebrain, which he feels as an exertion, and he looks to the external world for its effects because outward effects have been the result of all his felt impulses from the infancy of his life and of his race, and are his only criteria of consummated action. Instinctive behavior normally leads to physical achievement; and in unchanging savage existence practical activity, even with highly developed manual and technical skills, is still largely instinctual, though not purely instinctive, being helped or hindered at every turn by ideas. That incursion of ideas, envisagements, suggestions, and whims is constant in human life, yet in simple societies the basic patterns of self-maintenance are uncritically received and followed. Instinct is perseverative, conservative; the force of tradition is its modified version in mankind.

[33]"A Primitive System of Values" (1940), p. 385.
[34]Endicott, in *An Analysis of Malay Magic*, p. 26, realized—as few other writers seem to do—that causative practices do not necessarily rest on causal thinking, for he says: "Malay 'medicine' is almost entirely magical; even when procedures of real medical value are used, the reasons given are magical. The term *ubat* applies equally to remedies that work by magic and those working by chemistry. . . . Diagnosis is by divination, the causes of disease are supernatural forces, and their cures are the magical methods by which those forces can be controlled."

On this habitual round of behavior the dreaming, inventing, apprehensive mind imposes itself, giving all the familiar recurrent acts—shooting, fishing, planting, and above all the daily occasions of eating—a heavy cargo of symbolic functions. Being repetitious, their various detailed subacts have attained a natural economy and order; it is this fixed design of concatenated subacts, rather than the purposive act as a whole, that offers models for expressive gestures and manipulations. The emotional attitudes of people toward the plants and animals that provide their food, or toward the spirits that are thought to control them, are the contents of their hunting, gardening, and other protective or persuasive rituals; and the rites themselves usually involve some representation of the acts they celebrate. In our anthropological literature this is known as "sympathetic magic."

A better term, perhaps, would be "empathetic magic"; for the rationale of the practice appears to rest on a conceptual assumption which is probably unconscious today even in the lowest savage mentality, though its vestiges are still alive as the principle of such magic-making: the assumption that an act may be initiated by one being and picked up in its course by another. If this feeling (to use the least committal word) really underlies the mimetic performances which are expected to evoke responses of such agents as clouds, trees, rivers, or the yams in a garden, then the elements, at least, of enchantment by mimesis would seem to stem from the earliest phases of our existence as true human beings, a time of actual *"Menschwerdung,"* when instinct still held the main rule not only over behavior but over subjective reactions as well. At that time the bonds among fellow men were animal-like, and as the Hominidae are a gregarious genus, moments of empathetic feeling may have been frequent and familiar. An impulse starting up in one person would be naturally picked up from the smallest bodily sign, as it appears to be among many subhuman beings from bees to birds, and even wolves and dogs,[35] so the impulse seems to run through an intimate unity of beings; and the experience of empathy may have seemed as natural in that close-knit human society as it appears to be in a beehive or a school of herring today.

The question, why imitation of a desired event should serve to bring it about has often puzzled sociologists and anthropologists; the phenomena of "sympathetic magic" have even been regarded as evidence that savages not only fail to realize that certain events cause subsequent ones, i.e., the

---

[35]See the discussions of empathy in Vol. II above, especially, on Professor Lorenz's wolves, pp. 142–48.

law of cause and effect, but that they must even hold as a principle that "cause follows from effect."[36] From the point of view here proposed, however, no such absurdity need be imputed to the ritualists; for their action is not imitation, it is an incentive move to start the desired action of the natural or supernatural beings that have its completion in their power.

The relation between the intention and the realization of the act is supposed to be helped by imparting motivation to those divine or ghostly agents as some animals seem to pass an impulse from one ready agent to another.[37] In this way human beings hope to participate in the natural event, the work of clouds, winds, etc., before its overt phase has begun.[38] But if the ceremonial is, as here proposed, a mental push to get the impulse started and support it on its course, it is really the opposite of imitation; it is the priming and starting of an act, and the initiators naturally look for its continuance in the external world. They have handed over the initiated action, and the rest of it is expected to run on from agent to agent in the spirit-world, by its own impetus.

The great age of magical practice is attested by the chief elements in this so-called "sympathetic magic," empathy and mimesis. The former certainly goes back to the animal state of instinctive communion,[39] the

[36]Cf. Skeat, *Malay Magic*, p. 82: "I would draw attention to the strong vein of Sympathetic Magic or 'make believe' which runs through and leavens the whole system of Malay superstition. The root-idea of this form of magic has been said to be the principle that 'cause follows from effect.'" And he goes on, quoting Frazer (*The Golden Bough*, Vol. I, p. 9): "One of the principles of sympathetic magic is that any effect may be produced by imitating it."

[37]Cf. above, Vol. II, Chapters 14 and 15, *passim*, esp. p. 129 and also p. 313.

[38]The supernatural willed act is imagined as beginning with a covert phase, which is the typical act form as I conceive it. In fortuitous corroboration of that concept, Dr. Wilder Penfield, on the basis of his many electroencephalographic and surgical findings, has offered some interesting evidence that a voluntary act begins even before the impulse to it reaches an overt phase, i.e., with the intention. In "Mechanisms of Voluntary Movement" (1954), he explained that the "resting rhythm" of the sensorimotor cortex, the "β-rhythm," ceases in the area of hand control with movement of the hand, but the disappearance of the β-rhythm "is not due to the sensory effect of the movement, for when the patient is told to get ready to move his hand on a given signal, the β-rhythm also disappears with that warning. That is to say it disappears before the final signal is given, and before the hand is moved.

"It seems reasonable to conclude that the impulses which abolish the resting rhythm of the motor hand area reach the precentral convolution from some subcortical source, and not across the cortex from auditory or visual areas in the same hemisphere. It seems likely that these are the impulses which produce voluntary movement" (p. 8).

W. Grey Walter, too, said that the EEG pattern had been found to change about a half-second before a voluntary movement is begun. See "The Functions of Electrical Rhythms in the Brain" (1950), p. 27.

[39]Upon first thought it may seem implausible that human beings should have kept a

latter, to the dawn of conceptual thought. For the earliest, archaic, and doubtless deeply unconscious motive of the mimesis in ritual is intellectual: to comprehend the fears and expectations of life and thus make their impact as negotiable as possible. It is somewhat like speaking a newly learned word in order to produce, and thus feel as well as hear, its phonemic character.[40] The rite, like most major physical and mental functions, serves in several connections: to influence nature, to formulate ideas, to unite people with each other and with all spirits in their ambient in primitive communion, and to assure them of the power of their superlative asset, their humanity, their Mind.

The mimetic element makes "sympathetic magic" dramatic, and as its forms develop it becomes more and more so. Many anthropologists are well aware of this tendency, and have given it various interpretations. C. G. Seligman, largely following Geza Roheim and writing at a time when psychoanalysis was successfully storming the field of psychology, saw the dramatization of wishes as primarily a means of relieving emotional tensions.[41] Victor W. Turner, much more recently, characterized mimetic ritual as "the production of interaction between human actors of roles."[42] Jean Cazeneuve speaks of "the drama of initiation" in which a man becomes a magician.[43] Perhaps the most authoritative statement is that of Jomo Kenyatta, himself a Gikuyu tribesman, believer in magic, and adherent of his native religion (though hardly of all the superstitions it has adsorbed): "Religion is a dramatization of belief."[44]

The jumping of a spatiotemporal gap by the causal influence of the magician's performance is generally considered the essential mark of sympathetic magic. This is the criterion John Murphy—who fully real-

---

characteristic of herd animals—the contagion of feeling that causes an impulse to jump like a physical spark from one individual to another—so that the expectation of such a passage seems quite reasonable to them. But it may be a similar case to the extraordinary homing sense of the Aivilik Eskimos described by Edmund Carpenter and his collaborators (see above, p. 9, n. 11); a trait that has been preserved because it continues to have a function.

[40]Cf. Vol. II, pp. 350–51, in reference to Jarvis Bastian's article.

[41]"Anthropological Perspective and Psychological Theory" (1932), pp. 197–98: "experience of primitive peoples indicates that dramatization of an act symbolizing the performance of a desire, or avoidance of or escape from something repulsive, brings a great sense of relief, confidence and security."

[42]The Drums of Affliction: A Study of Religious Processes among the Ndembu of Zambia (1968), pp. 2–3.

[43]Sociologie du rite (1971), p. 189.

[44]Facing Mount Kenya: The Tribal Life of the Gikuyu, p. 316. The entire sentence runs: "Religion is a dramatization of belief, and belief is a matter of social experience of the things that are most significant to human life."

ized, and remarked upon, the empathetic character of a spectator's spontaneous gestures in watching an athletic feat, and also the use of such movements formalized in ritual—applied when he wrote: "The war-dance of many savages is a magical operation; it is also an elaborate gesture. It is the dramatic performance of the battle-action in all its separate acts, such as the ambush, the charge, the cast of the spear and so forth—every motor activity, in fact, involved in the coming fight, short of actual accomplishment—in other words, a very complete gesture. The difference from the realized, actual battle is one of time, since the war-dance is done beforehand; and it is a difference of space, since it may be carried through far from the ultimate scene of conflict; and therein is the magical character of the gesture, namely, that unseen power from it is believed to cross that intervening time, and that distance of space, and to affect, indeed determine, the event of the battle."[45]

But there is one further difference: the absence of any physically present enemy calling for defensive action. There is no falling, yielding, dying in the anticipatory dance. All the movements are aggressive, expressing impulses that arise from within, while none are triggered and also repulsed from outside, as in a real struggle. It is the offensive autogenic acts that are dramatized in the mounting fury of the war dance and perhaps in a final triumph scene, with the expectation that the warriors will be given extra strength by their totemic or other patron spirits who may be invisibly participating in the act, and that the spears and clubs carried by the dancers will cooperate in the actual battle.

In the context of motivational thinking there is nothing irrational about that expectation. When every eventuality, in nature as in society, is conceived in the act form, it is imagined as beginning in an intention, which gives shape and direction to a venture. The aim of a mimetic rite is to formulate and, indeed, to perform that stage of the desired act, with instinctive confidence that any visible or invisible agent in close proximity will fall in with it and realize the whole. Nothing "crosses" an empty space or time; but the driving impulse, and the act already coming to realization in its initial, in its mental phase, are expected to be taken up and to hold over in the consciousness of the spirits just as the concentrated excitement the warriors have whipped up in themselves is expected to carry their undertaking from the preparatory dance to the victorious consummation.

One writer, at least, took this view of sympathetic magic more than half a century ago, and he was not an anthropologist but a religious

[45]*Lamps of Anthropology* (1943), p. 67.

thinker, Alfred F. Loisy. In his *Essai historique sur le sacrifice* (1920), he judged the mimetic acts of savage tribes not in the behavioral, pseudo-scientific terms of our psychological and sociological records, but came to them through his own experience, especially by contemplation of the Christian sacrament of the Eucharist, the symbolic commemoration of the Last Supper. At once the so-called "make-believe" performances appear in their actual sacredness, even if on a more primitive level of conception than the expressive rites held holy in civilized societies. With such insight, he wrote: "For the outsider, the ritual action is a drama, if not a comedy. But for the believer the drama is real, the comedy is only apparent, for he is involved in an efficacious imitation of the represented thing. It is true that sometimes the fiction takes on such a character or such proportions that it looks like the most naive deception. When we see in many cults offerings made of paste figures or, as with the Chinese, paper images in place of live victims or real objects . . . it seems to us that they are trying to fool the gods or the dead. But the deceit is of much less account than we are inclined, at first sight, to suppose. . . . For to mystical thinking, and especially to a primitive mind, an image is not just a simple portrayal, but participates in the power [*vertu*] of the object represented; and as the representation holds the essential and characteristic aspect of the sacred action, a degree more or less of fictitiousness does not affect the nature of the ritual" (p. 60).

"The underlying idea of these rites is that the act symbolically performed by men has its repercussion throughout the universe—a small universe, such as the ancient religions had it. . . . When the forces of nature are personified and the magical idea of the sacred action accords perfectly with people's beliefs about the gods who are the initiators of [natural] phenomena, one may well believe that the earthly liturgy corresponds to a celestial one having the same intent, so that men by their ritual can take part in the work of the gods" (p. 65).

Here, I think, we have an interpretation of the primitive practice of sympathetic magic as a supposed occult event, thought to take its course without any gap in the universal rhythm which pervades the interpenetrating spheres of divinity and humanity. Magic, from this angle, is seen not only as a mystical relation between an earthly and an otherworldly activity, both its terms taken *in toto*, but a transference of each successive human behavioral impulse to the spirit or spirits hopefully adjured to consummate it. Perhaps this explains why the detailed subacts of vitally important actions, such as planting, gathering, sharing, and eating, are the substance of the formalized elements from which mimetic ritual is elaborately built.

Several writers who have recognized the dramatic character of primitive religious celebration have treated it as "playacting," theatrical entertainment.[46] On the same critical basis they have investigated magical actions of alleged healers and accused them of cheating and deceiving their patients. Sometimes they express surprise at the ease with which a shaman can fool his lay clients, who seem to accept the most obvious trickery as bona fide magic. So, for instance, Barrie Reynolds, in *Magic, Divination and Witchcraft among the Barotse of Northern Rhodesia* (1963), says: "An Nkoya, on the Kabompo River, divined with the aid of a whistling figure, the noise being produced through a castor seed wedged in his own nostril. A Kwandi diviner, in Senanga, was found practicing a similar deception" (pp. 118–19).[47]

The radical difference between the savage's and the European's thinking is never more apparent than when a pragmatically minded field worker argues with a native doctor about the efficacy of magic as a method to induce physical events. The tribesman does not see it the visitor's way, but cannot explain how he does conceive the magical process; neither his abstract thinking nor his language can encompass the problem, which has never been raised before. The inquirer, for his part, is prone to interpret the answer in his own terms, making the "doctor" either a knowing psychologist or a swindler exploiting the credulity of his

[46]The best-known advocate of this view was certainly John Dewey; see *Experience and Nature* (1925), pp. 78–79. There is a discussion of his treatment of religious ritual in *Phil. N.K.*, pp. 156–58.

Endicott, too, in *An Analysis of Malay Magic*, p. 26, classes dramatic rites with entertainments, though, contrary to Dewey, who held that symbolic value was subsequently attributed to playful dancing and comedy, he supposes the pleasure element to have gradually supervened, for he says: "Some of what must be called entertainments are the magical rites and feasts themselves, rites whose primary purpose is something other than amusement. The shaman's séance is especially popular and bears an interesting resemblance to the most elaborate of Malay entertainments, the shadow play."

[47]An elaborate instance of such ritual, reported by a white man who regarded its acts as psychologically convincing deceptions, may be seen in an essay by Claude Lévi-Strauss, "The Sorcerer and His Magic" (1967; orig. pub., 1949), telling of the making of a shaman: "his narrative recounts the details of his first lessons, a curious mixture of pantomime, prestidigitation, and empirical knowledge, including the art of simulating fainting and nervous fits, the learning of sacred songs, the technique for inducing vomiting, rather precise notions of auscultation and obstetrics, and the use of 'dreamers,' that is, spies who listen to private conversations and secretly convey to the shaman bits of information concerning the origins and symptoms of the ills suffered by different people. Above all, he learned the *ars magna* of one of the shamanistic schools of the North-West Coast: the shaman hides a little tuft of down in a corner of his mouth, and he throws it up, covered with blood, at the proper moment—after having bitten his tongue or made his gums bleed—and solemnly presents it to his patient and the onlookers as the pathological foreign body extracted as a result of his sucking and manipulations" (p. 31).

fellows, but in any case a sophisticate, thinking like the white man and manipulating the ignorant savages. An example of such highly probable misinterpretation occurs in Ronald Rose's *Living Magic* (1957), in the author's report and judgment on the cures effected by an Australian "doctor" of a Pitjendjara tribe. "There is no doubt in the native's mind," says Rose, "that there are physical objects of a magical nature in his body. There is no doubt in him that the doctor removes the objects; that the spot they come out is unmarked because the operation is a magical one.

"To the doctor, however, the real methods are, of course, known. 'Extracting' objects with his fingers is simple sleight of hand; 'sucking' objects out, he secretes them in his mouth beforehand; the blood that he spits out he gets by lacerating his own mouth and gums.

"Bluntly I put it to Fred Cowlin[48] that these were the methods he used, emphasizing my charge by 'extracting' a twig from the doctor's own arm. Smilingly he agreed, but immediately stressed the psychological point of view. 'They bin get better all the same,' he said" (p. 87).

What the doctor stressed was just as possibly and far more probably not a psychological point of view, but his faith in the perfect adequacy of his methods for ritual purposes. For mimetic ritual is a drama, and all its elements belong to the stage; but its stage is the world. Its elements are gestures, its acts produced as they would be in the theater: semblances, whose import is reality. They are presentational symbols; and as almost invariably is the case with such symbolism, there is no clear distinction between symbol and meaning. The image is the thing itself in the drama. The doctor's hidden objects—well known to most lay members of the tribe, at least the older men—are theatrical "props," symbolizing actual evils or remedies. Their symbolic nature, together with their actual existence, fills them with a magic which amounts to holiness, both wonderful and dangerous. But their sacredness and potency depend, to varying degrees, on the occasion of their use. White visitors have sometimes been shocked at the ribald way people of highly religious cultures may indulge in mock seances and horseplay apparently "debunking" magic action. In the book just cited there is a detailed account of a veritable farce carried out by two Pitjendadjara men, one of them a tribal elder, for the investigator's benefit that seems to bespeak the height of impiety and cynical disbelief; in fact, it was the prime exhibit that made the author assume that the initiated shamans and some other intelligent persons knew—"of

---

[48] A native doctor. Many tribesmen adopt English names because custom forbids their own given names to be spoken, so the English pseudonym saves troublesome circumlocutions like "father of so-and-so" or nicknames.

course"—that the value of magic rites was their psychological effect on amazingly innocent patients. His description runs: "I then witnessed an extraordinary pantomime with these two natives playing the parts of pointing victim and doctor. The two Pitjendadjara[49] men enjoyed their play immensely, roaring with laughter as they acted out, and at the same time explained, a native magical cure. There was no atmosphere of gloom as there probably would be in real life.

"Tjalkalieri lay in the sand and clasped his hands over his abdomen. 'There is a bone in me!' He moaned and groaned (and laughed); and his contortions whipped up the sand. 'I am dying. The bone is tearing the insides of me.' Then he said, 'The great and clever doctor, Maleiaba— he, he, ho—will cure me! Oh, the pain, oh, ah!'

"With serious face the little Ayers Rock man [Maleiaba] examined the writhing Tjalkalieri. He rubbed his abdomen, feeling carefully with the tips of his fingers. He applied his lips to the bare skin and pretended to suck. Tjalkalieri's contortions became less violent. Then Maleiaba felt again with his fingers and, with skillful sleight of hand, produced a short pointing bone (without wax or cord) apparently from the patient's abdomen. He held it aloft with a grin of triumph.

"'Yokai!' he cried.

"'Yokai!' I echoed the Pitjendadjara equivalent of 'Hooray!' and applauded the performance" (p. 41).

It is certainly not impossible, in view of the evident close contact of these two actors with white men, whose language they could manage in vulgar phrase, that they were insincere and frivolous about their own religious tradition; but I think there is a different explanation. They were performing as we would in, say, rehearsing a wedding—a solemn performance when it is actually intended, but neither sacred nor, for highly indecorous people, even serious in rehearsal. This alternative interpretation is borne out by the observation which mystified another anthropologist in a place where there could hardly be any question of insincerity or impiety, namely, in the harsh and remote spirit-world of Rasmussen's Netsilik Eskimos. Rasmussen wrote: "A curious game, a particular favorite among the children, was to ·näɳ·o·ʃArtut (the spirit game), in which they imitated and parodied shaman séances and the general fear of evil spirits with a capital sense of humor. They held complete and true shaman séances, fought with imaginary enemies just as the grown-ups do; in fact they even used the same formulas that they had heard their parents utter when really in fear and danger. Although this game was absolute

[49]The author's writing of the tribal name.

blasphemy the grown-up audience writhed with laughter, just as if they took a certain satisfaction in seeing the evil and inexorable gravity of life made the subject of farcical burlesque. Some hours later it might happen that an attack of illness, or perhaps a bad dream, would rally the grown-ups to a séance during which they desperately sought to defend themselves against hidden enemies, with exactly the same means as the children had mocked in play. When I mentioned this remarkable circumstance to my friend Kuvdluitssog, and enquired of him whether it was really prudent to mock the spirits, he answered with the greatest astonishment pictured in his face that the spirits really understood a joke."[50]

Obviously the children's game was not "absolute blasphemy," but quite innocent play by which their elders and even the supernaturals were entertained. The little mimics were using materials of ritual in a situation where these were neither religious nor magical—formulas for prayer where no one was praying. Their elders saw nothing wrong with putting the same words and gestures to a different purpose. It seems to be, for these people, like using words in second intension, that is, as items, not vehicles of thought; taking the ritual act as a theme and playing with it. In our society that would be deemed sacrilegious by most people, and by others at least bad taste; the action itself is considered holy and not to be played with. But the Central Eskimo moral valuation evidently permits it; the holiness of the religious form stems from the context, the address to the spirits, who enter into the serious communication and understand the human crisis just as, shortly before, in happier moments, they "really understood a joke." The same appears to be true in magic-making: the power of a magic rite, such as the Pitjendjara shaman's bone extraction, is the power of his mind to exorcise the evil symbolized by the bone that has been "pointed" or "sung into" the victim. Without the mysterious, invisible action of a commanding will the rite would have no force, but in the magic performance the "extracted" object symbolizes the pain and the source of sickness which the doctor has removed. The patient's recovery may really be from an imaginary incubus—there are many authoritative statements to the effect that savages, especially those native to Australia and the Pacific realm, are peculiarly prone to psychical trauma[51]—but

---

[50]*The Netsilik Eskimos*, pp. 68–69.

[51]Elkin, in *Aboriginal Men of High Degree*, p. 50, tells about the end of a man who had been "pointed" and consequently died, being told by the medicine-man that his (the patient's) ancestors wanted him to join them; on which the author comments, "he dies by suggestion, as Aborigines can, and as so many do."

Walter B. Cannon, well known for his studies of the physiological effects of emotion, especially fear and anger, on animals and his biochemical analyses of such phenomena,

the magician, far from thinking in terms of any such physiological and psychological facts, is the most firmly convinced of his own magic powers, because he feels the activity in himself as concentrated effort and strained attention.

Not all magic is as obviously pantomimic as dance, but its overt acts are nevertheless techniques of the theater, symbolic representations which mean real events and are identified as such. When a "clever fellow," or Australian medicine-man, extracts a bone that has been "sung" or "pointed" into his patient, he does not excite himself to an overt heroic attack like a fighter going into battle; yet he starts the act that is to be taken up by the illness he is exorcising and symbolically presenting in the theatrically produced bone. The initiation of that act is the mental concentration of his desire for the convalescence of the sick person. He may be a hired magician with little or no emotional feeling for the sufferer, but his concern for his own professional competence makes every test a crisis; what he is building up is his own sense of spiritual power, the power of his wish, his command to the spirit-bone that he imagines in the stricken body, coming out and passing into the tangible image he holds ready for it. The emergence of the phantom and its entrance into the physical proxy is an invisible process, and has to be effected in secrecy; his sleight of hand, which literal-minded European observers judge as a mean deception, is to him and his native audience a mystical moment.

The shaman is an actor in a sacred drama which is still entirely in the realm of actual belief, and his involvement in the histrionic creation is so profound that the dramatic idea supervenes over any factual condition. A

---

extended that research to the frequent reports of so-called "voodoo deaths" among people of primitive cultures. In a little essay, "'Voodoo' Death" (1942), he wrote: "Fear, as is well known, is one of the most deeply rooted and dominant of the emotions. . . . Associated with it are profound physiological disturbances, widespread throughout the organism. . . . great fear and great rage have similar effects in the body. . . . In the sham rage of the decorticate cat there is a supreme exhibition of intense emotional activity." He goes on to describe the behavioral symptoms: sweating, piloerection, excessively high blood pressure and blood sugar, tachycardia. "This excessive activity of the sympathetico-adrenal system rarely lasts, however, more than three or four hours. By that time . . . the decorticate remnant of the animal, in which this acme of emotional display has prevailed, ceases to exist." After a discussion of the physiological correlates of the symptoms he remarks: "A similar condition occurs in the wound shock of human beings." And further: "These are the conditions which . . . are prevalent in persons who have been reported as dying as a consequence of sorcery. They go without food or water as they . . . wait in fear for their impending death. In these circumstances they might well die from a true state of shock, in the surgical sense—a shock induced by prolonged and tense emotion" (pp. 176–79).

German commentator on the theater, Peter Richard Rohden, analyzing the German compound word *Schauspiel* ("stage play") into *Schau* ("sight") and *Spiel* ("play"), remarked that the "sight" was given not only to the spectators, as the external presentation, but also to the actor, as insight into the character whose part he is playing. The true comedian inclines to the "play" element; he enjoys changing roles and quite literally "playing" with transformations of his social self into other personages. The typical tragedian is apt to enter so deeply into the being he is incarnating that, as Rohden puts it, "whoever is personally acquainted with actors of this type has probably noticed that sometimes they keep the expression, particularly in their eyes, of a character they have represented, for hours after the performance."[52]

A shaman, priest, or magician usually plays no other role than his own, but in that role he is always acting, with full conviction of its seriousness and reality. There is no cleavage between the domain of fantasy in which he acts and the world of affairs wherein his mystic acts are efficacious. The demands of practical necessity give the continuous spiritual interpretation its adaptive twists and turns, as the guiding and constraining banks of a stream to the pressing waters, but they are the limiting framework in which daily life is lived, and their governing forces are ritually unadmitted.

It is the relation of magical, theatrical ritual to the round of practical life that bewilders the civilized observer, rather than this or that particular piece of inexplicable behavior in an exotic culture. Underneath every such exhibit lies the whole structure of that ancient human mentality from which our own conceptual scheme of causality and "natural law" is a special offshoot. One gets glimpses of the older pattern, which is still fully functional in societies where its typical traits have been cultivated instead of repressed and overborne, from incidental remarks in the writings of anthropologists reporting from the field. There one reads of the amazing ability of some savages—even children at play—to withstand pain,[53] yet of intense fear—in adults as well as children—of magical influences, especially "spirit abstraction"; their great openness to sug-

[52]"Das schauspielerische Erlebnis" (1926), p. 39.
[53]Meggitt, *Desert People*, writes: "At the death of her adult son, a woman singes off her pubic hair and cuts off her head-hair, gouges her scalp [with a digging stick] and sears the wound with a firestick, then wails for days" (p. 127). When a man dies, "the fathers and adult sons of his patriline, the men of his wife's matriline and those of his maternal kinsmen who are also his ritual friends, *bilarli*, at once gash their thighs deeply with knives, despite the attempts of the dead man's brothers and sisters' sons to prevent them. The men bind up the wounds with hair-string in such a way that they are forced wide open and the resulting scars will be very noticeable" (p. 320). The whole book is filled with accounts of circumcision, subincission, nose-piercing, earlobe-piercing, and cicatrization, usually borne without wincing.

gestion; their credulity and belief in the power of persons in the magic profession. The most important and striking of those findings seems to me to be the ease with which savages generally, and some people of high culture, especially in Asia, enter into states of altered consciousness that comprise all stages from dreaminess to genuine hallucination.[54] Apparently, the autonomous work of the mind in those persons is less constantly triggered and guided by the impingement of sensory "data" than that of the European, who upholds his empirical standard of reality at every turn by his experimental methods and logical thinking. The untrammeled imagination of savages and confirmed mystics is highly active, creative, and preemptive; that is why its activity is felt, so the thinker, dreamer, or fabulist naturally looks for some effect of his mental exertion on the tangible world.

It has often been said that some magical exhibits, such as sending a rope straight upward to heaven and climbing it (as Köhler's ape Sultan tried to climb a pole), or lying prone in a fire and rising from it unscathed, or cutting up a human being and reassembling the pieces into a

---

Dudley Kidd, in *Savage Childhood* (1906), an early study of the Kafirs in South Africa, tells of the way their children play the game of piling up their hands and pulling out the undermost to put it on top: "The native children play this game in the European fashion, and also in a rougher manner. One boy picks up a small piece of skin on the back of another boy's hand, pinching it between his finger and thumb; the next boy picks up a similar piece of skin on the back of the hand of the second boy . . . ; the next boy, or girl, follows suit, till a whole chain of hands is formed. Then all the children swing the chain of hands about while they sing, '*Mantsipatsipane, Mantsipatsipane.*' . . . Suddenly, at a given signal, they all jerk their hands away, each one pinching the skin of the hand he is holding as hard as possible. Large pieces of skin are frequently pulled off in this way, but no boy would dream of crying with the pain lest he should be laughed at for being girlish. . . . some children do not seem to feel the pain amid the fun of the game" (p. 168).

The worst reading is in the *Manuscript Journals* of Alexander Henry and David Thompson, published in 1897, on the self-torture of ecstatic American Indian penitents. To quote only the mildest acts: "The greater part of the men—Big Bellies, Mandanes, and Saulteurs—have lost a joint of several fingers, particularly of the left hand, and it is not uncommon to see only the two forefingers and thumb entire. Amputation is performed for the loss of a near relation, and likewise during the days of penance" (p. 443). Each man performs the surgery on himself with the iron barb of an arrow.

[54]Natalie Curtis, in *The Indians' Book*, tells of a Paiute prophet who arose in 1888 and taught a Christ-like gospel of brotherhood, on which she remarks: "Many were drawn to the new faith by the word that those who danced in the holy dance 'died' (fell in a trance) and went to the spirit-world, where they saw their dead loved ones. Any one familiar with the inner life of the Indians knows that, to this people, the trance condition is not uncommon" (p. 42).

Alexandra David-Neel, in *Magic and Mystery in Tibet*, after recounting a nightmarish story which purported to relate an adept's real experience, said: "Had that fantastic struggle not been purely subjective? Had it not taken place during one of these trances which are frequently experienced by Tibetan *naljorpas*, which they also voluntarily cultivate?" (p. 135). Mme. David-Neel was not speaking of savage or backward people.

living whole, can only be achieved by a process of mass hypnosis and suggestion. Such a claim may well be sound. The physiology of hypnosis is still very little known, as it is not readily amenable to neurological study, and other investigations tend all too much to slip into the shaky theoretical framework of "psychical research" with its assumption of "parapsychological" forces and talents. The alleged displays certainly admit of very little other factual explanation; yet they have too many witnesses to be brushed aside as meriting no explanation at all. A. P. Elkin, in his excellent book *Aboriginal Men of High Degree*, gives examples of the miracles just mentioned and of several others which are at least as weird. His accounts are a welcome source as to what the tribal audience claimed to have seen, and the beliefs they held about it. He reports (p. 64): "During their making in South-east Australia, a magic cord is sung into the doctors. This cord becomes a means of performing marvellous feats, such as sending fire from the medicine-man's inside, like an electric wire. . . . At the display at initiation time, in a time of ceremonial excitement, the doctor lies on his back under a tree, sends his cord up and climbs up on it to a nest on top of the tree, then across to other trees, and at sunset, down to the ground again. . . . Joe Dagan, a Wongaibon clever man, lying on his back at the foot of a tree, sent his cord directly up, and 'climbed' up with his head well back, body outstretched, legs apart, and arms to his sides. Arriving at the top, forty feet up, he waved his arms to those below, and then came down in the same manner, and while still on his back the cord re-entered his body" (like a vacuum cleaner).

As for the phoenix stunt of rising out of the fire, Elkin relates the following: "During one display in western New South Wales, after the bull-roarer had been swung, thus creating a mystic atmosphere, for it is the voice of Baiame (the sky cult-hero), the men present were told to sit around and stare into a big fire on the sacred ground. As they stared they saw a 'clever-man' roll into the fire and scatter the coals. He then stood up amongst the rest of the men, who noticed that he was not burnt, nor were the European clothes that he wore, damaged" (p. 63).

The hardest claim to authenticate is the cutting-up and restoring of a human being; Elkin offers no alleged instance of such a feat.[55] Yet the conception of this miracle is of greater social importance than any of the others because in many tribes it is assumed to have been part of the shaman's making. The initiation of the "clever man" involves being killed, usually by spirits but sometimes by living masters of the cult, eviscerated,

----

[55]Eliade, in "Remarques sur le 'rope trick,'" cites several episodes (curiously enough, mainly from Europe) purporting to be historical. See above, p. 10, n. 13.

The Dream of Power

and deprived of many bones as well, which are cleaned and replaced when he is given new organs and a generous filling of quartz crystals and lizards besides. The operation is usually supposed to have been performed by surgical means, but the restoration is by magic and leaves no external traces.[56]

It is, of course, the shaman himself who tells this story, and may incidentally reinforce it by a display of butchering, reassembling, and reanimating someone. That such a performance rests on suggestion in an induced hypnotic trance is an almost ineluctable conclusion. Since any hypnotist in our own society who conjured such a phantasmagoria would certainly be aware of his own trickery, white people who receive the medicine-man's tale judge him to be a charlatan feathering his own nest in society by shameless means. Yet it is not necessary to think of him as an unscrupulous impostor, hypnotizing his fellows to show them magical acts he does not really believe himself to be performing; he probably believes in them implicitly, being himself the first and most deeply hypnotized, speaking aloud out of his own dream to his receptive hearers.

Hypnosis practiced under conditions of savage life is not comparable to any that we know from our own experimental or therapeutic work. We have our techniques for inducing the trance condition; it takes no shaman or especially gifted person to hypnotize a subject, though not everyone is susceptible to the treatment as we practice it.[57] In savage society en-

[56]Cf. Elkin, *Aboriginal Men of High Degree*, pp. 28 ff., for a detailed account of such rites in various regions and tribes of Australia. In connection with the magical operations, he describes the mysterious, alleged taking of a person's kidney fat as a psychic experience on the part of the perpetrators: "The group of selected men led by a medicine-man, a psychic expert, visualize the body of the victim; indeed, they give it a pseudo-material form which they draw to their laps, and on which they operate for the kidney-fat, a cult heroine closing the incision. Having passed through a ritual which directed their thoughts on their victim, and holding the rope of human hair, reinforced by spirits of the dead, they would be in a condition of acceptivity and ready to work out the leader's suggestion in trance. . . . The Aborigines of the south-west, New South Wales and the Lower Murray maintain . . . that this causes a corresponding effect on the material body of the victim" (pp. 60–61).

Similarly, Meggitt, in *Desert People*, p. 325, suggests a conception of how objects can be "sung" into a person: "the medicine-man and the men of the deceased's matriline . . . 'sing' the killer. Their actions and curses [their songs] are projected through space and 'solidify' as lethal objects inside him."

[57]There is a considerable literature on the problem of hypnotizability among civilized people, though most of it goes back to the first half of our century and earlier. Little theoretical work on hypnotism has been done recently; perhaps the present recrudescence of mysticism and superstition has made psychologists shy of a subject which has often been found in bad company.

In a report from a veterans' clinic in 1951, "Personality Dynamics in Hypnotic Induction," Dr. J. A. Christenson, Jr., listed the results of attempted hypnoses as 6 percent failures, 47 percent light trances, 28 percent borderline states, 13 percent difficult or atypical somnambulisms, 6 percent easy somnambulisms (p. 224).

trancement seems to be universally feasible, which is not surprising where trance states are cultivated and part of the intellectual life—medicine, religion, myth, knowledge of the world. Our standardized procedures, such as making the candidate for hypnosis fixate a light and gradually relax his muscles limb by limb while hearing the monotonous, repeated, suggestive words of the hypnotist, are designed for the office or the laboratory, where the first essential move is to shut that prosaic, scientific environment out, and center the subject's attention solely on the voice that speaks to him. He and the hypnotist are usually alone; where the performance is a demonstration, so that other people are present, they are not involved in the act (it may happen that they fall inadvertently under its spell, but their response is also an individual one). But the most radical difference between a medical or academic session and a seance is that in the civilized session the suggestions for post-hypnotic behavior are not exciting, the inculcated beliefs not marvelous, so that after emerging from the trance the believer would naturally let his own fantasy continue the experience. If our aims are medical, the hypnotist's statements are practical—"It doesn't hurt," "You don't like candy and cake," "You can breathe freely again," etc. If they are experimental or didactic, the suggestions are usually trivial—small, silly acts, to be carried out with apparently insufficient motive, such as taking a plant from a windowsill and setting it on the floor. Sometimes a minor dishonest action has been proposed to see whether the agent could be influenced to commit it (which usually he cannot).[58] But there is no thrill of wonder or mystery, no revelation of superhuman powers, though subjects who reach the state of so-called "somnambulistic trance" do have visions and hear unreal voices or other sounds. In a brief article, "Hypnosis as a Healing Art" (1975), Dr. Manoochehr Khatami summed up the effects which even our methods, used under our usual conditions, have been known to elicit: "Subjectively, some patients report change or distortions in body image and perception of reality. Some subjects report feelings of floating, sinking, or moving outside of one's self." Subsequently, on the same page, listing the stages from light trance to somnambulistic, or deepest trance, he mentions "kinesthetic delusions" even at a medium depth and, at the greatest depth, both visual and auditory hallucinations.

[58]This topic, too, commanded most interest twenty or thirty years ago, so most of the literature on it stems from that time. Clark Hull, in his classic *Hypnosis and Suggestibility* (1933), remarked in passing: "It is usually difficult to secure the successful execution of post-hypnotic suggestions which are at all in serious conflict with the natural inclination of the subjects" (p. 34). For a much more detailed study of the rare cases of exploiting subjects for criminal purposes see H. E. Hammerschlag, *Hypnose und Verbrechen: Ein Beitrag zur Phänomenologie der Suggestion und der Hypnose* (1954).

A genuine fakir employing hypnotism operates in a circle of tribesmen who are all involved in the marvels they have witnessed up to the moment; the natural surroundings in moonlight and firelight, ·or even in broad desert daylight on cliffs and vast expanses, demand very little to be shut out by conscious concentration on a fixed focusing point. The magician provides that point, his chant repeats the suggestive words, and the hypnotic trance begins not in his fellows but in him. He has acted the part of priest and miracle-worker often enough in the usual ways, but in a grand seance—religious or just demonstrative of his powers—he hypnotizes himself until he feels himself floating, climbing, descending, carried on the drumbeat until the drummers succumb to his song and the drums talk slowly while the believers see his words come true, the rope produced, the man ascending. Or they may see him rise without any support and fly among fleecy clouds; or even, at some high point, cut himself apart, fall in pieces, and be reassembled before their eyes.

Such displays are extremes of ritual dramatization, made possible by the constellation of subjective and objective circumstances: the participants' openness to suggestion, their persisting susceptibility to empathetic transference of feeling, the whole motivational pattern of their conceptions, their typical lack of individual judgment, and the apparently limitless flow of every person's imagination, together with the natural environment full of voices and rustlings, human forms and ghostly motions and the muttering drums. Add to these conditions the well-established fact that the process of hypnotization is greatly accelerated by repetition, taking less time and effort on each successive occasion,[59] and it is not hard to believe that people who have been subjected periodically to hypnotic influences since puberty might require scarcely more than a "sign stimulus" to enter the trance state. Moreover, they might well have no need of a consciously operating hypnotist. In the mystical, expectant mood created by the seance, the presence of the awe-inspiring shaman and surrounding crowd ready for a miracle, each person could easily

[59]In a valuable essay, "The Process of Hypnotism and the Nature of the Hypnotic State" (1944), Drs. Lawrence S. Kubie and Sydney Margolin wrote: "The subject who has been hypnotized many times inevitably develops certain automatic or conditioned reflexes, by which a short-cut is established to the hypnotic state" (p. 611) and further, after a discussion of the reason for this great facilitation, which should certainly fit the celebrants in question: "That in any individual who has been hypnotized repeatedly the hypnotic state can be induced almost instantly by the mere presence of the hypnotist is not surprising, because the hypnotic reaction becomes a complex conditioned unit in the total Ego-*Gestalt*, an organized Ego-fragment into which the individual can be thrown in a flash, just as the patient with a specific phobia can be thrown into a panic by the appropriate danger signal" (p. 617).

learn his own technique of almost instant self-hypnotization, and the words of the magician weave the visionary scene for all alike. The hypnotic effect, familiar and prepared as the climax of a magic performance, spreads through the circle of watchers and listeners and draws them all into the one inescapable experience. So the shaman may work in perfectly good faith and impart his fantasy to his fellows, who meet it with their own self-hypnotic technique, embracing his suggestion as he sings his miraculous adventure.[60]

Now, what is the point and purpose of all these unrealistic claims and illusory performances? The answer is implicit in the primitive human scene. The world of nature is a theater of superhuman physical powers, against which the strength of every living species and, indeed, of every tiny separate life is pitted. Perhaps it is man's misfortune to know this; but since he does know it his primary desire is for power to hold his own amid the hosts of antagonists that surround him. Even their conflicts with each other, quite regardless of him, may crush him between them. In every case he must seek protection by one against another and, of course, try to take his stand under the wing of the strongest. In a cosmic arena where even the most impersonal events appear as acts he cannot but suppose that behind every thunderbolt, cloudburst, fire, or flood there is an angry agent willing it, as there is a benevolent spirit behind every good harvest, happy landing, or big drove of game animals. To counter the dangers of his haunted world and of particular foes—hostile tribes, witches, ghosts, offended ancestors, or whatnot—every person and every united group of persons seeks to build up its defensive and maintaining power.

The worship of power is not peculiar to primitive cultures, even if some conceptions of the origins and embodiments of power are. Civilized modern men are as prone to that worship as the crudest savages. It is built into our popular turns of speech: we speak of "the powers that be," "Money is power," "Knowledge is power." Our sovereign countries are called "Powers," and their dealings with each other "power politics." But intellectually we consider all "powers" to be reducible, by one analysis or another, to physical forces; most psychologists hold as a basic belief that psychological dynamisms as well as somatic ones are physiological, and

---

[60]The medicine-man quoted by Natalie Curtis in *The Indians' Book* (see p. 323) apparently hypnotized himself by singing all night (as another Indian described that process elsewhere). Medical hypnotists doubted the possibility of such a method until two English doctors, under pressure of need in war, discovered that hysterical patients could be hypnotized, though not very deeply, by a technique of overbreathing. Anything that could induce a hypnotic state in modern Englishmen, even under pathological conditions, could surely do so in a shaman who was whole in soul and body, especially as he could take all night for his overbreathing and probably attain any depth. See William Sargant and Russell Fraser, "Inducing Light Hypnosis by Hyperventilation" (1938).

involve no metaphysically distinct "mental energy" or spiritual substance, though we have certainly not mastered any but the crudest cerebral mechanisms. We work on the assumption that acts are causal phenomena which some day will be comprehensible in physicochemical
terms.

Not so the uncivilized thinker, to whom his own mental power is still
the most thrilling mystery, holding possibilities beyond any of the tangible things in nature. People generally have a fair idea of their own
physical strength and its limits compared to that of most animals of their
size, and know it is inferior (though, perhaps, not as pitiful as it seems to
Arnold Gehlen); but their mental capacity has no definite bounds. They
can imagine it as infinite, measured only by their subjective sense of
potentiality. So it is mental power they seek and hope to exercise in their
spirit-world. All the techniques of conceiving it—that is, finding or creating symbols whereby to imagine and represent it—make up their repertoire of magic: verbal formulas, sometimes long poems, manipulations,
animal voices and masks, miming and sundry less common means of
dramatization. With these the magic-maker shapes his intentions which
are designed to start off an act that is more than his own, as other beings
are expected to take it up and carry it to completion.

Magic power is the highest possession a person can boast in societies
that believe in its existence. Everyone has at least a small amount of it,
usually enough to make his curse on a personal enemy effective.[61] Some
people, however, are endowed congenitally with the power to harm others simply by projecting an evil wish from their minds to someone else;
such persons are born witches. Witchcraft may be an unintended function, and where it is regarded as such it is morally distinguished from
sorcery, which is always deliberate, as it requires accessories: plants,
bones, or parts of the victim—hair, nail-parings, blood, excrement,
etc.—to implement its work.[62] Anyone can perform sorcery, or "black

---

[61] See Elkin, *Aboriginal Men of High Degree*, p. 23: "The point to be stressed is that
while the medicine-man is considered to possess great power and faculties especially
developed, none of his powers is regarded as *extra-ordinary*, or abnormal. . . . in some
degree, though usually in a very slight degree, it is possessed by all."

[62] In *The Igbo of Southeast Nigeria* (1965), V. C. Uchendu, himself an Igbo and an
anthropologist, says: "Withdrawal, personal detachment, and fear of intimacy are traits
attributed to sorcerers. . . . Sorcery attribution—*nshi*—(not witchcraft) is the most feared
form of direct aggression and is directed at secretive persons who do not speak their mind,
who have 'something to hide'" (p. 65). On the other hand, Reynolds, in *Magic, Divination and Witchcraft among the Barotse of Northern Rhodesia*, says of another African
people, the Azande in Rhodesia (citing E. E. Evans-Pritchard): "Azande believe that
some people are witches and can injure them in virtue of an inherent quality. A witch
performs no rite, utters no spell and possesses no medicines. An act of witchcraft is a
psychic act" (p. 14).

magic," insofar as he knows a charm and can acquire the necessary objects to manipulate in support of it. In some societies the accusation of sorcery is a dreaded possibility, since every non-violent death is attributed to magic influence, and in each case part of the shaman's business is to find the culprit.[63]

There are degrees of magic power, ranging from the normal ability to use love charms bought from a magician who has them for sale, to the wildest exploits of shamans who kill persons at a distance by visitations of horrible diseases and tortures. Between these extremes there may be, in some cultures, ordinary men or women who own special "tabus," meaning in this case the ability to induce particular illnesses and the exclusive power to remove them.[64] Spells are passed on from one generation to another by inheritance; that is to say, they are family possessions. A person who has inherited a considerable store of such secrets is a rich member of the tribe.

But the holders of the highest magical powers have amassed their wealth in more strenuous ways. Medicine-men may be born to their calling, but in most societies they have also to be made, either by their prospective peers or by ghosts, human or animal ancestors, or deities. They may be ritually operated on, having viscera and bones removed and exchanged for new ones and having magic objects or creatures put into them at the same time;[65] or crystals, lizards, and magic cords may be "sung into" them as they lie entranced.[66]

The young shaman certainly believes in the experience he has had,

[63]Meggitt, in *Desert People*, pp. 324 ff., tells at length and in detail how the medicine-man reads the signs that indicate the killer who has "sung" or "pointed" the deceased.

[64]Fortune, in *Sorcerers of Dobu*, says: "Every disease is held to be caused by a *tabu*. . . . Each disease has its own *tabu* or incantation. Every man and woman knows from one to five *tabus*. . . . Thus Neddidiway, a middle-aged widow with two children, knew the *tabus* for incontinence of urine and incontinence of semen; Megibweli, an extremely old and once cannibalistic rainmaker [note: rainmakers are female], knew the *tabu* for elephantiasis; a man who gave me his knowledge of *tabu* knew gangosa, paralysis, tertiary yaws, and wasting in hookworm" (p. 138).

[65]Descriptions of all these procedures may be found in Elkin, *Aboriginal Men of High Degree, passim*. There we find the following enumeration of articles which are likely to be contained in the body of a practitioner, and lend him his power: "These are (a) *binji-binj*, or narrow pieces of pearl-shell about six inches long, pointed at one end; he is thought to have had these in him since his birth. . . ; (b) shiny white glassy stones (quartz crystals); (c) small bullroarer shaped sticks about six or eight inches long, called *koranad*, and kept in the small of their backs; and (d) a small snake, and perhaps a small dog, or a small kangaroo and so on" (p. 142).

[66]The idea of objects being "sung into" a person is not as far-fetched as it seems at first thought. The song holds an idea, and is immaterial; as such it can penetrate and invade a body. Inside the body it solidifies, and the physical object has thus been sung into the recipient (see Meggitt, *Desert People*, p. 325).

apparently in a deep hypnotic dream induced by his initiators, or even self-induced in a long, solitary fast—a dream that may have taken him to heaven, where the ordeal was conducted by spirits. When he returns he feels the invisible activity of his mind (which he may be locating in his stomach) as a vast power to meet the numberless occult powers that surround him and his people. His newly liberated talents come close to giving him a life-and-death control over many other people, for he may be hired either to cure or kill; he can interpret dreams and other signs of the future and provide magic defenses against its imminent threats.

Naturally, such a personage holds an exalted position and is constantly concerned to keep and augment it. The tribe relies on him to control rain and sunshine, avert disaster, and above all to cure disease. His status, in turn, depends on his success, which has to be sustained not only by sufficient happy outcomes but also by convincing explanations of the cases where nature does not do its part—clouds do not gather, or do not bring even a token shower, drought or blight destroys the gardens, patients die, hunters are unlucky, battles are lost, warriors meet death. The system of thought in which he lives and works fortunately allows for such exigencies, just as in our causal system some further reflection usually lets us explain events that disappointed our expectations. The medicine-man's interpretations are not lame excuses, as white observers too commonly rate them. They are reasonable modifications of common-sense judgment in motivational terms.

The possession of magic, however, is not an entirely comfortable asset. Pure superhuman power in itself is neither good nor bad; but as soon as it is put to a particular use it enters the realm of good and evil, which is the moral realm. And here its possessor may have to meet the hard condition that once he can use his special talent he must do so, or the power he does not choose to wield may turn against his own life. This condition accompanies even the natural endowment of witchery, and forces a born witch to practice her baneful spells on other people lest they attack their author.[67] But when we come to acquired magical power the situation is different: the danger inherent in its possession is a known risk, and the shaman who seeks to increase his magic repertoire expects to pay for each new acquisition. Since he has entered the occult realm of supernatural forces, he finds himself challenged by an inestimable host of willful, often invisible agents, and no amount of power that he can wield seems to be enough. His demonstrations in seances are as much to reassure him-

[67]Reynolds says regarding the "familiars" of witches: "The owner cannot refuse to let her *ndumba* kill, otherwise it will turn and kill her (*Magic, Divination and Witchcraft among the Barotse of Northern Rhodesia*, p. 16).

self as to impress his people, who are his moral supporters. The sense of his relative impotence in the spirit-world drives his desire for counter-forces of his own to the point of obsession, so that he will pay any price to have a new lizard sung into his belly or a new divine name revealed to him.

The conception of magic as a reification of meaning and consequent wielding of symbols as effectual instruments of will (one's own will or some other which they already embody) readily explains the extraordinary power attributed to words, and especially to proper names. Words are the paradigms of symbolic expression, for they have no other *raison d'être*. There is a whole great department in the world's religious literature dealing with the magical use of words and the mystical potential stored in verbal formulas, above all in divine names,[68] which may embody powers to kill or to save, in some high cultures even to beatify, and are sometimes held secret, like buried stores of "overkill" materials. In many tribal societies it is a serious breach of the most elementary manners to speak a person's name to his face, if not to use it at all; an elaborate system of relationship terms or pseudonyms serves to circumvent it.[69] The motivating feeling probably springs from the intimate connection of a person's

[68]A perfect example is given by S. Piara Singh, in "Shri Guru Nanak and Shaik Farad Shakar Ganj" (1971), quoting the Shri Guru Granth Sahib:

i) The world is ailing,
The Divine Name is the medicine,
One is polluted without the Truth.
(Dhanasri-I-786)

ii) The Divine Name is
Medicine for all the ailments.
(Gaur i Sukhmani-V-274)

iii) The Divine Name is the Pure Nectar,
It is the Quintessence of all the medicines.
(Sorath Ravidas-659)

iv) The Divine Name is the medicine,
Which keeps all the maladies away.
(Bilawal-V-814)

"In the *mul mantra* Shri Guruji has enunciated all the virtues and qualities of the Divine and Soothing Name. He has exhorted the people to meditate upon it constantly" (p. 6).

[69]Napoleon Chagnon, in *Yąnomamö*, pp. 10 ff., tells of several adventures that might have gone ill with him among those fierce people when he inadvertently spoke a tabooed name. As their names seem to be words of their language, this is an obvious danger for a stranger just learning it, for the word becomes taboo in ordinary use when it is tabooed as a name. It is odd that in South America, as in Australia, etiquette forbids the use of a person's name. Cf. above, p. 66, n. 48.

The Dream of Power

name with his sense of selfhood. Sometimes a child that has not been named is not considered a human being yet; if it dies the body is discarded without ceremony.[70] To use anyone's given name without traditional sanction is at best a gross invasion of privacy; such use is permitted only to specially situated people, as for Europeans the use of "thou" in address (still customary in most countries). Under tribal organization that permission goes with some age-class relationships, as it does for us with family relations, but it cannot—as among us—be extended to intimate friends. For savages, nearness and distance are characteristically social categories; a tribesman has near and distant sisters or brothers, mothers and fathers, grandparents, etc., the terms denoting generations, the distance the degree of blood-relatedness. In ordinary intercourse the name is replaced by such designations or by a descriptive nickname.

The power of a holy name is just about the greatest power a human being can invoke, since it carries the essence of the god himself; and it is, of course, correspondingly dangerous to speak. According to J. S. F. Garnot's study of some early Egyptian texts (Fifth and Sixth Dynasties), a man who wanted to get in touch with a god had to send his own name to heaven or to the underworld—wherever the god dwelled—through a priest; but he also had to know the right name whereby to address the god, who had several names. The priest apparently gave no help in that matter. Only a few powerful mortals knew the secret names of any gods, and thus could be put in contact with those deities.[71]

The feeling that words embody some efficacious force is not peculiar to primitive thinking, at least as the average civilized person would judge what is "primitive"—not his own thinking, of course. The belief in their efficacy is natural enough, since we all use words to command, beg, suggest, and generally direct each other's thought and action, and their influence in such intercourse is obvious. Where all happening seems like action, all nature may be expected to respond to our verbal utterances. "The Word"—the utterance of a god, of the civilized man's God—is the mightiest symbol today's religious thinkers can conceive: "In the beginning was the Word"; εν αρχηι ην ὁ λογος. Λογος means "reason,"

[70]See, for instance, Juha Pentikainen, The Nordic Dead-Child Tradition (1968), speaking of the pre-Christian custom of abandoning unwanted children: "A child that for one reason or another was not accepted into the family and who was not given a name, was abandoned. Abandoning a child with a name was already regarded as murder in the pre-Christian period" (p. 74). Elsewhere he speaks of the possession of a name as bestowing a right to live.

[71]See Garnot's article, "Les fonctions, les pouvoirs et la nature du nom propre dans l'ancienne Egypte d'après les textes des pyramides" (1948), quoted in Vol. II, p. 349n, in another connection.

"order," or "mind," as well as "word," but the English translators'
choice, "the Word," names the symbolic embodiment of them all; the
power of speech can stand proxy for everything mental, conceptual, or in
any way non-physical, of the spirit and the spirit-world.

Speech is the essence of symbolism; for the motivational thinking of
savages it holds the essence of magical potential. It can be marvelously
and elaborately manipulated, composed into poetic forms that are self-
identical yet immaterial, and when uttered, felt to spring from subjective
action, carrying the speaker's wish, the real mental force, through the air
(though the sound may vanish for ordinary ears) to its target. Verbal spells
are prized possessions among magicians, whether shamans, priestly di-
viners, witches, or laymen. They usually have to be recited word-perfect,
but accompanied by conscious wish; any formal error in their utterance
breaks the spell.[72]

Yet the employment of formulas which are pure abracadabra to their
users seems to be rare. I suspect that where we encounter such practices
we are dealing with a deteriorated culture. Among such people—de-
tribalized savages, or ignorant and superstitious persons in the backwaters
of our own civilized populations—one is likely to find completely un-
grounded, disconnected beliefs in good or bad forces inherent in charms
which are meaningless strings of syllables to be repeated a stipulated
number of times. That is a mental reversion to what John Murphy called
"the Primitive Horizon" of man's religious thought, and described as "a
simple belief in *power* in all things mysterious to him." This power may
dwell in phonetic patterns as such and in words or phrases distorted to
increase their cryptic character, as it does in lucky and baneful objects—
rabbits' feet, four-leaved clovers, opals, and other equally unlikely bearers
of good or evil;[73] such vague power, the author goes on to say, "has been
identified with the *Mana* belief ascribed by Codrington to the Melane-

[72]Cf. Jomo Kenyatta, *Facing Mount Kenya*, p. 287, speaking of the magic protecting a
hunter against perils of the chase: "It is very important to acquire the correct use of
magical words and their proper intonation, for the progress in applying magic effectively
depends on uttering these words in their ritual order."

The same requirement may appertain to the formality of religious rites. Curtis, in *The
Indians' Book*, quoted a Navajo statement: "The Navajo must never make a mistake or
miss a word in singing any sacred chant; if he does, the singing must stop, for its good has
been blighted. Even a whole ceremony will be given up if a single mistake occur in any
part of the ritual."

Similarly, Fortune, in *Sorcerers of Dobu*, p. 148, said: "Any spell of black magic, the
tabus included, is taught in several sessions. The greatest care is taken that the spell is
learned word perfect."

[73]A choice collection of such absurdities may be gathered from William J. Fielding's
Strange Superstitions and Magical Practices (1945), *passim*.

sians, and is found among the Jungle Tribes in India and the fetichistic tribes in Africa, and among many other peoples alongside their Animism or even more advanced religion."74

It seems that almost from the beginning of social life, on the lowest levels of culture, men tried to bolster their bodily strength with the additional energies they could feel but could not understand, their mental energies, given to their intuitive perception only symbolically as magic power inherent in all sorts of things, perhaps physiognomically suggested, perhaps derived from dreams and frights. But in the course of mental evolution on its broad, general front—however various its many separate advances and regressions may be—the symbolic forms which serve as the instruments of magic tend to become more and more vital and even psychical, until the magician himself becomes the chief symbol, possessing a wealth of specific powers to control nature and oppose spirit attacks on his life. Often these powers are thought to be quite literally in him, and still have such physical forms as the Eskimo shaman's *tunraqs* or the crystals, lizards, and other "helpers" inside a "clever man"; but also they may be purely felt powers bestowed on him by previous owners, inherited from his father or a maternal uncle or received, by virtue of sacrificial gifts, from benevolent ancestors, ghosts, or deities. A man may, in fact, become loaded with powers; at that point he resorts to the ancient principle, never quite abandoned, of crediting inanimate objects with mystical attributes, and sings or wishes his overload of magic into weapons, firesticks, pointing-bones, and *churingas*, which thereupon are charged with his spiritual potential.75

This brings up the problem of the grave dangers contained in all magic, which become imminent threats when the wielder of occult forces

---

74*Lamps of Anthropology*, p. 2. His four "horizons," or chief stages in the evolution of religion, are the Primitive, the Tribal, the Civilized, and the Prophetic.

75See, e.g., Cazeneuve, *Sociologie du rite*, p. 169: "Le charme est vraiment un objet magique lorsque sa vertu dépend surtout de celui qui le fabrique." In a previous passage (p. 154) he had explained the simplest technique of such power storage: "Le principe de contiguité se présente . . . souvent comme un transfert de qualités. Un objet ayant telle propriété la transmet à un autre par contact."

Victor W. Turner, in *The Drums of Affliction*, p. 85, says of the *mukula* root, which exudes a dark red, fast-coagulating sap: "Mukula, regarded as a medicine, is at the same time a shade manifestation and a mystical power. Part of its mystical power derives from the 'mystery of the red river, the river of blood.' . . . Redness, like whiteness and blackness, is conceived by Ndembu as a primary and eternal power, issuing from the supreme being, Nzambi himself, and pervading the phenomenal world with its quality. It is impossible to draw the line here between animism and dynamism. All one can say is that Ndembu try to tap many sources of power (ngovu), treating their dominant symbols as power accumulators."

[83]

acquires too much of such a dynamic cargo. B. W. Aginsky has recorded his findings on that subject; to the Pomo Indians (a northern Californian tribe), he noted, "every death and misfortune was the result of indirect or direct retaliation either from (1) the 'supernaturals,' or (2) from some individuals. . . . The supernaturals retaliated either for the infringement of a taboo or for the calling upon them for too much power. . . . Almost every masculine phase of Pomo life was on the status of a profession. Each member of a profession (some of which were money-manufacturing, gambling, fishing, deer-hunting, and doctoring) had a collection of out-of-the-ordinary objects which were potent in their ability to store up power to be used for the successful participant in an undertaking, and the power and techniques, which he had received from an older relative. All the objects were kept in a 'bundle.' Any individual could increase the potency of his bundle by accumulating objects and putting more and more power into them.

"Aside from the 'poison men' (sorcerers), gamblers were the most fearless and at the same time most dangerous men in the community. Some gamblers made themselves so potent before a gambling match that their children died as a result. That is, the 'supernaturals' caused their deaths. Some of these men could not have children because they were so full of power. The same statements were also made concerning the other Pomo professionals, especially the hereditary doctors."[76]

Another American anthropologist, M. E. Opler, who studied some groups of southwestern Indians, found that while their alleged belief in a supreme life-giving, ruling God was probably a product of missionary influence, their real metaphysical conception was that of a vast, pervasive Power. Of this more native and convincing idea he said: "Power is thought of as a mighty force that pervades the universe. . . . Nothing is barred a priori from being a conductor of supernatural power, though the tendency to expect transmission through traditional and well-known channels is strong. . . . every Apache, man or woman, is a potential recipient of supernatural power. . . . One day a person may have 'something speak to him.' It may be in a dream; it may be when he is alone in camp; it may be when he is with a crowd of his fellows. . . . The words or the vision are for him alone. . . .

"An Apache may accept or reject the power thus offered. If he accepts he is given directions for conducting a ceremony. . . .

"At a later date this same Apache may be approached by another and

---

[76]"The Socio-Psychological Significance of Death among the Pomo Indians" (1940), pp. 1–2.

different power, and he may accept this second ceremony too. . . . Thus it is that an Apache becomes 'loaded up with powers,' as one informant put it.

"If a power is successfully practiced by one man for many years, he or a near relative must die for it. If he consents to sacrifice a relative, that person will die by disease or accident very soon."[77]

Far away from these people, in Africa, Barrie Reynolds found a similar relation of magic power to death, but here it was not so much the danger of being overwhelmed by the greatness of one's own potential as the price of its acquisition. After a discussion of the art of divining by the use of a conglomeration of symbols shaken together in a basket so they form a pattern on the surface of the pile, much as tea leaves do on the bottom of a cup, he observes, "The training of an *ngombo* basket diviner must be both difficult and arduous. No doubt it is also expensive. An interesting point about this training is that the novice must first kill a near relative before his basket is able to function properly."[78]

Men can become "drunk with the sight of power." Where the notion of magical control over other men and magical propitiation of "supernaturals" prevails, they vie with one another for possession of such assets and feel themselves ever pitted against each other and against invisible presences, spirits of evil, in self-defense. There are always greater forces threatening, so their desire for more magic potency may become obsessive, like the pathological avarice of a person craving more money no matter how much he has, or of an Alexander, a Napoleon, or a Hitler for conquest far beyond anything he could hold and rule.

Now, what is the basic reason for this magic-madness that is apt to develop in savage societies, this extreme and constant fear and defense? The cause, I think, lies deep in a tenet which many anthropologists have recognized and recorded,[79] but which does not betray its pervasive influence at once: the belief that death is always an infringement and violation of a life, no matter what may be the sufferer's age or general condition when it occurs. It is always brought upon one by a hostile act of a human or superhuman agent. Death is not something natural. Aginsky's statement to that effect was quoted above; where people hold that conviction, every illness or accident is a challenge, just as truly as an enemy onslaught. Every approach of death is to be met in the same way, not with the idea of merely stemming and delaying it, but of really conquer-

---

[77]"The Concept of Supernatural Power among the Chiricahua and Mescalero Apaches" (1935), p. 66.
[78]*Magic, Divination and Witchcraft among the Barotse of Northern Rhodesia*, p. 102.
[79]See n. 1 above.

ing it, winning the battle, for there is no notion of an ineluctable end to each individual life. So, no matter what the circumstances, the smitten person, often supported by his whole kind, will rise to contest every attack, whether alleged to be by earthly foes, witches, ghosts, angry ancestors, gods, or demons; no matter how long the battle has already been waged, the weakness of advancing age is of itself no ground for defeat; all one needs is more devices, more gifts of magic. Such personal assets, if not at one's own hand, are stored in the potent material objects which every magician has in his possession as well as in himself. In any emergency the doctor can be called to diagnose the trouble and, one hopes, to exorcise the troublemaker.

This attitude explains not only the high value set on magic in savage cultures but also the radical difference between the primitive view of life and any more advanced conception. To the true savage, life appears as an indefinite course of adventure with no foreseeable end but, like a battle, with a constant chance of death—the sort of death that is a forfeit of one's bravely risked life, and the end of the gaming contest when it comes. The loser is not eliminated from the tribal scene but only lays down his finished role; he lives in a new role as an elder, an ancestor, with responsibility for the succeeding generations and the power to punish any acts of theirs that he disapproves. In the constant earthly tug-o'-war he (or she) is still involved, but in a higher capacity, i.e., only in major issues where the ancestors are called on for power or guidance. The image of life is that of a stream, which gathers up all trickles and rills that enter it and carries them along, mingled but present; the individual is imagined—perhaps one can hardly call it "thought"—in the same way, with a distinct beginning in the rather spectacular act of birth[80] but no distinct end. It may be true that each person is defeated sooner or later; but without defeat by human or superhuman force nothing would bring about his death, however long he might have lived already. This is, indeed, the phylogenetic form of life, the vital pattern of the stock, going back to times when organisms ceased to be generated from chemicals in the earth's surface and envelope, and survived only if they were already procreative enough to continue in endless lines. Perhaps it is quite natural for unreflective minds to impose the same image on the living individual as on the presumptively deathless tribe.

A civilized person may wonder, indeed, how even the most naive, isolated group existing today could fail to realize the inevitable decline of

---

[80]Most savages, no matter how low their cultural level, have some myth of origin, at least human if not cosmic.

every old person who has escaped illness, violence, and accident to senility and, gradually, death. Does not the pattern of exits balance that of entrances in a steady-state tribal society, such as most native communities in wild countries seem to have been before the European adventurers invaded them? Generations may be shorter among savages—their brief life span has sometimes been remarked—but there are always some relatively aged members who are obviously going to die on their beds before long. How could people ignore that evidence? Through a surprising condition of nature, which has come but lately to the notice of biologists: that if there were no end of life without murder, accident, or acute sickness, the pattern of mortality would not be radically changed. It is perfectly possible to fit the belief in a potentially endless individual life into the existing order of successive, though overlapping, generations. Their length might be a little different, but—given the same vulnerability of human beings—sooner or later each one would meet his end.[81] The assumption that any slight or offense committed against an ancestor will induce that worthy to retaliate by sending fatal illness to the offender is an adequate substitute for physical causes in the frame of the spirit-world and completes the system of unnatural demises, from getting eaten or ensorcelled to ghostly visitations, making old age a theoretically dispensable factor in thanatology.

Nothing, perhaps, is more comprehensible than that people—savage or civilized—would rather reject than accept the idea of death as an inevitable close of their brief earthly careers. If they can maintain a confident hope of going along with an endless stream of life, their way of feeling their own vitality can really take the form of the phylogenetic continuum, a completely open-ended progress, punctuated by brushes with death but always expecting to triumph or escape, without end. In many of the world's hinterlands such an attitude really seems to prevail; contacts with civilization bring in new ideas, missionaries set up new

---

[81]George Wald, in a short and somewhat whimsical essay, "Origin of Death" (1973), remarks on the hypothetical effect of an equally hypothetical absence of natural decline, as follows: "Over the centuries and the millennia, one has searched for the Philosopher's Stone, the Fountain of Youth, all of those efforts somehow to abolish death.

"That age-old quest for fleshly immortality is a hoax. Peter Medawar has a book called *The Uniqueness of the Individual*, and in its first two chapters you will find this all laid out. Peter Medawar points out that if we already possessed every feature of bodily immortality that one could want, it would change our present state very little. . . . Every time you cross a street you risk your life; there are cars, trucks, trains, and planes; there are viruses and bacteria. . . . There are electric circuits, and all the other hazards. All the insurance actuaries would have to do is hang around for awhile, and pretty soon they'd send you the new rates."

gods, but ideas and powers are assimilated at once to the basic feeling of life itself, and take its primitive form.

Yet gradually, reluctantly, humanity comes to recognize the closed form and the brevity of each personal life. It is a complex, problematic insight, as even an elementary study of comparative religion and eschatology evinces. It meets with resistance and "ritual ignorance" where it has certainly dawned. The interesting fact is that it does dawn, inevitably, on people who do not discuss it and do not seem to think about it; and that wherever and whenever they come to realize that death is not, in essence, an extraneous force pitted against the vital impulse but is inherent in the form of human life itself, there is a momentous change in their experience that marks no less than a phylogenetic step in the history of Mind.

21

Dream's Ending: The Tragic Vision

Ach, wie dunkel ist es in des Todes Kammer!
Wie traurig tönt es wenn er sich bewegt,
Und nun aufhebt seinen schweren Hammer,
Und die Stunde schlägt.
                                                    —Matthias Claudius

AT FIRST thought it seems strange, even fanciful, to regard a conceptual insight like the realization of natural mortality as a milestone on the road of man's evolutionary advance. On longer consideration, however, one can see many reasons to class it as such, both because of the conditions which its attainment has required and the influence it has had on the subjective and objective course of human life wherever it has taken root as a genuine conviction. It marks no direct physical change, though indirectly and subtly it may produce many; its historical significance and its crucial function belong to the advance of mind, not of physique.

Yet that mental advance is of one piece with the rest of human evolution. Despite the vastness of time and change that must have prepared what we call "the Mind" today, I hold that the elements of that marvelous structure may all be found in nature, and the principles of its formation are those of organic chemistry, electrochemical action, or whatever substitutes for such current concepts the progress of scientific thought may dictate in future. If this is an audacious assumption, I can only plead that it seems to me the most promising to open, and keep open, a way to a rational concept of human mentality.[1]

[1]The study of mind is a central interest of the existentialist school today, and some of its adherents are excellent psychologists; yet I cannot follow their lead, because it seems to me a basic mistake to think that to correct the simple-minded reductionist theories of life one has to add some non-physical element to our scientific thinking. An adequate study of

The basic principles by which that mentality has arisen are, then, the principles of biological action, from the most primitive to the most advanced, complex, and deeply structured. These vital foundations of mind have been discussed in earlier chapters, especially 8 and 9;[2] the latter one, indeed, is a preface to the theory to be dealt with here. But the making of mind has been such a weaving of coincidences, asynchronous changes and readjustments, and especially chance opportunities for new realizations of potential acts that it is only after the whole foregoing survey of animal life that this strangest of vital phenomena—Mind—can appear in its biological setting; and even when we see it in that context, its own, unparalleled history has only begun to emerge for us. We have to follow its course a long way before we come upon the origins of its characteristic products: society, religion, conceptual thought, and personal intent and action.

It is in a fairly recent phase of that evolutionary course that the realization of death as the inevitable finale of every life has overtaken mankind; in fact, it is not entirely complete in some of the remotest corners of the earth. In most of the present world population it has been met and dealt with in various ways—religiously, philosophically, and sometimes (though not widely) by simple admission. Its long preparation, however, has been as natural as the wholly unplanned developments which culmi-

---

psychological and social phenomena in progressively developed scientific terms is more apt to correct the faults of hasty generalization and simplistic conclusions than is any resort to acts which are "not processes," "not in space and time," and similar metaphysical chimeras. But of this, more below.

[2]Since their presentation goes back to Volume I, the reader is not likely to recollect them too clearly or have the text readily at hand; so it may be helpful to recall the main points that will figure in the present context. (1) Acts are natural events of a specialized form, beginning in a discharge of energy (impulse) due to chemical reactions; a completed act has rise, acceleration, consummation, and cadence; its cadence is, or enters into, the build-up of a subsequent act. (2) One act may entrain another, either by stemming from a stronger impulse or by being further advanced on its course and involving some of the same mechanisms as the entrained act. An entrained act becomes a support and an elaboration of the entraining act. (3) Since an act is a change in a material substrate, such as a chemical transformation or change of electrical potential, its passage is recorded in that substrate, and a cumulative system of cyclic acts constitutes a matrix of activities from which acts of growth and articulation of forms arise by the process known as individuation. (4) Individuation has degrees and may proceed at different rates in different directions from a single matrix. (5) Tendencies to individuation or the opposite process, progressive involvement, are characteristic of organisms. (6) In animals, behavioral acts arise from the matrix; all external stimuli that have effects on an organism affect the matrix, i.e., the organism as a whole, and through it motivate reactions, including reflexes. (7) Feeling is a phase of acts of high intensity and (usually) great complexity; numberless acts are performed unfelt. (8) The growth and elaboration of feeling is our index to the evolution of mind in man.

nate in the peacock's ornamental tail or the beaver's landscape architecture; for it is an implicit consequence of a basic evolutionary process, individuation.

The persistent tendency of acts to nucleate and form matrices of mutually involved, integrating, and ever-augmenting acts gives rise to individuals, long-lasting or transient, partial or self-sufficient, to all degrees. Their possible degrees and varieties have been discussed above in Chapter 9. The avenues of physiological development, progressively opening up new options, lead to the tremendous proliferation of organic activities that have recorded themselves, since the beginning of life, in the complexities of even the simplest vital mechanism, simpler than a cell. Roughly in parallel, sometimes in dialectical progression with that "complexification" (to borrow Teilhard de Chardin's apt neologism once more), runs a tendency of strong impulses to gather up smaller or weaker ones, and for acts in the accelerating phase to assimilate lesser acts in progress or seem to commandeer incipient ones to serve them as elaborations of their own development. That is the principle of entrainment, which simplifies the tangle of separately directed impulses by massing their expressions into a few organizing acts.

Entrainment is the fundamental process of individuation, as it is of nucleation and inward coherence. How an act arising from one impulse can exert a force on other acts from equally original impulses so as to pace and plot their courses is a puzzling question; yet there can be little doubt that there are autonomous physiological rhythms which not only mesh in very intricate ways with others from different sources but also seem to control a creature's larger, facultative acts, its behavioral cycles adapted to ambient conditions, and even unique responses. The difficulty of explaining them lies, I think, in a tacit common-sense assumption that the energy mobilizing an act must be supplied from outside the organ (or organelle) which performs it, and ceases when—and because—"the need of the organism" is served. But if every living structure does all it can at any time, the nature of entrainment may not be the effect of a force *a tergo* at all, but rather the opening of a way for small impulses to find expression in the wake of a great and vigorous one, whose progression from moment to moment proffers and limits the opportunities of many lesser impulses in the agent's vital advance, which would otherwise be smothered, but can adapt to those opportunities to fit into the larger unit as elaborations of its passage.

As the entrainment of small spontaneous impulses by greater ones, especially by such as are already launched on their realization, organizes a center of cyclic biochemical rhythms, the matrix, so it also makes the division between the vital organism and the world in which it exists. The activity of the matter involved in a life is hard to conceive; it holds its environment at bay by living, somewhat as an eddy in water keeps its distinct shape, perhaps even while traveling downstream, by the centripetal motion that feeds surface water into it and the centrifugal phase that keeps its funnel expanded. The vortex is a very simple dynamic form which dissolves again, leaving the water unchanged; but the organism, being built of acts—in themselves highly complicated events—makes permanent changes in the material it exploits. The elements it retains are metabolites which enter into the biochemical round and create the distinct protoplasmic structure which is functionally centralized and thereby divided from its environment. That is the process of individuation, the counter-aspect of the integration that establishes the matrix.

In the course of this process the variations of living form appear which distinguish taxonomic groups, for there are crowding and competing started lines of development within a living system, each seeking its own chances of growth and expansion and maximum activity. It is the same dynamic pattern as individuation, wherefore some earlier biologists, notably Charles Manning Child and N. S. Shaler, called every limb, tentacle, or even transient pseudopodium an individual.[3] I think better to call them articulations, since the impulses of their outgrowth and formation spring quite directly from the central organic complex. But the phenomenon of bodily articulation into distinct limbs, organs, and other special parts is a result of the unit character of acts, the inherent push of each impulse to its own expression, and the consequent general imbalance of tensions in an organism. This ever-changing yet ever-renewed condition drives forward the process of individuation whereby a being is formed, a process which has stages and directions, and very different rates in its various reaches. Individuation may go far in some plant or animal species and remain incomplete in others; and in the ontogeny of specimens the same principle governs the formation of their features.[4]

Any internal strain or external impact on living tissues seems to be a trophic or functionally activating stimulus; the autonomic function of an organ, usually a lifelong workload, is enough to promote its continued development and potency,[5] so it tends to increase and variegate unless its

[3] Cf. above, Vol. I, pp. 309–10 and notes.
[4] John Murphy wrote, in Lamps of Anthropology, p. 95: "Individuality is something that develops; and this implies that there are degrees, and possibly even hierarchies, of individuality."
[5] In this connection it is interesting to note a remark made by Dr. Paul Weiss at a biological symposium at Shelter Island in 1956: "Perhaps the mere act of discharge of the

career is checked by other developing processes, and if it happens to find an uncommonly long free course it may eventuate in some very uncommon species-specific feature, which may have a radical influence on the life of the specialized stock. Consider what the elephant's trunk means to the possessor of that fantastic nose! It must have had much the same anlage as the tapir's, the anteater's, and perhaps even the pig's snout, which are all put to a secondary use beside their primary olfactory function, namely, grubbing for food. The double task, guided by smell but bringing more than the olfactory sense into play, stimulated the external development as well as that of the chemically sensitive inside membranes, so the grubbing animals have long noses which are also refined tactual organs.[6] But a prehensile nose—one that can seize and uproot a tree, draw up water by a precisely started and stopped breath and squirt the water over its manipulator's back or into his mouth, and double for the vocal apparatus by serving as a trumpet—is really a far-reaching overgrowth and endowment of the oldest and lowliest special organ! The elephant's life is as different from that of other long-snouted mammals as his nose is from theirs; that versatile and powerful appendage gives him almost the benefit of a hand. Not the least of its advantages may be that he can feed himself by large, collected mouthfuls instead of browsing by day-long nibbles. In any case, the elephant carries around a spectacular exhibit of what can happen when circumstances favor one organ very much above others in the evolutionary rise of a stock, and thus produce a specialization, particularly one that creates many new potentialities.[7]

---

thyroid product stimulates the thyroid gland to produce and/or accumulate more of its product" ("The Compounding of Complex Macromolecular and Cellular Units into Tissue Fabrics" [1956], pp. 789–830).

[6]Frederick Wood Jones, in his well-known book *The Principles of Anatomy, as Seen in the Hand* (1942; 1st ed., 1919), wrote: "It is the sense of smell that guides the primitive mammal about the world. But . . . further knowledge . . . is derived from the sense of touch. There is no doubt as to the manner of touch-testing with most primitive mammals, for it consists of the familiar process which may best be described as 'nosing.' . . . Vibrissae, or 'whiskers,' and sensory papillae are added to this nosing area to heighten its tactile sensibility; . . . and even in the absence of vision such an animal is kept informed of its surroundings by the sensation of touch derived from its muzzle" (p. 327). "The snout of the tapir is that animal's great tactile organ, and the trunk of the elephant might almost be regarded as an extreme specialization of the same thing" (p. 328).

[7]One of the circumstances in this case was probably the fact that the lengthening and strengthening of the nose without involvement of the mouth let the nasal structures acquire new functions at short intervals; such shifts would be apt to provide repeated optimal conditions for change and growth. Whether the new organ promoted his allegedly high intelligence is hard to say, but it certainly is not improbable.

There are other examples of such uneven development; prehensile tails, the lemur's "toilet claw," and the wryneck's remarkable tongue all are cases in point, and have been mentioned above.[8] But the one that concerns us here is the most far-reaching in natural history: the overgrowth and hyperactivity of the opercular lobes of the human brain. How this might have resulted from the combination of general primate traits with the peculiarity of man's upright stance and bipedal gait has already been discussed at some length, as have the most fundamental psychological changes which evidently followed from the overabundance of cerebral acts;[9] but the most radical product of his symbolific mentality, his cultural life—in embryo, perhaps as old as his existence—has been meeting a crisis piecemeal, partly in prehistoric and partly in historic times, so it is not utterly impossible to trace it even to an evolutionary source.

That source is a particular phase in the process of individuation which seems to overtake every human society sooner or later, paced by the rate at which the activity of the cerebral cortex outruns the needs of the animal organism, as it typically does. For no matter how adequately those needs are met, the great neural complex does not come to rest; it goes on producing its figments, dreams and thoughts, wishes and emotions, apparently below as well as above the fluctuating limen of feeling. The possibilities of varying, combining, and deriving further images and conceptions from prior intracerebral acts are practically endless, and lead the brain on to more and more symbolic play. But every act also leaves its trace in the action-built matrix, the physical organism; every metabolic rhythm in its somatic structure, and especially every behavioral act, from a whole performance down to each muscular movement or tension, inscribes itself on the cumulative formation of the historic individual. And so does every act of mentation. Since countless mental acts are started and finished in the brain, their main effects are likely to be on that organ. The material involved in their passage seems to have very little bulk; after a few childhood years, growth of the brain stops and leaves a free field for elaboration of structures and functional patterns.[10] Since the

---

[8]In Vol. II; see esp. pp. 228 ff.

[9]In Vol. II, Chapters 16–18.

[10]In a brief article, "Entwicklung und Leistungsfähigkeit des Menschenhirns während der Menscheitsgeschichte" (1955), J. Gottschick pointed out the alternation of periods of growth with periods of elaboration and progressive use. After noting the obvious increase of potentiality with periods of organic change, he says further: "Aber auch das Prinzip der Leistungsentfaltung ist nicht zu übersehen. Es will sogar scheinen, als ob es gerade erst im Anschluss an rasche und hochgradige Massen- und Formveränderungen des Menschenhirns während der Phylogenie, nicht aber gleichzeitig mit ihnen, zur einem beachtlichen Kulturanstieg kommt und evolutiv-organgestaltende Prozesse auch in der Phy-

cerebral cortex seems to be the most intensely active center in the normal human makeup, its self-contained activity tends to build a matrix of its own, wrought mainly of memory traces and consequently composed in large measure of residual feeling, thought, dream elements, emotional and intellectual experience. The brain, in other words, tends to individuate, and to establish a dependent yet distinct pattern of mental life within the physical life of the organism, even while it serves that organism as a vital part. It achieves a partial individuation, a functional matrix, which appears subjectively as a sort of homunculus or autonomous "inner man," the Mind.

There are some indications of this semi-independence of the brain, or rather of its readiness to form a relatively closed and isolated system, which, with abnormal evolutionary advancement, might produce something close to an autonomous matrix. C. J. Herrick observed that in the salamanders studied by Coghill "the behavior of the adults of these lowly vertebrates exhibits so simple an action system that one might expect a corresponding simplicity of pattern of reflex arcs in the central nervous system." Instead of that, however, "it is hard to find in the brain of a salamander any well-defined reflex arcs at all. The nervous elements have widely ramified fibrous processes which interweave to form a nervous feltwork or neuropil of baffling intricacy, and the main lines of transmission which serve the standardized behavior-patterns are threaded through this tangle of cells and fibres in so disperse formation as to be recognized with great difficulty. In the higher centers these interwoven fibres are mostly unmyelinated, and since every contact is a synaptic junction the entire feltwork may be activated diffusely by every nervous impulse that enters it from any source."[11]

So it seems that the brain, even in rather low animals, amphibians, is more complex than their behavior betrays, and has reserves of very plastic and reactive tissue only half-committed to special functions, but ready to take them on.[12] The tendency to develop somewhat apart from the needs

---

logenie (wie in der Ontologie) des Menschenhirns seine Leistungsentfaltung sogar zeitweilig verzögern können. Das wird durch die Tatsache verständlich, dass Entwicklungs- und Entfaltungsprozesse auf teilweise verschiedenen biologischen Umständen beruhen und damit auch unterschiedliche Zeitspannen erfordern. . . . Die phylogenetische Entwicklung beruht auf plötzlichen Erbänderungen (Mutation) . . . ; den 'sprunghaften' Mutationsfolgen verschafft erst der jahrtausendlange Ausleseeinfluss bleibende Bedeutung. Die Ontogenie wie die Phylogenie bringen aber immer nur Körper*formen*—und organe zustande. Erst wenn diese vorhanden sind . . . kann sich physiologisch eine Leistung anbahnen und entfalten" (p. 273).

[11]"Mechanisms of Nervous Adjustment" (1951), p. 81.

[12]A few pages later Herrick concludes: "In higher vertebrates . . . tissue of this sort is

of the organism seems to be an ancient trait of central nervous systems, which may be found where it is of no apparent importance to the survival of the stock. Another sign of the brain's readiness for an independent course of development, seen in more than one class of vertebrates, was pointed out by Tilly Edinger on the basis of her paleontological studies of fossil crania and their evolutionary changes in comparison with the concurrent changes in the skeletons to which they belonged. From these studies it is quite evident that the growth and general form of brains advance at rates which may differ, sometimes even extremely, from the rates of progress of other parts shown in the fossil record. In the evolution of birds the brain lagged behind the avian form and remained reptilian when the creatures were no longer reptiles;[13] but for the history of the horse—a paradigmatic fossil series—she claimed that "in the first five million years of horse evolution *the brain advanced considerably without concomitant progress in specialization or size of the other known parts of the body.*"[14]

Not only in phylogeny but in present-day existence the brain often reacts in ways of its own, not like other organs; so the same author wrote in another article: "The foxhound bitch injected by Benedict *et al.* [with pituitary growth hormone] grew to 150 percent of the weight of its sister, yet the difference in PB [pituitary body] weight was only 7 percent; uterus and ovaries were 300 percent, thyroid and spleen, 100 percent heavier; the difference in brain weight amounted to no more than 3 percent." So she states the interesting conclusion: "We are here facing a phenomenon which has an extremely important bearing on our present investigation: the fact that brain growth follows other laws than body growth and PB growth"[15] (yet may have some effect on pituitary body growth; the pituitary body is an attachment of the brain).

---

segregated and specialized, and this process culminates in the associational tissue of the human cerebral cortex. . . . Here there is spread of excitation in patterns which change from moment to moment. There are vast reserves of latent energies and some unknown kind of organization which preserves vestiges of past experience in patterns which can be recalled. . . . And this cortex exhibits, not only plasticity and modifiability, but also a measure of 'central freedom and sufficiency' (Bentley) which is our human birthright of intelligent adjustment and creative power" (p. 83).

[13]See above, Vol. II, p. 341.

[14]"Paleoneurology versus Comparative Brain Anatomy" (1949), p. 19.

[15]"The Pituitary Body in Giant Animals Fossil and Living: A Survey and a Suggestion" (1942), p. 32. Not only hormones but also extraneous chemical inputs may affect brain tissues, especially that of the cerebral cortex, and other body tissues differentially. So, more than thirty years ago, a research team reported: "The local application of acetylcholine to the exposed cerebral cortex of the cat produced a period of depression of electrical activity followed by acetylcholine discharges. The depression of activity is inde-

The anlage to separateness, then, lies in the physical mechanisms of vertebrate nervous systems, ready to come into play when unusual opportunities invite the human brain to outgrow its original cybernetic functions and develop something like interests of its own, accommodating the tremendous excess of its burgeoning impulses to each other by building whole systems of ideas and emotional attitudes centered on them, units of motivational power. That such systems comprise more than felt acts has been long established as a result of psychoanalysis; a mind is something more solid than any "content of consciousness," or, on the other hand, any pattern of "behaviors." It is a physiologically based, intraorganic functional entity, a relatively independent complex of vital rhythms supporting facultative mental acts.[16]

The tendency of that complex to nucleate into something like a subordinate matrix of activities is at the same time a tendency to become an individual being, to emancipate itself from the organism in which it developed. That, of course, would be a fatal achievement; the service of the brain to the rest of the body is of its own essence. Yet the partial individuation which can take place only in the confines of a complete animal economy is the same biological process as the individuation of the whole.

To think of individuation as an intraorganic process makes for a somewhat different concept of individuality. The most natural way to define that term is, of course, through the criteria whereby we judge its exemplifications; so the concept of individuality is usually based on the traits which distinguish a given organism from most others of its kind, and the particular assemblage of unusual features or actions provides a unique

---

pendent of systemic effects of acetylcholine. . . . The depression of electrical activity spreads over the cortex, and apparently not along neural pathways but in all probability in linear fashion. Depression appears in distant areas in which the acetylcholine discharges did not appear. . . . This type of cortical depression is not due to stimulation of suppressor areas, nor to mechanical stimulation" (F. M. Forster, W. J. Borkowski, and R. H. McCarter, "Depression of the Cerebral Cortex Induced by Applications of Acetylcholine" [1946], pp. 28–29).

[16]In this connection, D. B. Lindsley, studying the most active of all cells, the neurons in the cerebral cortex, wrote: "Apart from the actual phasic discharge of a neuron, there appears to be a rhythmical property of the cell body depending upon the rate of chemical reactions taking place in it. Such a rhythmic waxing and waning of activity seems to be accompanied by an electrical effect, the summation of which in many neurons, somehow synchronized, gives rise to the spontaneous (alpha) rhythms of the cortex" ("Psychophysiology and Motivation" [1957], p. 75). The "somehow" of their synchronization is through entrainment of random acts by dominant ones, which has been intensively studied in recent years, particularly for rhythmic activities. See Jürgen Aschoff, ed., *Circadian Clocks* (1965). Such studies are still going on. The relation is still intriguing.

characterization. Such distinctive attributes are undoubtedly our main indices of what we call an individual. Even in the minimal case—recognizing a plant or animal as a specimen of a particular taxon—similarity to a standard form, in taxonomy usually a "type specimen," determines the kind, and the sheer distinctness of location in space at any time makes the exemplar an individual instance.[17] But in a human context, of course, the word "individual" means more than a physically separate entity. It even means more than a being endowed with traits deviating from the ordinary pattern exemplified by most members of a population. The word has an aura of superior strength, in our society, moral superiority.

The fact is that to define a phenomenon in terms of the criteria whereby we recognize it as such may be conceptually crippling. There are some clear and highly important concepts which have application to reality, yet have no sure criteria for cases of their applicability,[18] for instance, where the decisive signs are not directly observable, as in this case, where they are (for our present ignorance) covert events. We can only construe them from what we do observe. But if we accept deviation from an accepted standard as the measure of individuality, then that all-important property becomes the same as oddity, and a person extolled as a "great individual" appears to be honored essentially for his abnormalities, which cannot go very far without putting the "great individual"'s life in jeopardy. Also, deviations may be acquired in many circumstances, through ambient conditions or organic disturbances, and lead to alienation, which usually seems to impair rather than increase the subject's individuality, such as it is, great or small.

A better criterion of individuality seems to me to be the origin of all a being's acts in a highly organized matrix of impulses. It is the organic unity that makes its acts strong, by linking them all on the level of their embryonic impulses, so that the organism is ready to go into action at once with a complex response to a fairly high challenge, because the deep linkages prepare minor impulses to follow greater ones in large expressions. In that way the forms of the agent's acts are characteristically and peculiarly its own.

Individuality, in this sense, belongs to every living being, and may be present in great numbers of organisms that are as like each other as

---

[17]In logic and epistemology, such distinctness is sufficient. C. I. Lewis, in an untitled lecture (1949), made the statement: "Only individuals exist; and individuals I conceive to be continuous bounded parts of the space-time whole." Similarly, Bertrand Russell's article "Le principe d'individuation" (1950) has nothing to do with any biological process of individuation, but with criteria for the logical distinction of particulars.

[18]"Truth" is such a concept. But that issue belongs to the last part of this essay.

Dream's Ending: The Tragic Vision

Tweedledum and Tweedledee. If they are alike in their genic makeup their normal appearance and actions should be similar by being true to the pattern of their respective natures. Of course, no two genomes in different beings are really identical, not even in uniovular twins, nor their separate products impervious to external forces, especially early in life. Yet there are species-specific degrees of individuation. A crayfish is more of an individual than, say, an alga, such as a ribbon of kelp, though the alga often differs from others of its kind much more than a crayfish ever does. That is because the alga has a weakly integrated system of impulses to growth and articulation, so its shape, its adult size, proportions of stem and root-anchor and leaf, thickness and color are much more dependent on ambient conditions than the bodily form of the crayfish, which suffers little distortion except by extreme pressions.[19] As somatic activities become more numerous and devious in a living system, their record in its tissues becomes highly intricate and the fabric of its life increasingly dense, until it is tightly woven into a distinct and central agent, a coherent individual.

If, now, the activity of the human brain so far outstrips that of the rest of the body that its symbolic renderings form an internal situation which motivates more and more mental impulses, the pseudo-matrix which the covert consummations of those impulses tend to establish will be composed largely of symbolic elements, traces of such cerebral acts. The psychical phases they are apt to attain differ rather radically from those of somatic, muscular, or even perceptual acts, where these last are purely alertive and directive, built into behavior as in animals. Consequently the partial individuation of the mind produces a peculiarly non-physical appearance of what seems to each person the essential agency within his own body.

Among people of very communally organized cultures, that agency is but vaguely conceived; their interest is in acts, and the most interesting acts of their daily lives as well as special occasions are tribal affairs. Every actor in such a horde feels the effort he is putting into the current undertaking more as the power of the working, fighting, or dancing group than of his separate body; through him the power of the whole is flowing. A man's (and even more, perhaps, a woman's) private routine of chores

[19]Yet low animals, such as crayfish, are more variable than higher ones, at least in functional respects; a physiologist, Joseph K. Hichar, in a research article, "Spontaneous Electrical Activity in the Crayfish Central Nervous System" (1960), stated as a finding: "ACh content of abdominal nerve cords of completely normal-appearing animals was found to vary by as much as 6,000 times. Most cords had 6 gamma ACh/gm tissue but three cords, also from 'normal' animals, had 0.001 gamma/gm tissue. Electrical activity was found to vary by as much as 30 times" (p. 204).

[99]

does not evoke enough feeling to make the person so engaged aware of any particular achievement. But in communal work, hunting or fishing, and even agriculture which is ritually performed so it creates at least a modicum of emotional tension most persons experience a lift of a general vital feeling which some German writers have called *Lebensgefühl,* "sense of life." In the most primitive societies this sense seems to be somewhat diffuse and impersonal, like the acts which inspire it; the agent is not really "I," but "we." The homunculus is not strongly felt as a single being, but at best as a great, continuous power, the Mind of a human tribe, set in the midst of natural forces it seeks to control by thought and magic mastery; the "doctor" or priest speaks for the tribe, and when he dies (by influence of a hostile magic) he joins the great company of ancestors who are still involved in tribal affairs, and someone else of the lineage steps into his place to continue his acts. It is the human society whose life is felt by each member as a power streaming through his limbs.[20]

In such a stream, an individual death is an episode, not a finish. The *Lebensgefühl* may rise and ebb with war, expeditions, disasters, or the seasons, but it has no real form of its own. What it does seem to bring with it, however, is the intuitive conviction that every creature "has" its life, as we "have" our mind (and may lose it). A person may change form, become a spirit or a were-tiger or what not, but his life—his identity—continues. The distinction between the mental homunculus and its incarnate appearance has already begun in the most backward hordes we know; long before it is conceived as an indwelling agent that leaves the body at death or even, perhaps, in sleep, it is quite unconsciously expressed in the notion of metamorphosis.

[20]The fact that savages have more communal than personal conception of life has been stated so often that one is in danger of accepting it as an anthropological cliché. Their proverbial carelessness of life, however, which is empirically unmistakable, does bear witness to it, and in many societies their use of language does likewise. One of its most recent confirmations appears in a study by the missionary Hermann Strauss of a fairly large native population of New Guinea who were not discovered by white men until 1933, so his linguistic findings should still be undistorted. These people have an unusual totemic system involving a sacred object, different for each group and known as its particular "*Mi,*" wherefore they are referred to in his monograph *Die Mi-Kultur der Hagenberg-Stämme im Östlichen Zentral-Neuguinea* (1962) as "Mi-communities." Of these people (who were, at the time of his researches, still in the stage of regarding every death as magically induced), he writes: "Die Lebensmacht, die durch das Mi allen Gliedern der Mi-Gemeinschaft zufliesst als Zeugungs-, Vermehrungs- und Wachstumskraft der Gruppe, wird von den einzelnen, hier zwar in gradueller Abstufung, auch als magische Seelenkraft erfahren und von jedem als na-na- min-i 'meine Seele' bezeichnet. Es ist aber nicht die Einzelseele in unserem Sinn, sondern ist der *Anteil*, das *Anteilhaben* des einzelnen an der *gemeinsamen* Lebenskraft und Seelenmacht der Gruppe, an der alle Glieder der Gruppe irgendeinen Anteil haben" (p. 137).

Dream's Ending: The Tragic Vision

In the higher non-human animals, any pervasive feeling stirred by behavioral action or its frustration is probably a general body-feeling together with the play of emotions triggered by percepts and other, even more casual, impingements. Such bodily sense is apt to be dormant, ineffectual, apart from the particular felt acts of the moment; animal feeling, therefore, is likely to be episodic, though its episodes may often be intense.

Human *Lebensgefühl*, by contrast, is a sense of continuous activity, because it comprises something more than body-feeling, something added to it by the cerebral function of "primary imagination": the vague but constant adumbration of potential action, from which arise intentions, wishes, or simply fleeting half-conscious ideas with various cathexes to keep them close to the limen of feeling, often playing across it. Those merely conceived possible acts are a large part of the mental matrix, i.e., of that integrated *substantia* of inner stirrings and outer impingements we call "consciousness"; and so are the acts we have forgone in performing the ones we did, for every realized option entails the rejection of an alternative, which thereupon is no longer potential, but negated. The existence of conceptual alternatives in the mind makes the behavioral options in human lives choices, not automatically decided on physiological and purely sensory grounds, as animal reactions are.

With the development of the mental quasi-matrix by the constant activity of a brain that far outruns the needs of the somatic system for cybernetic control, the basic feeling of life becomes centered in that organ, too, and attains a distinct holistic form. As a German "existentialist" psychiatrist, Kurt Schneider, noted in an early article, the *Lebensgefühl* gradually becomes a unitary phenomenon in which various phases can be distinguished, all of a dynamic character, such as rise and decline, vigor or weakness, health, illness, etc.; and also autonomous, influential activities, because the feelings of which a subject is capable anticipate the effects of stimulations by predetermining their possible values, the experiences they could elicit if they should occur: the special qualities of the fear, desire, thoughts, and other tensions they might evoke in that particular human being.[21]

In the context of the present theory of mind built on the act-concept, it is unfortunate that Schneider, like most, if not all, other disciples or

[21]Schneider wrote, in "Die Schichtung des emotionalen Lebens und der Aufbau der Depressionszustände" (1920), pp. 282–83: "Das Lebensgefühl ist ein einheitlicher Tatbestand. . . . Im Lebensgefühl fühlen wir das Leben selbst, *in* diesem Fühlen ist uns etwas gegeben, 'Aufstieg,' 'Niedergang,' 'Gesundheit,' 'Krankheit,' 'Gefahr' usw. . . . Sinnliche Gefühle sind nur Begleiterscheinungen, sie sind gleichzeitig. Das Lebensgefühl antizipiert den Wert der möglichen Reize diesen selbst und ihrem Eintritt: Angst, Furcht, Ekel, Appetit, vitale Sympathie und Antipathie."

followers of Max Scheler,[22] regards an act as "timeless" and "not a process." If such it were there could, of course, be no further research into its etiology or physical functioning. But Schneider was also a psychiatrist who based his reflections on clinical experience as well as on Scheler's peculiar doctrine (which has found wide acceptance among existentialist philosophers today); and his observations of the nature of vital feeling point even a sober naturalist to the source of man's inescapable recognition of his own mortality. The articulation of the *Lebensgefühl* with the progressive individuation of the Mind lets each person feel the rise and expansion of his life, its gathering impetus and the establishment of his world with maturing interests and commitments—but also the decline, past the zenith, when he finds that the life-long continuum of choices and the renunciations they automatically entail are slowly infringing on his sense of boundless potentiality, and many major options no longer exist. This emergence of biological form into feeling comes with the progressive elaboration of mental acts, as they have to adjust to their own increase by more and more integration and mutual concession; so, with evolutionary advance, the fabric of cerebral acts becomes so close-woven that it makes the individuated mental life seem like a single, all-embracing act.[23]

Wherever this point is reached, the *Lebensgefühl* of the subject takes shape as a sense of personal agency, not tribal power flowing through an instrument of human action, but the mental power of one human individual activating an obedient body of inexactly known ability and readiness. That inexact knowledge of one's own capacity is enough to stake out a rough general limit for the act of living, which now is felt to emanate from the quasi-matrix of mental activity, as every act expands from its

[22]Scheler's first highly influential book was *Der Formalismus in der Ethik und die materiale Wertethik* (1921). Among his adherents are Kurt Schneider, Kurt Strasser, F. J. J. Buytendijk, Melchior Palagyi, and an increasing number of more recent writers in America as well as Europe.

[23]This conception is most convincing where it is least formally stated, i.e., where it is simply assumed in use; as Harry Gersh, in *The Sacred Books of the Jews* (1968), did, apparently without sensing any difficulty or novelty in it, when he ended a long account of the pessimistic doctrine of Koheleth, in the book of Ecclesiastes, that all man's acts are "vanity of vanities" with the words: "Why do the satisfactions men find in life, however temporary, appear to have value to man? Perhaps because life itself has value, because there is a kind of wisdom in the act of living" (p. 96).

Stephan Strasser presented it more explicitly, as itself a philosophical issue, in his article "Zur Gefühlsstenerung des menschlichen Aktes" (1953), p. 189, where he proposes his solution to the conflict of subjective and objective approaches to human experience: "Daraus ergibt sich für den Philosophen die Notwendigkeit, die typischen vorprädikativen Auffassungsrichtungen noch ein drittes Mal zu untersuchen, und zwar diesmal vom Standpunkte jenes Aktes, den das menschliche Leben *als ganzes* darstellt."

impulse to its consummation and cadence (which may be obscured by entrainment, dispersion, etc., in other acts). The sense of life becomes concentrated and reduced to a feeling of selfhood—the *Lebensgefühl* to *Ichgefühl*, as the German phenomenologists would say. And with the rise and gradual conception of the "self" as the source of personal autonomy comes, of course, the knowledge of its limit—the ultimate prospect of death.

The effect of this intellectual advance is momentous. Each person's deepest emotional concern henceforth shifts to his own life, which he knows cannot be indefinitely preserved. Instead of the typical savage carelessness of death as an episode in the course of communal acts, personally only a change of status, one finds a new seriousness meeting "the blight man was born for"—the impending relinquishment of all power, the end of the Self.

As a naked fact, that realization is unacceptable; there are few societies, savage or civilized, that admit it today. Consequently, where it has been met or its recognition is in progress, it is often possible to follow the ways people are dealing or have dealt with it, from their earliest evasions and simple rejections of the unwelcome knowledge to the most fully developed religious eschatologies. All stages of the defensive counter-action are still to be found in living populations. Even the state of undisturbed faith in the accidental, unnecessary nature of death certainly existed until recent times, and seems still to have some strongholds. So, for instance, the inhabitants of the Andaman Islands in the Sea of Bengal—little Negritos, who are perhaps the lowliest men in the world as far as social institutions and material conditions go—are not at all amazed to hear that someone has died and come back to life again; most of their medicine-men claim to have done just that when they received their initiation to their art. They have visited "the spirits," the people who have died and not returned to the village, but gone to live with their peers in the jungle, or, if they came from a coastal village, to live in the sea. "The spirits" are so much a part of the living community that the more primitive among these islanders do not assign them any realm of their own, but consider it quite possible to meet them in the hunting or fishing grounds. There seems to be no very coherent belief about the dead except that they can send illness to the living or endow them with magic powers. Only one thing is sure: they are not very dead. They have died, by overt violence or black magic or ghost magic, but they are still there to be reckoned with.[24]

[24]A. R. Radcliffe-Brown, *The Andaman Islanders*, pp. 168–69, found it best simply to reproduce individual reports, such as: "When a man dies he becomes a *Lau*, and wanders about the jungle. At first he keeps near the grave or the place where he died, but after a

The next step is to give the spirits a dwelling place—underground, with a known cave for entrance, or somewhere beyond the horizon, or in the sky. Some of the Andamanese have progressed to that stage, but their idea of the spirits is still of people very little changed by death.[25]

In some societies still clinging to the belief that death is always a contingency not really necessary in the course of nature, one can see signs, none the less, of the dawning knowledge and fear of death as inherent in individual life. Since in every past generation people have sooner or later met their end, whether by magic or bloodletting, why should it matter so greatly how they died? To the minds of highly active men, hunters and warriors, and their intrepid women, bearing child after child, it is not the constant threat of violent or magical death that is intolerable and unbelievable but the prospect of death without a "fighting chance"—passive, inevitable, expected death. That is what they unconsciously resist with tacit but adamant denial. So M. J. Meggitt reports, for instance, that among the Walbiri a person who quite obviously has died of senility is quietly and unceremoniously removed.[26] His end was not in the orthodox pattern, and to preserve the ritual value of that pattern the aberrant case had better be bypassed as lightly as possible. The motive is certainly unconscious, but felt as a depressing inhibition blocking the usual responses of sorrow, active vindictiveness toward an imputed killer, or intensified dread of supernatural agents. It is like a fearful glimpse of

---

while he finds that is no good, so he goes to live with the other spirits. If he is drowned he becomes a *Jurua*." This was from a northern tribesman. Another member of a northern tribe added to it, "If he be a jungle-dweller he becomes a *Lau* and lives in the jungle. If he be a coast-dweller he becomes a *Jurua* and lives in the sea. All the *Aka-Cari* become *Jurua* when they die. The spirit stays in his own country. The spirits of a man's own country . . . are friendly to him, but those of another country are dangerous and will make him ill." (Make him ill, even after death!)

[25]*Ibid.*: "An entirely different statement frequently made to me by men of the Northern tribes is that when a man dies the spirit (*Lau*) either immediately, or after the lapse of some time, goes to another world that lies under this one and is called *Maramiku*. This world of spirits is said to be just like the actual world, with forest and sea, and all the familiar animal and vegetable species. The inhabitants spend their time just as the Andamanese do on earth, hunting, fishing and dancing. Still another statement that is commonly made in the North is that the spirits of the dead go to live in the sky.

"Turning now to the Southern tribes, one informant of the A-Pučikwar tribe gave me the following account: 'When a man or woman dies the spirit goes away to the east or north-east and goes over the edge of the world, remaining in a place called *Lau-l'uŋ-ciŋ*. . . . Beyond the home of the spirits is *Puta-koiča*, the home of the sun and moon. The rainbow is the path by which the spirits come to visit their friends on earth, which they do in dreams. The rainbow is made of canes (? a cane).'"

[26]*Desert People* (1962), p. 322: "I was told that, when a very old man or woman dies, the brothers simply inter the body in a shallow, unmarked grave, with the head pointing towards the lodge-dreaming or the conception-dreaming country."

the normal end; a secret conviction that no magic could have obviated it, that it would have happened anyway.

Another symptomatic reaction, obviously unconscious in that it is found characteristically in the children, who have not yet completely absorbed the religious doctrines assumed and fixed by ritual and therefore are still open to intuitive insights, is that among the Kafirs of South Africa the young have a horror of old age. They know that it can happen, that one may die slowly, inevitably, without magical defense because there is no opponent, no challenge to be met. But, being naive and straightforward, the children simply ask the ancestral spirits not to let them grow old as they grow up.[27]

Adult savages, meanwhile, who still resist the belief in the natural finitude of human life, have found many ways of bolstering their counterconvictions. Yet the defensiveness of their attitude toward the idea is sometimes evident in the very lengths to which the denial goes. R. F. Fortune tells how the Manus in Melanesia treat their dead as if they were alive—advising them, during the funeral ceremonies, to marry another recently dead person who is ritually (i.e., by totem and family relationship) eligible, and announcing through a medium when the new ghostly couple has a child. In his *Manus Religion* (1935), he says of these macabre unions: "Every ghost is married off, or rather encouraged to do so during the last rites over the corpse. News of marriages consummated between particular named ghosts is frequently announced by the mediums. At fitting periods thereafter, corresponding roughly to the periods within which such things occur to mortals, news of births to ghosts so married comes from the oracles."[28]

---

[27]Dudley Kidd, in *Savage Childhood* (1906), p. 140, wrote: "Prominent among the fears of Kafir children is that of old age. Death in itself does not seem to frighten the children, for they do not think about it very much; but they have a great fear of old age, and do all they can to ward it off. A boy gets a friend to pull out any hairs which appear prematurely on his chin . . . and little children pray most fervently to the *amatongo* (ancestral spirits of the clan) that they would keep them from growing old. They are immensely keen to grow big, . . . but they have the greatest dread of old age."

[28]Pp. 18–19. Later in the same work the author relates an instance of such a marriage: "The ghost, the daughter of Pokenas, had been married, as a ghost, to a son of Pope, a ghost. Pope had paid a bride price on the mortal plane to Pokenas for the ghost wife for his ghost son. Pokenas had repaid it with wedding finery, dowry, sent with the bride to Pope's house. This dowry . . . must by custom be sent on the bride's person with the bride when she goes to her groom. As the payments were material, substantial and ponderable in this case, . . . whereas the bride was an insubstantial ghost, a living daughter of Pokenas impersonated her dead sister's person. She became 'ghost' for the purpose and shortly after was allowed to resume her mortal, distinct personality" (p. 269). Here we have the familiar theatrical practice of an understudy's substituting for an incapacitated actress.

It is not possible, with our present knowledge of the human mind, to know at what point in social evolution the realization of mortality really begins to dawn on people; much earlier, probably, than they admit or even know. In some very backward societies that seem to give hardly any thought to death and the dead, that theme may be found to haunt their dreams, in quite disarmed and cheerful guise. The Yir Yoront in northern Queensland, from whom Schneider and Sharp gathered their collection of dream protocols,[29] are by their observers' account Australian aborigines of a very naive and rudimentary culture,[30] yet those protocols betray a deep anxiety permeating the ostensibly ignorant minds of the dreamers, for an inordinate proportion of the dreams deal with death and resurrection—"standing alive" after dying by accident or being killed, even killed and eaten. The displacement of the idea from possible conceptual thought to dream (which several of the informants rather insistently declared to be meaningless, "merely a dream," though other dreams might be significant, often prophetic) and, therewith, the repression of the emotions usually evoked by the thought of death are so complete that not only are the dreamers protected against the unacceptable truth, but their civilized investigators were equally deluded into believing in their manifest indifference,[31] though they realized that the occurrence of so many dreams of dying and "standing alive" again does bespeak a special preoccupation with the subject of mortality.[32] The very "playing down" of the subject and especially the dreamers' indifferent attitudes toward the frequent fatalities, as they tell their dreams, show the

[29]D. M. Schneider and Lauriston Sharp, *The Dream Life of a Primitive People.* Cf. above, Chapter 19, p. 12, n. 21.
[30]*Ibid.*, p. 10: "In the field of conduct, there is no distinguishable social organization for economics, for religion, or for government. The Yir Yoront are a people without sovereignty, without hierarchy outside the family, whose whole life operates through the familial institution—they are a people without politics."
[31]Schneider and Sharp remark that "as many as one third of the total number of deaths occurring in dreams are treated as minor events" (p. 42); and subsequently: "Although death is treated as a major event in the dreams twice as frequently as it is treated as a minor event, we consider that its treatment as a minor event is notably frequent. Taken together with the fact that the dreams of death are noticeably lacking in intense affect and the fact that the dreamer is resurrected so often after he dies, we are tempted to infer that the dreamer's attitude toward death, and his view of death, is matter-of-fact. In a sense the Yir Yoront do not appear to have a grave emotional reaction to death" (p. 53).
[32]They realized, in fact, that the dreams of "standing alive" served to obviate the danger of pursuing unacceptable ideas, for they say: "If the deaths of others . . . arouse little emotion, the actor is faced with the problem of what his own death means. In the dreams, at least, he seems to dodge this question by denying his own death as a possibility, for he is so often simply resurrected" (*ibid.*).

success of their subjective defenses; above all, perhaps, the fact that in waking thought they have no conceptions of life after death.[33]

However deep the repressions go and however high the bulwarks against the threatening truth, the process of individuation goes forward with the overgrowth of the cerebral organ, and gradually the defenses break down. In one society after another—and within each, over the centuries, for one mind after another—the central *Lebensgefühl* takes on an articulated form, the act form, until it presents as one act of living that spans all other acts which arise from the mental quasi-matrix, the Mind; and the rest of the organism, requiring only a part of the Mind's activity, seems to belong to it rather than to possess it as an organ. With that development, a human individual feels his own agency no longer as the stream of tribal life flowing through his limbs but as his unique, autonomous Self living its unique, inviolable life.

With the idea of such a personal, single act of living comes the understanding of the place of death in nature. Death is inherent in human life itself, and as life is power, so death is defeat of man's power. The defeat may come soon or late, but come it will for every individual.

If that insight were to break in suddenly on the old dream of limitless power, it would be shattering. But the mind has its filters and screens as the body has its skin. It takes centuries, if not millennia, for such a diffuse and nameless feeling to become common in a society, so people are quietly taking it for granted, and even then its admission may be stayed through ages by ritual ignorance or taboo. Nevertheless, of course, one intelligent person after another would know when his life was waning, and either fight hysterically against some unconvincing, alleged hostile influence or—more and more frequently—lose faith and interest in magic at that juncture, and resign himself to death. Then people would accept such mythical explanation as priest or medicine-man provided so they could dispense with the inquest and vengeance expedition.

Finally, the small scope of any possible individual life-act has become a terrible, inescapable fact. When that realization is accepted, no one is aware of the crisis that has occurred because evolutionary crises are longer than oral memory which covers a half-dozen generations. But the change in feeling and outlook is radical. No longer is the joint tribal act, whatever it may be at any hour, the prime interest of each participant, but his own life-act, his one and only life. Instead of undergoing a meta-

---

[33]"There is no explicit, verbalized idea of resurrection in waking life belief. This occurs only in dreams, so far as we are aware" (*ibid.*).

morphosis into a spirit, handing over any act in process to other persons to become an ancestral elder controlling their behavior, each person must expect to leave his unfinished works or parts undone, his grievances unavenged, and, above all, his potentialities cut off, his world and his self dissolved. Most societies today have been through it, as the truly naive ones who have not faced it yet are dwindling in our world. But none, perhaps, have remained in that state of conviction very long; there is too much emotional necessity to deal with it conceptually and somehow give it a tolerable semblance. Meggitt, in his careful study of the desert-dwelling Australian Walbiri, observed the deep trouble of a people with an unmitigated belief in death. According to his account, "they do not believe that the human personality long survives unchanged the destruc-tion of its corporeal shell or that it sojourns happily with departed kinsfolk in an intermediate after-world while awaiting rebirth. Instead, they see death as something final that marks the end of each individual personality as they know it. The previously unified personality disintegrates into its basic components, and the conception- and lodge-totems return to their spirit-homes, while the matrispirit soon dissipates completely.

"Consequently the people are unable to regard the inevitability of their own or their relative's deaths with any philosophical detachment or resig-nation." Even before a man is dead, when he is generally thought to be dying, "the women of his patriline and matriline, and his mother-in-law tear off their garments and sit straight-legged on the ground while they gash their scalps and toss handfuls of dust and ashes over themselves.

"A concerted shriek goes up when the medicine-man or a brother announces that the man is dead. . . . The fathers and adult sons of his patriline . . . [and other near kinsmen] . . . at once gash their thighs deeply with knives, despite the attempts of the dead man's brothers and sisters' sons to prevent them. . . .

"Most of the deceased's close kinswomen wail unceasingly and again gouge their heads. The women of his matriline, his widow(s) and moth-er(s)-in-law first hack off their hair and then sear the wounds with fire-sticks. . . . The man's own mother, his widow(s) and mother(s)-in-law also singe off their pubic hair. His sisters and m.b.d. [mother's brothers' daughters] stand by, ready to intervene if the women are likely to do themselves serious harm."[34]

What these people have discovered by their growing intuition and subjective insight, and, apparently, not yet found a way to deal with

---

[34]*Desert People*, pp. 319–20, 317. The matrispirit is the dead person's ghost; it is feared during its short existence as possibly bringing ghost-sickness, but is soon lost in the sky.

religiously to their own consolation or resignation, is one of the great basic rhythms of the life process, which is felt only in a fairly advanced stage of mentality, certainly not below the human plane and not universally even above it: the inward rhythm of each individual life. Each life is a rhythmic structure, as its every smallest act is drawn into its passage and enters the next situation, which motivates subsequent acts to meet the new condition. The inward rhythms of different individuals vary widely and provide the groundworks of their separate personalities. Yet despite their uniqueness they all exemplify one deeply felt rhythm which goes beyond the familiar *Lebensgefühl*: the rising impulse of the single life-act, its great spanning tensions from youth to age, and the cadence, the decline to death.

This sense of wholeness is a new feeling of a dynamic pattern which is not itself new, but has newly risen as a whole to psychical phase; and our bitter experience of it is the price of our advanced individuation. We have, indeed, two ways of feeling the passage of life itself, one the old continuum of acts which may be dimly felt by all biological forms, being simply the rhythm of action that belongs to the undying stock, and the other the highly articulated rhythm of the death-bound life of man.

The recognition and expression of these two contrasting dynamic forms is certainly not within the range of tribal cultures, however vitalistic their rituals and their thinking may be; it is today outside the scope of most scientifically oriented civilized people. Its only sure grasp has been by creative artists, namely, poets, and not early in the development of their art, but first, I think, in the great "golden age" of Greece—certainly not a primitive phase; it makes its appearance with the conception of tragedy and the consequent distinction of that dramatic form from the much older one of comedy.

Greek tragedy is, I believe, the first conscious presentation of the tragic rhythm of life, the movement of the greatest act whereof a human individual is capable, his single life-act. Its form is one overarching parabolic curve from youth to death—symbolically, of course, from birth or even conception, through the prime of life, to its close. The classical "fatal error" committed by the protagonist is not a realistic story element but a dramatic device to signify the turning-point from the expanding, upward course to the downward, the cadence, literally the "descent." The hero's or heroine's death in the drama is not necessary; it is only the usual finale. In Ibsen's *Ghosts*, the tragedy is completed in the last scene with the breaking of Oswald's mind, when he says: "Mother, give me the sun.— The sun.—The sun." The death of the mind is the end of a human career.

The rhythm of comedy creates a different frame; it is the rhythm of society, more anciently felt and apprehended than the passage of an individuated life. In the realm of literature it figures as the "comic" rhythm in contrast to the "tragic,"[35] but in life, and as a fundamental form of life, it were better called the "social" rhythm, for it belongs to the indefinitely self-rejuvenating life of the stock. The word "comic" is derived from a Greco-Roman god, Comus, whose festival was a processional celebration of life; "comic" does not originally mean laughable, but denotes the feeling of that joyous rite, which moved from rise to rise with a lilting progress, every rise tending to break into laughter as waves break into whitecaps. But the laughter may be of very different kinds; for there is not only merry comedy, but also heroic, like the dramatic art of India, in which the high moments are exalted, not trivial and humorous as in our popular comic theater. The term applies to the vital rhythm, not essentially to the subject matter of the drama.[36]

The stage is a mirror of human feeling, and gives us an abstractive, concentrated, and intensified image. The first recognition of the tragic rhythm—the first clear tragic vision—was expressed in its starkest and simplest outline. Nothing could be more pared down to essentials than *Oedipus Rex*: two actors—Man, and the Seer of his fate; the chorus—the magnification of that fate as something universal, embracing every individual, but each one alone.

The natural reaction to the growing and widening insight that no magic can overcome or indefinitely stem death is despair of human power. But mankind does not easily succumb to despair. As every creature and even every living tissue responds to stress with heightened activity, so the mind meets the challenge its own evolution has created by a radical deepening of religious feeling and dawning of religious ideas. If a man's own power seems minuscule beside the dreamed omnipotence he no longer sees in possible reach, where is real power to be sought? From the Supernaturals, of course. They have always possessed more of it than

[35]In Part II of this book, where the theory of art from which the present theory of mind is derived was recapitulated, the discussion of dramatic art was unfortunately omitted because at the time of that writing I was not aware that it would have any relevance to the evolution of mind, as it now proves to have; so at this point I cannot but refer the reader to an earlier book, *Feeling and Form*, Chapters 18 ("The Great Dramatic Forms: The Comic Rhythm") and 19 ("The Great Dramatic Forms: The Tragic Rhythm") for the background of the present analysis.

[36]In the Indian *Nataka* the characters are normally drawn from the *Ramayana*, and therefore are gods and semi-divine heroic beings. Milton's masque, "Comus," is a serious and decorous work. Dante called his great religious poem "The Divine Comedy."

mortals and dispensed it as they pleased, so the human hope is to borrow strength and luck from them.

With the progress of individual feeling to the point of personal self-awareness, the relation of men to their gods becomes more subjective, too, so they no longer perform the old efficacious rites only in a tribal fashion, to ward off illness and public disasters, but each person also tends to pray in his private interest. That leads him to think of the being he is imploring in a more intimate way as his particular guardian ancestor, ghost, or herm, and his chief concern, therefore, is to find his protector equal to the task and always willing to perform it.[37] So he imagines his deity more and more powerful, and at the same time tries to win his or her grace by praises and by protestations of his own dependence and trust. But as long as there are other spirits hearing other people's prayers, perhaps with incompatible requests, the special patron cannot have full sway; and the best solution men find is to assume a still higher power and finally a ruler of the world, and to delegate all human power and all forces of nature to that supreme being, giving men an infinite reservoir of power on which they can draw by prayer.

[37]This stage of religion is clearly illustrated by Fortune in *Manus Religion*, where he records many pieties, but also many insecurities, of a surprisingly literal and primitive ancestor worship by a not-very-savage people. There we find: "Each Manus man worships his father, not in Heaven but in his house front rafters. . . . The skull of the father of the house owner has an honored place in a finely carved wooden bowl hung high above, and just inside, the entry at the front of the house." This personage—invisible, but represented by the skull—is referred to as "Sir Ghost," more specifically, as the house owner's Sir Ghost.

"The name of Sir Ghost is hallowed. The house owner often talks to his father's ghost, and honours the name of his father in his manner of speech. When he, in his turn, dies, his son or heir will honour him similarly, but . . . never a ghostly grandfather, saying that Sir Ghosts deserve to become anonymous and dishonoured when they fail to protect their sons from death.

"Sir Ghost gives a man his daily fishing upon which he depends for his existence. To punish sin a Sir Ghost may either bring illness in his ward's house, or remove the potency, or soul stuff, for catching fish from his ward's nets and traps" (pp. 1–2). And further: "The Manus dramatise death as Sir Ghost's final betrayal of his compact, in spite of all his ward's great benefits to him. . . . The lack of any really self-sacrificing devotion to Sir Ghost is most reasonable, considering the way in which one Sir Ghost after another fails his ward. The Manus put a price upon their devotion to their dead; but it is an impossible price. They want life, long life, and no accidents. . . . they realise very clearly that too optimistic demands from life are not always met. It is well to persist in such demands, for they may work to some extent. It is well to be outraged when that extent proves to be limited" (p. 19).

The Manus are evidently in transition from belief in the endless possibility of life to recognition of natural death, and their religious concepts are at odds with their knowledge.

This development of religious ideas has often taken place, notably, of course, in the great monotheistic religions—Judaism, Christianity, and Islam—but also in some smaller spheres. It is easier to achieve in societies which conceived of a highest god even before they lost confidence in their own infinite magical potency than for people whose spirit-world has no central godhead but is a conglomerate of unrelated beings—flying heads, were-animals, the moon, ghosts, night witches, vampires—with no Jove-like image to dominate the assemblage. Such a world is built up for the exercise of magical powers, to meet opposing forces piecemeal in the old manner of conquering death; there is no real deity to whom human power could be delegated. True, the idea of a highest god, just in itself, is by no means that of a one-and-only god; it is a fairly widespread conception, especially in Africa,[38] but such a supreme being is apt to be purely a creator, who has finished his work and withdrawn from the world and has no further interest in man or beast.[39] Yet the possession of even that concept is an asset toward the next religious advance because it provides some orientation for a hierarchy of powers culminating in the creator God, whose image can then be developed. This may be all the easier for the fact that such otiose gods have few, if any, previous rites to define them; they are available to be endowed with new traits and functions. Where people's attitude toward the Supernaturals is mainly defensive, benevolent deities generally receive scant attention.[40] But as soon as all

[38]C. M. N. White, in "The Supreme Being in the Beliefs of the Balovale Tribes" (1948), said: "A belief in a High God or Supreme Being is usually said to be characteristic of the Bantu, but the conception of a High God is not uniform in all parts of Africa, in fact the exact nature of these beliefs is often of a very elusive character."

[39]According to V. C. Uchendu, *The Igbo of Southeast Nigeria*, pp. 94–95, "The Igbo high god is a withdrawn god. He is a god who has finished all active works of creation and keeps watch over his creatures from a distance. The Igbo high god is not worshipped directly. There is neither shrine nor priest dedicated to his service. . . . He seldom interferes in the affairs of men. . . . He is a satisfied god who is not jealous of the prosperity of man on earth."

Arundell del Re, in *Creation Myths of the Formosan Natives* (1951), describing the eight-story cosmos and its *anito* (spirit) population, says: "The divinities of the first [highest] plane live in a region above the firmament and seem to form a special category of their own. . . . These gods have no direct relation with the Yami who neither invoke nor make sacrifices to them. Some believe, however, that should the tribe be guilty of some exceptional misdeed, the gods would afflict the island with some terrible natural disaster. . . . Generally speaking, however, the conduct of the tribe does not concern them" (p. 58). There are many other findings, among other peoples, of the same attitude toward the highest power; for instance, M. E. Opler ("The Concept of Supernatural Power among the Chiricahua and Mescalero Apaches") states that their high god, the life-giver, is a remote god; K. T. Preuss ("Die religiöse Bedeutung der Paradiesmythen") says that Nanderevuçu, the creator-god of the Matotela in Rhodesia, has retired from the world.

[40]Christoph von Fürer-Haimendorf states the reason for this general neglect of the

power has to be begged from them, there is reason to cultivate and honor particularly the gracious ones, the father and mother images raised to the status of an infant's omnipotent parents. With the acceptance of an all-cherishing highest god, the obvious works of the old, demoted dispensers of wrath and punishment—the gods who had to be placated—have to be somehow accounted for, too; this has sometimes been done by giving the god an opponent, Ahriman, Satan, or any other embodiment of all evil, whom he is supposed to conquer at some future end of the devil-ridden world; while his present tolerance of man's terrible ills is accredited to him as his justice, and the responsibility for them assigned to the sufferers, whose sins incurred whatever pains and terrors he permits. Or, again, both good and evil may be attributed to one great power whose existence has both aspects, like the supreme god of the Lugbara, Adro, whose evil aspect is immanent in nature while his perfection resides in heaven.[41] In the oldest well-known religion of our historic civilizations, Brahmanism, it is the material world itself, the world of illusion and deception, that militates against the life of the mind; but that concept has such great implications for the whole pattern of religious and ethical values which has taken shape in India that it really belongs to the next chapter.

The reason why a highest god, where such a being is postulated, is so often regarded as a remote power not in direct touch with humanity is that most people, civilized or savage, cannot imagine it as a presence in their daily lives. The creator is an abstraction, not a personage; they cannot make a guardian and helper out of it. So they continue to address their prayers to the old, trusted ancestors or to some traditional local spirits, who become intermediaries between them and the cosmic life-giver and death-dealer. In a great world-wide religion like Christianity, these tribal Supernaturals are replaced by canonized saints who assume the role of intercessors.[42] The characteristic conservatism of ritual (es-

---

highest god very simply and frankly: "Sämtlichen Naga gemeinsam ist die Erscheinung, dass das Höchst-Wesen im Kult und in der Bedeutung für das tägliche Leben hinter dem Heere der erdnahen, stets Opfergaben heischenden, niederen Geister weit zurücktritt. Die höchste Gottheit ist zu ferne und meist auch zu wohlwollend um dem Menschen gefährlich zu werden" ("Zur Religion einiger hinterindischer Bergvölker" [1936], p. 274).

[41]Cf. above, Chapter 19, pp. 16–17.

[42]It is interesting to see this shift reversed where people try to square the teachings of Christian missionaries with their own religious tradition. So Jomo Kenyatta, in *Facing Mount Kenya*, describing a sect of holy men and women, the Watu wa Mngu, who are trying to assimilate those teachings, says: "Their prayers are a mixture of Gikuyu religion and Christian. . . . In their prayer to Mwene-Nyaga they hold up their arms to the sky facing Mount Kenya; and in this position they recite their prayers, and in doing so they

pecially in speech formulas, which above all uphold articles of belief) helps to tide people over the dangerous changes of thought, for under its "cultural lag" new meanings can grow up and permeate the old symbols, to which the most modern thinkers in any age can resort to shield them from their own fear of change.

There is, however, another problem that arises with the conception of each individual life as an act, the single life-act of the personal agent at its center: that is the fact that the definite form thus given to his life also defines the form of its negative, the time before and after his existence. Before him was the long chain of lives in which his own was implicit—represented by the ancestors, going back to the origin of humanity in the dreamtime or in some mythical act of creation; but after? Logically, of course, nothing more in the way of individual experience or action, if the soul is now thought to join the ancestors. But once the feeling of life has become personal, the impersonal existence of those ancestral spirits offers no substitute for its lost embodiment;[43] it is hard to conceive the non-being of a person once known, and for most people it is quite impossible to imagine their own annihilation. At that point and thereafter, an individual existence beyond the grave is spontaneously and quite unquestioningly assumed; and the shift of feeling from general act-consciousness to self-consciousness makes each soul want its own happiness and fear its own frustration. This leads to all kinds of anxious speculations about the

---

imitate the cries of wild beasts of prey, such as lion and leopard, and at the same time they tremble violently. The trembling, they say, is the sign of the Holy Ghost, Roho Motheru, entering in them. While thus possessed with the spirits, they are transformed from ordinary beings and are in communion with Mwene-Nyaga" (p. 274). "As to communion with ancestors, it is argued that since the Church recognizes the sacredness of saints, who are but ancestors of the *mzungu*, and if the deity can be addressed by saints and can listen to their intercessions, it will be the more likely that the spirits of the Gikuyu ancestors will act effectively" (p. 276).

43John Middleton, in *Lugbara Religion*, p. 194, makes the statement: "Ancestors are to a large extent collectivized, whereas ghosts are regarded as individuals." Going further in the conception of ancestors as a collectivity, M. C. Jedrej characterizes the "village ancestors" of a Sewa Mende village in Sierra Leone "among whom no particular spirit can be identified nor from whom is any attempt made to trace a genealogy. Usually they are described as the original founders of the village, from whom the present inhabitants vaguely feel themselves to be descended. They live in an undifferentiated collectivity under the lands of the village and are sometimes specified as *ndowuhla* (under-ground-people). . . . Secondly there are local kin group ancestors, most important among whom is the common antecedent linking the households of the local group and lately deceased senior members of each household, especially a dead father or grandfather" ("An Analytical Note on the Land and Spirits of the Sewa Mende" [1974], pp. 39–40). But the generations move on, and the recently dead persons do not keep their individuality beyond the memories of their living descendants.

future state. Some envisagements are clearly wishful, others based on fear or simply on reluctance to give up life, which in itself makes any ghostly existence seem like a reduced, deprived condition.[44] E. O. James tells of ancient Mexicans who postulated distinctions among the dead according to the ways of their dying, which, except for the heroic and sacrificial deaths, are hard to relate to any status distinctions in their social life, which were separately observed. Of the fate awaiting the great majority of people, he reports: "The rest of the people were destined to pass at death to the dreary subterranean region, Mictlan, 'a most obscure land where light cometh not and whence none can ever return.' There they were sunk in deep sleep, but class distinctions were maintained, the lords and nobles being separated from the commoners in the nine divisions into which it was divided. At the end of the fourth year of residence in this cheerless abode the ninth division was reached, and in this its denizens were annihilated."[45]

However one's future state was decided, it was entirely in the hands of the gods or other non-human powers; and as people had always looked to these for the means of daily living—rain, growth, fish or game—and

[44]This conception of death as a reduction of the spirit to a shrunken, bloodless condition in a crepuscular place is found in both savage and civilized cultures. Strauss, in *Die Mi-Kultur der Hagenberg-Stämme*, p. 150, says: "Das Leben nach dem Tode stellt man sich ganz ähnlich dem irdischen Leben vor, aber nicht besser, sondern schlechter. Die Sprache gebraucht Ausdrüke der Nacht, des Dunkeln und Finsteren, um das Dasein der Toten zu beschreiben. Es ist ein Schattendasein. Die Toten hungern und frieren, haben nur schlechte Nahrung, sind Wind und Wetter, Regen und Kälte ausgesetzt." And further, he quotes a native's statement: "'Die Toten schauen von draussen neidisch herein. . . . Sie neiden uns das durch wippenden Federschmuck, glänzenden Muschelbehang und rauschendes Gesässdecklaub beschwingte Lebensgefühl. Nur wir, die Lebenden, erfreuen uns noch der Frauen, Wertsachen und Schweine.'"
At the other extreme of the cultural scale is the Greek conception of the nether world, the realm of Hades, where again the dead are relegated to a shadowy existence in a sunless, joyless place, though not as sorry a "hereafter" as Strauss' informants projected.
[45]*Prehistoric Religion: A Study in Prehistoric Archeology* (1957), p. 138. These apparently honorific ways of dying and their special rewards are described as follows: "men killed in war or offered as victims on the sacrificial stone, and women dying in childbirth (who were liable to become malevolent goddesses), joined the emperor and nobility in the Elysium of Huitziopochtli in the eastern part of the sky where honeyed flowers and luscious fruits abounded in shady groves, and hunting was enjoyed in the parks. Dressed as warriors they accompanied the sun daily on its course and fought mock battles till it reached its zenith. Then it was transferred to the charge of the celestial women (e.g., those who had died in childbirth), who lived in the western part of the sun-house, where merchants who died on their journey also dwelt. After two years of this Elysium the souls of warriors were transmigrated into birds of golden plumage, and either returned to the earth or lived in the celestial gardens. Those who were struck by lightning, drowned or died of contagious diseases went to a happy paradise (Calocan) on a mountain in the east" (*ibid.*) (There follows the account of the common people's fate given above).

assured themselves of divine favor by sacrifices and other ritual acts, so now the future of each soul seemed like another individual life, with no means of influencing the conditions of that new existence by anything one could do in preparation. No ritual act seemed great enough to cover all the exigencies of that new life; sacrifices had always been made in view of expected dangers or undertakings, and to divorce a rite or a prayer from any particular situation was beyond most of the traditional worshippers' thought. It would require too great a rite.

That seems to have been the most persistent motivation of the revolt against the prospect of death, once speculative thinking had reached the realization of man's utter helplessness in the face of divine omnipotence. As the belief in the finality of death was intolerable to savage minds whenever they began to foresee it, so the idea of passive acceptance of an unmitigable future state, decreed by an absolute, unswayable deity, was to the followers of more advanced religions. Surely there must be something one could do to steer one's further fate. Or—had mankind delegated too much of its power to the gods?

As often happens in nature, the same condition that creates an impasse for a living stock also produces the means of its solution. This biological principle extends to the evolution of the mind, and is involved in the imagined greater situation to be met by the surviving soul after death. In life, a pious person wins the favor of his deity by acts which please that holder of all power: prayer, praise, and sacrifice. The god is the judge of the worthiness of such devotional acts, and rewards them if he finds them good. With the progressive forming of a whole life as one act, that life attains a unity which allows it to be judged as a single act, and to be found holy or unholy, clean or unclean, good or bad; and at death or at some juncture in the hereafter, that whole life can be thought to be presented to the god (or gods) as a sacrifice. Such a ritual gift can surely be deemed great enough to meet the needs of the whole future state.

What constitutes "the good life" is highly variable within the compass of human society; but in keeping with the progress of cultures to civilization it tends to take in more and more non-ritual elements and gradually become a pattern of moral actions, with the religious performances as its framework. This life can be presented to the god, with or without priestly or mystical mediation, to win his favor and be rewarded by a happy existence in the hereafter. Then the conceptions of man's afterlife become clearly defined by the priesthoods, which use them to bind their laities to a system of moral dictates by hopes of heaven and especially by fears of hell. So there is, indeed, something that mortals can do to shape their expected future, by conforming in all their behavior to the will of their godhead.

Here is the link of mortality with religion. In naive religious thinking there is generally only an incidental connection between these two elements of social life, in that certain trespasses such as a break of tabu or any neglect of a deity or ancestor require ritual atonement; the condition awaiting the dead, however, is the same for good and bad people.[46] But once the shift is accomplished from the easily offended spirits (with or without the distant, unconcerned high god) to a supreme god who ultimately judges the quick and the dead, a really momentous change has also occurred in every individual's feeling of responsibility; for the incubus of guilt, which in savage society is carried only from an episodic sin to the expiatory sacrifice that cancels it, now is laid to account as a part of the whole moral life, even if modified by penance and pardon.

The price of our individuation is a heavy one in many ways, but heaviest, perhaps, in this deepened consciousness of personal continuity and, therewith, of cumulative responsibility. It is a product of phyletic maturation which repeats itself in ontogeny with every passage from infancy through adolescence to adulthood. A young child, forgiven a misdeed, is wholly forgiven, without carrying any stigma; in later youth he can still achieve such a reversal of mind that he "lives down" many wrongs, though really serious past delicts will sear his conscience and cloud his image in the public eye; as an adult he has to carry his transgressions. He may atone for them, even reform his ways, be religiously absolved and socially reinstated, but the stain on his inner life is there.

The awakening of one people after another from the old dream of magic power to the gradual dawn of the tragic vision of human life is a

---

[46]The attitude of the Netsilik Eskimos described by Knut Rasmussen has been discussed above (Chapter 19, pp. 11–12). Another instance is given by Radcliffe-Brown in *The Andaman Islanders*, p. 174: "I did not find any evidence whatever that good men and bad men (in any meanings in which those words could be used by the natives) receive different treatment after death." Even so moralistic a religion as that of the Jewish Torah did not carry the idea of retribution beyond the grave; according to Harry Gersh (*The Sacred Books of the Jews*, p. 77), it was one of the late prophets, Zephania, who introduced the Persian eschatological notions of a day of judgment and of heaven and hell into Jewish doctrine. In Greek philosophy the idea of moral retribution in a future life enters only tentatively with Plato, and takes the mild form of better or worse conditions of reincarnation—a concept that never touched the populace. As H. J. Rose stated in his *Encyclopaedia Britannica* article "Greek Religion," "The Greek religion was for the most part . . . completely free from otherworldliness. It was a religion of everyday life, which sought for temporal blessings such as good crops, deliverance from enemies, health, or peace within the community."

long, sobering experience, especially in its side effects such as the concept of death as inevitable, the god (or gods) as omnipotent, and the work of meeting the divine demands as a lifelong task. It has many elements of a defeat of human mental power. Yet it is a forward step in the very development of that power. As biologists have found in their studies of evolutionary changes, the most radical advances seem to take place in epochs when the evolving species is "defeated"—small in size and numbers, poor in territory.[47] So it seems to be with the evolution of mind too. The reduction of human feeling from the expansive sense of tribal action filling each individual agent's consciousness to the small, centralized awareness of his own being has been (and in some cases, still is) at once the cadential close of one phase—a great imaginative phase—of man's mentality and the upswing of that eternal pendulum, history, to the next, a phase of elaboration and realization of his teeming brood of ideas.

[47]Cf. Vol. II, p. 39.

22

The Ethnic Balance

ETHOS is the fundamental quality of acts in human conception. It is wider than their evaluation as right or wrong or even as good or bad; it includes the spontaneous perception of acts as important or trivial, holy or profane, instrumental, obstructive, intentional or not, dangerous or not, noble or base—all elements that modify our estimate of their ethos, by virtue of which they enter into the human scene. An act may be good without being noble, as ordinary peaceable behavior usually is, or terrible, like many religious sacrifices, without being base, and even without being received as evil. The finer gradations of value are made with increasing intellectuality in the course of mental life; the two primary reactions, approval and disapproval, may rest on moral or various other grounds. These grounds—often tacit, unformulated assumptions and beliefs—and the traditional pattern of accepted action against which specific acts are seen and evaluated by any given community constitute its ethos.

Approval and disapproval, primitive as they are in social life, do not exist for animals. For them there are only reactions of tolerance, conflict, or (especially in gregarious species) falling in with the action, which are limited to directly given situations and such as concern the agents themselves at the time. There is no impersonal critique of what other creatures do or fail to do; there is no ethos. The phenomenon of ethos marks the departure of man from the common animal estate of the other high vertebrates. Its beginning probably goes back to the very origins of that departure when symbolic communication—speech—first opened the vast realm of ideas which could be shared by a whole population. Then acts could be conceived and talked about before and after they had been performed or even without any instance, and in contemplation they could appear as good or bad, to be approved or disapproved as something that should or should not be done. Ethos arose with the feeling of mental potentiality that makes our *Lebensgefühl* seem to reside in the mind rather than in the body.

The perception of quality, as that of form and relations, is an intuitive perception, a datum for human sensibility. It seems to be directly given, like the famous "pure sense data." And so, perhaps, it is, on the empirical level of knowledge, though it may take a highly elaborated nervous system to create such an apparently direct presentation. Also, like sense data, it can change with ambient changes, so a later intuition does not necessarily match the first. Evaluation of acts is a constant process that normally goes on near the border of consciousness, springing from deep activities and rising above the limen of feeling, sometimes barely, sometimes acutely to culminate in a judgment.

The perception of values alone would not beget an ethnic society, were it not met and entrained—that is, used and thus promoted—by another advance, the growing sense of agency, both actual and potential, in each individual mind. Even in communities in which the mental individuation of their separate members is still somewhat incomplete, so they tend to act and think in concert rather than singly, the inward consciousness of action exists in each one; and although any larger intentions and impulses are generally directed to some joint undertaking, each agent is realizing the whole venture and, in case it miscarries, suffers the whole failure.

This meeting of two evolutionary trends has led to a new attainment, the really crucial step in humanization: the sense of responsibility. In the dangerous course of the mind's individuating out of the physical organism, this common concern for the acts of other persons as a context and continuance of one's own, felt subjectively as such, is the deepest bond holding each independent self to the generative stock as its society. It is not a tie between particular persons but an indirect and unbreakable union, comparable to the internal bonding of an organism by the repetition of its genome in every cell.[1] Yet a society, though organic, is not an organism; it is a community of minds, activated by symbolic thought and symbolic communication. Its whole integral being is a product of the novel elements engendered by the new functions of human forebrains which have advanced to the stage of pseudo-matrices in mental interaction with each other. In the course of each life, the physical intimate unity of mother and child does not simply melt away as it does with the maturing of young animals, but is transmuted very gradually, one tie after another, into a conceptual understanding of the maternal-filial relation, which is a permanent, socially recognized element of family structure.[2] The comprehension of a relationship which lasts whether the instinctual attachment does so or not requires words, such as forms of address and

[1] Cf. above Vol. I, Chapter 9 *passim*, esp. p. 367.
[2] It has often been stated that each person's first social contact is with his mother or mother-surrogate. The opposite is probably true; she is the last being to become a "socius," or objective personage, in that person's world.

terms of reference; and such comprehension, no matter how it is learned (i.e., how it is triggered), is intuitive. Its acquisition makes the shift from instinct to intuition.

The same is true, of course, for other human relations; their recognition and abstract conception gives them the permanence of a formal framework, in which the persons as personages find their orientation toward one another first of all as members of the natural family, but soon—as a result of the statuses realized by each actual union or birth— in the greater pattern known as the expanded family. This pattern is capable of wide elaboration and is the basic form of tribal organizations, which exist (or have existed) in many varieties.

The original quality of ethos is the fitting of acts into the frame of statuses based on the interwoven lines of descent and cross-relationships in a familial community, the elementary ethnic unit, or society. The distinction between a society and an animal colony is immediately apparent by the fact that the human, conceptual order includes not only all of each person's living relatives but the dead as well. The dead, in fact, are apt to be the real holders of power; in many traditional cultures the ancestors inflict all punishment for serious wrongs, which are mainly of a ritual nature—neglect of sacrifices whereby the ordinary sins of social living are wont to be expiated. The punishments for omissions of these constant symbolic penances are not purely symbolic at all, but quite physical and visited on the family, the village, and the tribe or tribal segment as a whole: sickness, drought or flood, no game, no fish, no harvest. Extensive sickness is the most usual chastisement.

The hazards and difficulties of life are, of course, world-wide; but why their interpretation as supernatural punishments should be so common that it is really a normal phase of human conception, somewhat higher than the primitive notion of magical powers in people or things accounting for personal bad luck but essentially an extension of that same idea to the realm of the Supernaturals once these are imagined, is a philosophical challenge; for it involves the much-mooted but little-understood basic concept of punishment itself.

The function of punishment is a very complicated topic, for in the course of its evolution it has gathered many secondary aims deriving from different sources, and consequently has received at least as many interpretations. Yet its central and universal motive has rarely been recognized because it lies too deep in emotional feeling—far below the level of rational thinking—to be easily apparent. Some great thinkers have even rejected the corrective value of punishment altogether; Spinoza, for instance, held that regret and repentance, which punishment is supposed to engender, only compound the evil of wrong already done.[3] Others have seen it as a regulated form of vengeance, saving society from violence which might spread and turn into wholesale internecine blood-feuding.[4] The most widely accepted purposes today certainly are correction of the offender's behavior and prevention of similar acts in other people by threats of the same consequences, two aims usually entertained together. The preventive power of punishment is small, the corrective even smaller, at least as it is practiced through our courts; prison only brings felons together to abet each other in their antisocial intents. Yet in our society any major offense that is allowed to pass without the infliction of punishment on the culprit or culprits fills a normal, law-abiding public with deep misgiving.

Even these obvious uses, however, are accessory; the idea of punishment is older, and prevails in cultures where its personal corrective effect serves only for childhood training and is hardly distinct from simple adult intolerance, or sometimes is not used at all.[5] Its primary conception has a historical origin in the very shift to human life, and a growth concomitant with that long physiological process. The tendency to individuate and develop a paramatrix, the mind, with interests of its own, always threatens to lure the mental organ from its primitive function of steering its possessor through the hazards of physical existence. The danger in every aberration from the instinctive round of hereditary behavior is that it is an act of self-assertion, and self-assertion is an overt sign of the agent's

---

[3]See *Ethics*, Pt. IV, prop. 54: "Repentance is not a virtue, or does not arise from reason; but he who repents of an action is doubly wretched or infirm. . . . For the man allows himself to be overcome, first, by evil desires; secondly, by pain." Yet Spinoza supported the use of punishment to keep the balance between evil done and evil suffered, for which it was to be imposed by a vested authority, which "should not be said to be indignant with the criminal, for it is not incited by hatred to ruin him, it is led by a sense of duty to punish him" (*ibid.*, prop. 51, note).

[4]René Girard makes this interpretation his main thesis in *La violence et le sacre* (1972). A concrete instance of such a social safeguard is presented by Napoleon Chagnon in his book *Yąnomamö*, on a people that prides itself on its fierceness; speaking of their frequent duels, he says: "Duels are formal and are regulated by stringent rules about proper ways to deliver and receive blows. Much of Yąnomamö fighting is kept innocuous by these rules. . . . The three most innocuous forms of violence, chest pounding, side slapping, and club fights, permit the contestants to express their hostilities in such a way that they can continue to remain on relatively peaceful terms with each other after the contest is settled" (p. 118).

[5]So, for instance, Dorothea D. Lee, in her article on the Trobriand Islanders, "A Primitive System of Values," following up Malinowski's previous researches, says: "In a society such as that of the Trobrianders, extraneous inducements to good conduct are naturally absent. We find no use of punishment, for example, in the bringing up of children. If a little boy tries to fondle his sister—thus infringing on the supreme taboo— the adults around him will appear so horrified, that the situation in itself will be fraught with unpleasant emotion and become undesirable" (pp. 372–73).

growing individuation. It is that basic, unconscious gesture of selfhood
that has to be balanced by some display of the biological claims of the
stock upon each living generation.

The true intent of punishment, therefore, is symbolic, not "condition-
ing." Its practical effect only underscores the element of disapproval so it
cannot be ignored or defied. That is why, under relatively primitive
conditions, the penalizing power belongs to the Supernaturals and is
exercised against the community, which is "Man," and why vicarious
punishment may redeem the actual offender; why young princes sometimes were not punished for naughtiness, yet punishment had to be dealt,
so it fell on a hired "whipping boy"; and why, to this day, one person may
pay another's fine for a civil offense, such as a breach of traffic rules, and
why fines are the same for rich and poor, though the penal burden is
not.[6]

Since, as aforesaid, most wrongs which tribal gods or ancestors are
wont to punish are ritual faults—insufficient sacrifices, errors in recitations, the utterance of tabooed names or eating of tabooed food, etc.—
they are themselves concerned with symbolic gestures, which have the
same basic motivation as the supernatural penalties for their neglect or
distortion, namely, the expression of every individual's commitment to
his human responsibility, not only in his transgressions but in his normal
independent acts. It is the advance of mentality that has to be held in
check so it shall not outstrip the support of its soma. A brain which
produces such fantasies that it drags its bodily self into a fictitious world
and gives its whole allegiance to the postulated beings of that world and to
their demands soon loses its realities and is alone, literally "alienated"
from the greater human life that engendered and still carries it. This
danger exists not only for individuals but even for whole societies. In all
evolving species, there is always some function ready to take the lead in
growth and elaboration and, in so doing, to throw the cycles of instinctive
life of the mutant strain out of balance. Then a rival impulse or some
limiting condition has to retard the excessive advance until the rest of the
evolutionary process can catch up with the needs which the radical
change is creating, or the stock becomes unviable.[7] The great shift from

[6]No educational principle could be more dangerous to morality than the teaching that
"crime doesn't pay"; for it shifts the basis of right and wrong from the recognition of the
moral structure to the problem of successful personal operation within that structure.

[7]This probably happens far more often than we can observe, especially in low forms of
life such as protozoa, molds, and smuts, in which species are often difficult to establish
and change so radically that their taxonomy tends to be elusive. Since the unsuccessful
forms have a short history before they disappear forever, we have no knowledge of their
unbalanced traits unless their rise and decline is inscribed in the fossil record. Cf. above,
Vol. I, Chapter 10, especially pp. 381–82.

animal mentality to human, conceptual mentality is no exception to that law of life. Since the beginning of our cerebral overgrowth—whenever that was—the odd human specialty has led and largely constituted our natural history. A new potentiality launched on the course of its realization tends to flourish at the expense of other functions, not only in other organs but even in the organ in which it is itself originating; and for the human brain so many new potentialities opened with the rise of symbolic imagery and expression that it must often have been in grave danger of becoming possessed by its own creations, to the loss of its life-preserving essential work.[8]

But with the beginning of the imbalance between the overactive cerebral cortex and the less progressive, sometimes even regressive limbic parts, there arose—from the very same developments which led to the dangerous tension—the conceptual talents that gave a symbolic function to the products of imagination and intuition, and made the complexes of communally held ideas that imposed themselves on mankind, everywhere on earth, as patterns of culture. There is no speech-gifted horde, however crude and backward, that does not have some cultural rule to live by; and the acceptance of the rule is undiscussed, unquestionable, simply manifest in sacred custom. The sacredness of custom derives from the punishments that descend on the community in the case of a breach. Since imperfections can be found in every ritual performance, and bad luck is always present in some degree, these two evils could easily be linked so displeasure at the former was generally imputed to the Supernaturals, whose overt response was seen in the latter. What prompted this world-wide interpretation was the growing sense of agency together with the naive conception of all events as acts, which led almost ineluctably to the assumption that natural occurrences, especially disasters, were motivated acts of conscious, willful agents. The need of doing something in defense against such misfortunes could usually be met only sym-

[8]How extreme the danger of excessive ritual enactments of fantastic ideas can become to the human race is horribly set forth by E. O. James in his account of Mexican sacrifices to assure the daily return of the sun: "the sun and the maize crops required perpetual regeneration, which could be obtained only by the offering of the hearts of human victims in the prime of their vigour as revitalizing agents. . . . This led to endless wars that the altars might be supplied with a constant stream of virile victims, and it may have been one of the causes of the break-up of the Toltec Empire in the middle of the eleventh century A.D. before the incursions of Chichimec hordes." And further: "When the Aztec warrior-god Huitzilopochtli was transformed into the solar divinity, he was thought to require a colossal supply of human hearts to enable him to perform his vegetation functions, demanding an extensive campaign into northern Oaxaca to obtain no fewer than seventeen to eighteen thousand captives as victims at the height of the holocaust" (*Sacrifice and Sacrament* [1962], p. 78).

bolically;[9] hence the ritualistic form of service and appeal to the controlling deities, ancestors, or local spirits, and even in societies that could hardly be called religious, the symbolic character of their magical practices to counter the inimical mysteries of nature.

The bare possibility of linking two events would not be enough to establish an explanatory connection between them if such connections were really found by empirical methods, but they are not. They are parts of an imaginary scheme, which is imposed on the world by seeking and finding exemplifications of its formal elements in actual experience; and quite trivial experiential items will do to verify the scheme. The explanation in terms of motivation thus provided for natural events is only an incidental achievement in the course of such thinking. Its real aim is to maintain the equilibrium between the drives of mental individuation and the integrity of the biological continuum, the rhythmically self-perpetuating stock. That equilibrium is the ethnic balance.

The principle of balance runs pervasively through all human life. The significance of punishment as a symbol of censure and recall to the social sphere is only one—albeit a primary one—of the many expressions of that basic principle. The whole advance of mind proceeds by piecemeal, dialectical movements, for every fully competent human brain strives, even without conscious intent, for emancipation from its somatic and reciprocal organic duties and for freedom to shape and follow a purely mental life of its own. Yet the physical organism in which that mental life is rooted has to be functionally represented and guided by the same organ that creates the mind. The higher the cultural expression of a society rises, the more tenuous becomes the balance between the physical security and strength of the stock and the autonomy of its members. Every behavioral act carries the possibility of upsetting the equilibrium of the social order in which successive generations are born, mature, and age, think, command, negotiate their conflicts and develop their separate minds, each unique, unlike any that ever was before. The primal and perennial work of social organization is not to fix the bounds of behavior as permanent lines, which would make all evolutionary process impossible, but to retrieve the vital balance every time some act, public or private, has upset it.

Meanwhile, the traditional rituals practiced in most societies—"rites of

[9]Arnold Gehlen, in an essay, "Über die Verstehbarkeit der Magie" (1963), p. 84, refers to Pareto's theory that magic springs from the need of making some overt response to any startling or abnormal impression in situations where only symbolic acts are possible: "das von Vilfredo Pareto genial erkannte *'besoin de faire quelque chose'*: das Bedürfnis, irgend etwas zu tun, um diese Eindrücke irgendwie aktiv zu beantworten."

passage," as Arnold van Gennep called them—marking the stages of life and its normal achievements by acts of name-giving, initiation, marriage and funeral rites, superimposed on the round of sacrifices or other regular religious services, are not expiations of sins, yet their social meaning is closely allied to that of punishment. They are expressions of the claims of society on the individual (often its first acknowledgment of his individuality), symbolizing his inherited responsibility for the welfare and continuation of the interwoven lineages, his people, that represent humanity to him.[10]

There is a very ancient rite—how old we cannot tell, for its existence goes back further than our earliest historical records—so widespread in the world that it must have a primitive symbolic function: the rite of circumcision. Like punishment, it is rarely, if ever, seen in the light of its basic meaning but has been given various interpretations in the different cultures where it is practiced. It has been interpreted as a sign of membership in this or that particular society or religious cult; but Jews and Moslems carry the same mark, which is also borne by many Australian, African, and even American tribesmen[11] and is said to have been known in Egypt before the infiltration by the Israelites in Joseph's day.[12] So it has figured as the mark of Abraham's covenant with God and as a badge of fortitude which boys had to receive on the threshold of manhood;[13] the

[10]The name of a tribe, in its own language, often means "mankind." G. B. Schaller, in *The Year of the Gorilla* (1964), p. 58, says that the natives of the region called themselves *"Batwa,"* meaning "men." The name *"Yạnomamö"* means "people" (see Chagnon, *Yạnomamö: The Fierce People,* p. 1). There was a notice in our newspapers some years ago that the Canadian "Eskimos" objected to that term because it means "raw flesh-eaters," and demanded to be called *"Inuit,"* meaning "human beings" (*New York Times,* June 23, 1973). According to M. J. Meggitt, "The Walbiri refer to themselves in general as *jaba,* 'people,' a term that may also include other Blackfellows, as distinct from White-and Yellow-fellows" (*Desert People,* p. 233). The list of instances could be extended to greater length.

[11]See the casual mention of this rite as found performed on Peruvian mummies in W. R. Dawson, "Mummification in Australia and in America" (1928), p. 137.

[12]See the *Columbia Encyclopedia* (1947 ed.), *s.v.* "Circumcision": "Circumcision of males was practiced in Egypt before it was introduced among the Hebrews by Abraham (Gen. 17:9–14). Among Mohammedans, the rite is older than Mohammedanism. It is or has been practiced by African, Australian, and American Indian tribes. The decision that Christians need not practice this Hebrew rite is recorded in Acts 15. It is practiced, however, by Coptic and Abyssinian Christians. Similar ritualistic operations are performed on Mohammedan women and the women of some African tribes. Explanations of the origin of circumcision are conjectural."

[13]M. J. Meggitt, in *Desert People,* gives a detailed account of Walbiri initiation ceremonies subjecting the boys to pain and terror. The brutal nature of their rites of circumcision, subincision, and chest cicatrization makes it clear that they are primarily a test of fortitude. Cicatrization appears to be optional, yet few men forgo it because "they do not

The Ethnic Balance

Watut of northeastern New Guinea, whose very simple former culture Hans Fischer has tried to reconstruct after its almost complete destruction by Christian missionaries (who even burned the little native villages to herd the inhabitants into larger settlements for easier surveillance and control), had their own rationalization of the practice, which also affected their method: its purpose in their eyes was to drain out the feminine blood which male children still carried by derivation from their mothers.[14] The Walbiri in western Australia, meanwhile, interpret it in a very different spirit, as a means to increasing sexual pleasure, although the elaborate terrors and pains under which the rite is borne by the young initiates clearly defy such an explanation.[15] The theory of a test of fortitude, however, though it might apply here, can hardly be accepted universally, in view of the fairly venerable custom of infant circumcision practiced on babies a week to a month old, especially by the most famous users of the rite, the Jews. Its motivation must lie deeper in primitive human feeling, where it may have the same significance for many unrelated societies.

It bespeaks, I think, a darkly apprehended intuition of the danger that lurks in an excessive spiritualization of man, the tendency to develop a mental life in defiance of the biological mainstream and let the physical stock degenerate or even cease.[16] Circumcision is the branding of the

---

want to be the object of a clearly-expressed satirical sanction. Uncicatrized men are likened to 'cleanskins' or unbranded cattle, or to children. Sooner or later, in an all-male assembly, someone will comment on their smooth chests and will question their courage. A quarrel is bound to follow, for no man can suffer this imputation with equanimity. The Walbiri place a high social value on the capacity of adults to tolerate without flinching or outcry, physical pain caused by others" (p. 316).

[14]Fischer reports, in his book *Watut:* "Sie umwickelten das Glied mit einer Brennessel, bis es gefühllos wurde, dann wurde die Haut mit einem Obsidiansplitter abgeschnitten. Dann nahmen sie einen spitzen Knochen vom fliegenden Hund und stachen in das Glied und pressten das Glied, bis all das weibliche Blut den Jungen verlassen hatte. Bei den Watut und Wampar ist die Angst vor dem weiblichen Blut bei den Männern sehr gross. Die alten Männer beschneiden. Der Grund dafür ist, dass die Kraft der Alten auf die Jungen übergeht und das kindliche weibliche Blut ersetzt. Das schwache Blut von der Mutter soll verschwinden und die männliche Kraft herauskommen, die zum Kriege fähig macht" (p. 86). The alleged purpose is supported by the highly extraordinary use of the anesthetic nettle, which shows that the rite is not intended as an ordeal; the boys had passed a milder test of hardihood in the face of heat and smoke before.

[15]A vivid and detailed description of that ceremony, too long to recount here even in summary, is given by Meggitt in *Desert People,* pp. 284–309.

[16]The extent to which an asocial attitude in favor of egocentric spiritual values may go is illustrated by the willingness of some religious zealots like the Albigensians or the Shakers to desist from all sexual activities and let their societies die out, being fed only sporadically with new non-procreative converts.

The lamas of Tibet seek a still greater spiritualization not simply by abstinence from

organ of procreation as a possession of society. Wherever this rite obtains, it symbolizes the necessary balance between the development of individual minds and the continuously creative matrix of social life, the slower, broader advance of mankind. Like many vital safeguards, it anticipates by long ages—probably millennia—the occurrence of any conceptual insight into its basic significance. Yet that unrecognized, purely felt function imbues the rite with sanctity, no matter how inadequate its conscious rationalization may be.

If the interpretation here proposed is accepted, a fair range of other practices may be viewed in the same light, namely, as branding the individual with the mark of his tribal or national involvement. The symbol may not be placed on the sex organ but in the face, such as a quill or other decor worn in the pierced nasal septum, like the ring in a bull's or boar's nose; as the animal's freedom is thus effectively curtailed, the human being's subjugation is symbolically attested.[17] Not improbably all cicatrization and tattooing had a similar ritual origin, though the visual qualities of the imposed designs would quickly make them marks of status, enhancements of personal appearance, and in some cases—like the Maori's very painful tattooing on the tongue—a show of fortitude, which is somewhat like an individual's defiance of society's eminent rights in him even as he surrenders to them. The essential process is to effect some visible symbol of the young person's socialization, the limitation of his selfhood, to be borne on his body for life.[18]

The growth of the mind, however, goes on even in the confines of its natural duties, which it gradually comes to feel and conceive as moral impositions; and as the vague feeling becomes more and more conceptualized, the permanent physical symbol may no longer be required (provided it has not, meanwhile, taken on a supplementary patriotic or religious meaning), so a person's identification with a purely mental kindred may be ritually established without a bodily sign—by a promise,

---

sexual indulgence but by strenuous exercise of mental concentration on images formed in their own minds. According to Alexandra David-Neel (herself a Tibetan lama), "the different kinds of exercises in this training aim at utilizing the energy naturally expressed in animal manifestations connected with sex, for the development of intelligence and super-normal powers" (*Magic and Mystery in Tibet*, p. 283).

[17]Hitler reverted to this practice in having his bodyguard, the Schutzstaffel, tattooed with the swastika.

[18]How vague in conscious thinking the motivation of such practices is apt to be is evident from Radcliffe-Brown's *The Andaman Islanders*. Telling about their custom of scarifying their babies, gradually, all over, he remarks: "The only reason that the natives give for this custom is either that it improves the personal appearance, or else that it helps to make the child grow strong" (p. 87).

The Ethnic Balance

an oath, a spoken commitment. The accompanying rite may be a sacrifice or a manipulation of sacred objects, a transient ordeal, or a presentation with or without priestly or choric dance and prayer.

A familiar example of such entirely symbolic attestation of a moral status is baptism. The fact that in its most common form today it is given to very young infants who cannot even take an active part in the commitment which is made for them by their elders shows with peculiar clarity that it expresses a social claim, even though it is consciously thought to bestow personal salvation. That putative efficacious power keeps it in the mystical realm, so it is not felt to be a conceptual symbol but a religious event.

Every rite that has traditionally marked the progression of a person's life from one phase to another gives expression to his inescapable involvement in the greater life of his lineage and the still greater life of humanity. But that does not mean that this inherence is the most important meaning of every rite of passage, as it is of birth and puberty ceremonies. In most cultures the usual next sacrament is marriage; and in all tribally organized societies marriage is more than a commitment to an established pattern: it is the making and upholding of the pattern itself, which is the skeleton of the social order.[19] Before the existence of state or priesthood or army, or any formal establishment, the only permanent

[19]The seriousness of connections made by marriage was generally not appreciated by those church missions and colonial administrations which could, and did, simply forbid any customs they did not approve, as the British authorities in Nigeria forbad the Tiv custom of "exchange marriages," i.e., the procedure whereby two men gave each other their respective younger sisters in marriage. Exchange marriage was not an ideal arrangement, as Laura and Paul Bohannan make quite clear in their account, but it had a comprehensible, physical structure that was not replaceable, on the level of Tiv understanding, by the principles of choice and sentiment introduced by the European conquerors (for a discussion of the effects see the Bohannans' *The Tiv of Central Nigeria* [1953], pp. 69 ff.).

Similarly, the demand made by the missionaries on the people of Kenya that, before they could receive baptism and Christian education, they must accept monogamy and even put away all but one of their wives if they were already polygamously married, broke up the native social structure fatally, and offered no new political scheme in its stead. As Jomo Kenyatta wrote: "the African could not understand how he could drive away his wives and children, especially in a community where motherhood is looked upon as a religious duty; the children are regarded as part and parcel, not only of the father, but of the whole clan (*mbari*), and without them the *mbari* is lost. It was also terribly hard for a woman to be driven away, and to lose her status in the society where she is respected as a wife and a mother. However, the African, having no other choice, superficially agreed to fulfil those conditions in order to get the little education which the missionary schools afforded him. The education, especially reading and writing, was regarded as the white man's magic, and thus the young men were very eager to acquire the new magical power; a fact which undoubtedly had escaped the notice of the Europeans" (*Facing Mount Kenya*, p. 272).

[129]

relationships of people to each other were their natal links: siblinghood, or cousinship in various degrees, among members of the same generation, and between successive generations the equally natural linkage of direct or indirect descent. It has often surprised administrators and anthropologists to find that totemic classifications in the most primitive human tribes were intricately complex even by the standards of educated civilized men, although the people who made and used them could not count by specific numbers beyond two—i.e., "one," "two," and "many."[20] The fact is, I think, that they recognize quite abstract symbolic contents where a natural form is presented and anciently familiar, perpetually repeated or sustained; then words are gradually coined for all its aspects and drawn together by the process of association that builds language in the first place, until a very elaborate relational system grows up through centuries, and is directly, intuitively, perceived as a pattern. Yet its originators cannot freely invent a systematic symbolism, so the complexity of their social structure seems utterly out of keeping with their crude cultural life. The apparent difficulty is, perhaps, even greater than the actual, because while they still think of each separate relational nexus among particular persons under a special name (as we speak of "nephews" and "nieces," "parents" and "grandparents," but with greater particularity) and let the named categories fall in with each other as they will, we are wont to think in a few terms which we use in dizzying combinations in analyzing the Australian's genealogical scheme.[21] The scheme is, indeed, more complex than ours because agnatic and affinic relations differ from each other and exogamic rulings cut across them,

[20]Alf Sommerfelt, in *La langue et la société; caractères sociaux d'une langue de type archaïque*, p. 158, expressed this surprise, saying: "L'Aranta ne connait pas de veritable système de noms de nombre, mais il est capable de retenir les détails d'un système de parenté extrèmement compliqué, système qu'un Européen n'arrive à saisir qu'au prix de grands efforts."

[21]*Ibid.*, p. 154: "Si nous écartons les termes identique à ceux qui ont déjà été mentionnés en vertu du principe que frères et soeurs ont le même nom, nous aurons les mots suivants: '*antara* (*iruntera*) 'fils et fille du frère de la mère de mon père'; *mbana* (*umbirna*) 'fils et fille de la fille du frère de la mère de ma mère'; *amba* (*umba*) 'fils et fille de ma soeur'; *mara* (*mura*) 'fils et filles du frère de la mère de ma mère' et 'fils et fille de la fille du frère de ma mère'; *namara* 'fille du fils du frère de la mère de ma mère'; *tjimia* (*chimmia*) 'père de ma mère,' 'soeur du père de ma mère' et 'fils et fille de ma fille'; *kamuna* (*gamona*) 'frère de ma mère' et 'fils du fils du frère de ma mère' et aussi, . . . 'fils et fille de la soeur de mon père.'" There are also single words for assorted groups of relatives, e.g., "*ebmana* (*ipmunna*) 'mère de ma mère et son frère,'" and for relatives by marriage; thus "*iliarra, iliara* (*illiura*) est un terme special pour 'le mari de la fille de la soeur de mon père' . . . et pour 'le mari de la fille du frère de ma mère.'" The list is longer, but this excerpt should make the point.

The Ethnic Balance

but the expanded family is a fairly fixed, slow-changing image which each individual learns to use as his symbol of society. If, however, the rules of marriage are suddenly abrogated or changed by a conqueror's fiat, not only domestic security but even political authority lose their footing in tribal tradition and find no other principle of allocation and support.

Finally, there are the rites that confirm the end of each individual life on earth; and these mark the point that is really the growing tip of the "Golden Bough," the point where religious ideas take shape, using whatever ritual practices there are to suggest meanings, and sometimes elaborating these into mythical eschatologies—fragmentary and inconsistent, yet offering a general background for any particular speculation a thoughtfully inclined person might pursue. In some societies more than in others such imaginative flights are pursued, and a general scheme of divine powers gradually finds acceptance.

There are today very few societies which have not produced some such scheme and carried it to the extent of conceiving the powers as personal wills, which naturally leads to their envisagement as physical individuals more or less manlike, though often supposed to be able to take on the bodily form of an animal—a swan, a bull, a fish, a serpent, or what not. Yet in deep jungles or other isolated regions there are still laggard communities on the road to religious conception who have not reached even that low resting place in the ascent. The mental gestation that leads from the first awareness of outside forces to the notion of such forces as living agents is not achieved in one step but is synthetic, like all important vital processes, and its contributing elements may look strange if one sees them in isolation. The first objectification of external power may be not by its attribution to a living being (real or imaginary) at all, but to a concrete ritual object that is thought to influence events which are beyond human control. Such an object is a fetish, and from the atavistic remnants of fetishism that still exist one may gather that it was once a phase in the origination of abstract thought.

In western Africa, in Nigeria, two anthropologists had the belated good luck to find a surviving tribe, the Tiv, which had not outgrown that phase, but imagined the fortunes of its little society—to its members, "mankind"—directly controlled by a contrived display of objects, a genuine fetish which seemed to represent no god, devil, or ghost. Their belief in the magical potency of their "Akomba," which appears utterly bizarre to a European, to them was implicit and reasonable, because unquestioned, a rude (perhaps original) symbolic projection of the nameless feeling of mind-action into an arrangement of such things as potsherds and a hoe handle;[22] the fetish represents human mental power and, characteristically, is supposed to contain and exercise the efficient "principle" it embodies for its user. This visible representation of the conceptual function of mind may not merit the name of religion, but it is the first stage of mystical, non-physical thinking, the forerunner of all conceptions of supernatural forces on which religion is built. From these most rudimentary beginnings still extant in our world to the highest theological doctrines, just about every possible stage and variant of religious belief is to be found in some society today. Even as the power of symbolic thought creates the danger of letting the mind run wild, it also furnishes the saving counterbalance of cultural restraint, the orienting dictates of religion.

The typical expression of religious feeling is sacrifice. This in itself is a highly suggestive fact. Literally, "sacrifice" means "making sacred," "hallowing"; it has no connotation of destroying the dedicated object, but only of sanctifying it, as by giving it to a holy being or power whose acceptance of it lends it holiness. Yet wherever the word is used in its religious context it carries the idea of renunciation, yielding something, giving over, depriving oneself. In secular use it has lost all other meaning. Commercial advertisements announce that such-and-such goods are to be "sold at a sacrifice." No one thinks they are to be made sacred, but only that the seller will take a loss of his potential profit to sell them at all. Obviously the idea of forgoing, yielding, is essential to the meaning of the word, even though its Latin form lays stress exclusively on the element of sanctification.

Popular usage, which commonly confuses and degrades the real sense of words, in this case seems to have preserved a primitive content which points to the fundamental nature of that basic rite, perhaps the most ancient in the world, and provides a cue to its biological source and function, its wide dissemination and variability, and its apparent deathless persistence.

The original motivation of sacrifice was, I believe, a sense of danger in the performance of an autonomous overt act that changed the agent's situation. Any such act, initiated by a single or multiple agent, is an exercise of mental power, and as such demonstrates the individuating

---

[22]See *The Tiv of Central Nigeria*, p. 83. The thinking of this large tribe is so unlike that of other people, not only European but African, that this rather small, clearly and factually written book requires very close reading and often re-reading, and one can understand the difficulties the authors encountered in translating words that have no equivalents in other languages.

activity of mind. It made the performer (and his witnessing fellows) feel a shift in the balance of power between him and the tribe or, if the tribe was the doer, between it and the powers of nature, at whatever stage of mystical representation or deification the latter might be. Something had been autonomously done; to restore the biological balance something would have to be yielded;[23] and the readiest symbol of submission to the claim of the greater, ancestral life force is to give up some precious thing to it, i.e., to make a sacrifice. That sacred transaction expresses the continued responsibility of the individual to his kind, represented for him by his lineage, his society, or, in higher cultures, his deities. Sacrifice is *par excellence* the means of restoring the ethnic balance;[24] and in this capacity it is never without a basic sense of loss and surrender.

Since the ultimate, intuitive aim of sacrifice is to symbolize the re-trieval of a balance, its magnitude is determined for each occasion by that of the committed self-assertion. An act of self-assertion is not the same as an act of aggression; it need not be directed against any other creature, although aggression is, of course, always self-assertive, and therefore most obviously requires ritual compensation. Any bold thought is at the same time a gesture of independence; so are all our decisions, choices, volun-tary acts.[25] It is in these normal ways that the mind takes its own course,

[23]The belief that every good must be paid for, not necessarily with something to benefit the bestower of it, but with something suffered by the receiver, is an ingrained conviction that seems to require no justification. So Victor Turner, for example, states that "running through most Ndembu rituals is the belief that one must suffer to obtain benefits. Psycho-analysts claim that many of their patients unconsciously think that any voluntary suffering entitles them to the privilege of a compensating pleasure. The same ideas are expressed in the attitudes of sacrifice and prayer in the higher religions" (*The Drums of Affliction*, p. 266).

[24]The Bohannans, in *The Tiv of Central Nigeria*, analyze—as best anyone can—the Tiv concept of *Akombo*, an omnibus term which means the fetish they employ to invite their luck, the disease or other affliction to be removed by its magic power, that power itself, the ritual performed with it, and its effect, and the restored well-being of the person or people involved. It is this last aspect that shows the true nature of the symbol: it restores the balance between mind and the powers of nature, wherefore the native term for the ceremony means "repairing the *Akombo*." The sacrificial rite may be elaborate, or very reduced and formalized, depending on the importance of the occasion (see their final chapter, *passim*).

[25]The realization of this condition has led some existentialist thinkers, especially re-ligious ones, to hold that the very act of living is inevitably sinful. So, for instance, Pepita Haezrahi complains: "It is our fate and our tragedy that we can neither achieve (as statesmen, social reformers, patriots, citizens even) nor fashion (as artists, craftsman [sic], scientist [sic]) anything without in the process incurring the guilt however slight of moral transgression, and that every transgression mars the nature of our persons and our achieve-ments, both. We oscillate between a law we *must* break in order to grow and a growth vitiated by the guilt of the broken law" (*The Price of Morality* [1961], p. 276).

and develops the self-feeling that has to be balanced *in toto* by an equally generalized ritual of maintained communion.[26]

One of the advantages of sacrifice as a pattern of holy rite is the range of its possible enactments, which makes it capable both of generalization and of adaptation to specific contexts. Its values can be formally matched against those of great or small transgressions, from homicide to the most trivial liberties taken in the course of everyday life; for the importance of the religious act is expressed by the greatness of the sacrificial gift, on a scale of inexact but accepted degrees which may be symbolically handled to compare and generally compute the balance of action and obligation. This makes it possible to classify the sacrifices commonly required to keep society on an even keel between these two limits and let the mind grow in the frame of social responsibility. Furthermore, sacrifice may be adjusted to the special dangers which in higher cultures beset individuals or small groups such as couples, comrades, or siblings acting together. The range and adaptability of sacrificial rites allows them to be systematized not only on a scale of magnitude but also of relative generality. In ancient Israel, a society with strong religious controls, there were traditionally fixed thank-offerings, sin-offerings, peace-offerings,[27] and sacrifices to effect purification after passing through crises, such as childbearing and the child's own first struggle, birth. Every abnormal situation requires the being at the center of it to muster its strength and carry through the winning act, which—even in a fetus—is a vigorous piece of self-assertion, and as such is a specific move toward individuation; to the religious-minded Jews such a morally innocent act was nonetheless polluting and had to be countered by a stipulated purifying sacrifice. For not only might people be made "impure" or "unclean" by natural and necessary acts[28] but they might incur guilt in ignorance, which required sacrificial atonement; and it was, in fact, particularly sins of inadvertence, and of the tribe as a whole which could not be laid to anyone's personal account, that were expiated by the daily services in the sanctuary. Both the "pollution" resulting from contact with things or beings deemed impure and wrongs committed in ignorance required a particular sin-offering.[29] In the early

[26]Arnold Gehlen, in the previously mentioned essay "Über die Verstehbarkeit der Magie," introduces the concept of "unbestimmte Verpflichtung," i.e., "unspecific obligation," which appears to be the consciousness of oneself as a generally responsible being, or a sense of responsibility (p. 84).

[27]For such regulations see especially Exodus 29 and Leviticus 1:10.

[28]For instance, in Numbers 19:11, it is written: "He that touches the dead body of any man shall be unclean seven days." Obviously, someone had to touch it to dispose of it.

[29]Roland De Vaux, in *Studies in Old Testament Sacrifice* (1964), p. 94, has summarized the sacrifices deemed appropriate, saying: "Prescriptions rather different from those

days of Yahweh worship, the demands of the Lord were not so much moral as ritual, and unintended sins were sins nevertheless. This aspect of the ancient ethos has often puzzled modern moralists but is found throughout the uncivilized tribes of man and well into some high civilizations; and if one regards sacrifice as a symbolic restoration of balance between individual freedom and hereditary responsibility, it is reasonable. Blunder as well as wickedness can upset the equilibrium of life. One trespass for which there was no saving ritual was deliberate sacrilege; murder, theft, and adultery might be expiated by sacrifices and gifts to the tabernacle, but sacrilege was a capital sin, for which the guilty person was "cut off from the congregation" and killed. Religion was what held the nation together, and sacrilege of any kind its gravest danger.[30]

The Old Testament stands halfway between savage conceptions of the supernatural and modern moralistic religion. The concept of sacrifice as the fulcrum of the ethnic balance runs through its primitive mythological phases much as it does in tribal societies today, for ancient Israel, in the days of Exodus and the possession and settlements which followed, was tribally organized, and in many ways—especially religious ways—remained so for centuries even under its own kings and foreign rulers. Its early records show an attitude toward God which is chiefly one of deference to a supreme power who demands above all to be honored, held in awe, assured every day of his human flock's obedience and humility, and endlessly worshipped. Such a divinity naturally makes for a ritualistic standard of virtue.[31]

An evolutionary history of sacrifice if carried out in sufficient detail might be a revealing contribution to the history of mind; for the unfolding of mind in all corners of the earth—in the heart of Africa and the remote headwaters of the Amazon as well as in India, China, the Mediterranean, the white man's Europe, and its global reaches—has recorded itself in a mosaic (or better, perhaps, a pointillist picture) of locally evolved tribal rites which, for all their differences, have a common element, a central

---

of Leviticus are given by Numbers xv. 22–29. In this text . . . it is a question only of the sin of the community or of an individual; inadvertent faults of the community are wiped out by the holocaust of an ox and the sacrifice *ḥaṭṭā't* of a he-goat, the inadvertent faults of an individual are wiped out by the sacrifice *ḥaṭṭā't* of a young goat. . . . When it is a matter of deliberate fault, it cannot be expiated by a sacrifice and the guilty one must be cut off from the community" (p. 94).

[30]See, e.g., Leviticus 24 (death for blasphemy); Numbers 15:32–36 (death for Sabbath-breaking).

[31]It is interesting how these early foundations of Judaism (and, consequently, its Christian and Moslem derivatives) resemble the morality of many savage societies today. Meggitt, in *Desert People*, writes: "transgressions of jural norms generally take the form of

act of sacrifice.[32] In large ways they are all comparable. Even the purely magical Akombo involves a little tribute of food and incense left, not for god or spirit, but for the Akombo itself, as if to feed its magic power.[33]

While the Judaic cult went back to a savage or at least semi-savage conception of supernatural power as the chief attribute of God, it also developed intellectually through phases of prophecy and mystical emotionalism until it could harbor such refined doctrines as those of the Essenes or the sophisticated Sadducees. This continuity of the historical record of sacrifice makes the biblical account an invaluable display of religious expression, change by change, age by age, where each impinging exotic influence has inscribed itself; for the rise of Christianity as well as the unbroken life of Judaism has carried it on to the present day, when it has become an entirely symbolic action, as it did a thousand years earlier in the minds of Chinese sages.[34] But throughout all shifts from

torts or private delicts. . . . one individual or group injures another who directly or through a surrogate retaliates in a prescribed manner. . . . There are, however, some misdeeds (those we might loosely term sacrilege) that are crimes or public delicts. The people regard them as attacks on the religious system itself, as undermining the bases of the law and the society as a whole. It is significant that their retribution is sometimes thought to follow automatically, without the intervention of other people" (pp. 259–60). And John Middleton, in Lugbara Religion, p. 100, makes equally clear that the aim of sacrifice is to restore the lost balance between a trespasser visited by "ghost sickness" and his society, with the statement: "Once God has shown that he accepts the promised oblation, and once the sickness is removed by the ghosts, then the sacrifice and communion are made . . . as a recognition that its ties are restored. The visible sacrifice is the sign of an invisible reality, lineage order. Oblation marks the return to lineage order, by the resolution of conflict within the lineage."

[32]In Australia, religious ritual had apparently not developed to the point of burnt offering at the time when Spencer and Gillen, Tylor, Durkheim, and other early anthropologists made their direct observations. Northcote W. Thomas, in his essay on "Sacrifice" in the Encyclopaedia Britannica, the eleventh edition of 1910–11, referred to "Australia, where sacrifice is unknown." But as research grew, and with it the researchers' knowledge of sacrifice, the Christian standard ceased to be the measure of what could be so called; surely pouring out one's own blood on the sacred stones in which the dreamtime kangaroos dwell belongs (at least somewhat obliquely) into the category. To give blood is to give part of one's life.

[33]See Bohannan and Bohannan, The Tiv of Central Nigeria: "Akombo are not shrines, for a shrine assumes a spirit of some sort, and akombo have no spirits associated with them in any way. Akombo are non-human forces, established by the Heavens at creation. . . . Akombo are not primarily guardians of morals or ethics. . . . Swendegh catches a woman just as thoroughly if, unknown to herself, she steps over a dog's grave as if she kills a person" (pp. 85–86).

[34]Cf. above, Chapter 19, pp. 35–39. The Chinese masters, unlike the orthodox European theologians, did not conceive of their rituals as efficacious, but as personally and socially expressive gestures of recognition and respect toward their ancestors. A few modern Jewish and Christian sects have given up the mythical conception of rituals as directly efficacious acts, but most of them have made it an article of faith.

magical to ideal status every phase has had the central purpose of holding the individual members to the lineage.[35]

Culture, however crude, is an essential safeguard to regulate the advance of mind in its present state of functional elaboration. The first phase of that evolutionary step was the terrifying growth of imagination, which provided a flood of emotional stimuli, probably more than the organism could deal with, and also kept itself activated by the envisagement of more and more unrealities. This may have driven the human species to articulate utterance and laid one of the foundations of speech; but speech, in turn, allowed fantasies to be shared, and in that way augmented the load on each brain, until the tendency to form a pseudo-matrix, the mind, and let it individuate beyond its physical supports became a lethal threat to the race. At that point, however, the widening possibilities of symbolic expression offered a saving device, probably well ahead of any intellectual use, the ritual demonstration of each individual's yielding and subjugation to society, however that greater felt life presented itself—as the tribe, the tribal ancestors, a family of divinities like the Greek and Roman gods, or a single divine ruler, Yahweh. In every case the intuitive sense of the balance between man's mental activity and the claims of his physical nature has been upheld by the offering of sacrifice in one form or another.

Religion, even the most primitive and superstitious, is inevitably a beginning of culture. It is not possible without some kind of symbolic expression, at least on the non-discursive level; and evidently it does not long remain on that level, but breaks over into communicative speech and begets dramatic gesture, dance, and chant, feelings of heightened power, and ideas of surrounding invisible beings. Under the protective restraints of religious actions, especially dance and the many forms of sacrifice, the shift from herd life to social life could take its jerky, piece-meal course through all the rocky rapids of fantastic thinking. It was fortunate for our kind that one of the first intuitions was the projected and metaphorized sense of imbalance, which held back the mushroom growth of imagination and let other functions—memory, reasoning, judgment—catch up with it; for in the evolution of mind imagination is as dangerous as it is essential.

So great a phenomenon as religion has, of course, more than one part to play where it prevails. Its original function may have been to keep men's minds in balance with the rest of nature, but what has led to its

35The ritual bond is usually emphasized much more for men than for women because the latter are held visibly and psychologically by their biological bonds.

own elaboration is a purpose it soon acquired: the denial or masking of death. When finally the recognition of death as not only natural but inevitable breaks through all defenses, the tenor of human life changes. In the civilized world this has happened so long ago that we all take it for granted, and normally are taught from infancy how to deal with the tragic image of our existence and its shocking brevity: how to soften it and deny its importance as an episode in a mythical world of everlasting life. This task has provided a challenge to reason as well as to imagination and served as a disciplinary guide in the development of thought, using the floods of spontaneous fantasy as materials instead of final products of mind.

But a much deeper change came with the realization of mortality, too—unperceived, biological, a new orientation that overtook one people after another until almost all but the most unenlightened savages have experienced it: the gradual shift from the ideal of boundless personal power to a demand for the highest degree of vital action in the small possible span of earthly life. No matter how firmly we may hold to the interpretations which would make death trivial or unreal, its actual constant approach has its unconscious psychological effect—so completely unconscious that it might better be called neurological, cerebral. The desire for maximal experience is easy enough to understand, but it is not the whole story; the part that one might not expect is that with the wish for fullness of life there comes a higher potentiality for action, a great new mental potentiality.

A little reflection on the rhythms of growth and change, however, makes this accelerated gain not really surprising. Every change of internal as well as external conditions tends to activate an evolving stock subjected to it, and elicits intensified, even new, reactions. The fact that the crucial stimulus in this case is not physical but conceptual, yet reaches to the very matrix of each organism shows that by this time the intellectual functions of the brain are well in the lead in directing and shaping the conative and emotional life of humanity, even though actual lures and threats play over its surface in an everyday pattern.

The present races of *Homo*, self-styled *"sapiens,"* live in the long consummation of the evolutionary "great shift." The radical change from animal life to human is still in progress and, I suspect, far from the limit to which it may ultimately go. Meanwhile, each major loss and replacement takes its separate course, and usually the loss of the old, animalian function outruns the development of the new, symbolically negotiated one. We have lost many valuable instincts. The directly elicited instinctive act of swimming when plunged into water, which puppies and kittens perform at the first trial before they are really firm on their feet, is no longer in the infant repertoire of a being built for a bipedal walk, and even its substitute learned version is not something everyone acquires— like acts of lifting, carrying, etc.—with natural childhood development. And not only such whole instinctive acts but our muscular reflexes have largely changed, and left only vestigial traces of their ancient useful forms. The "righting reflex" of animals in falling, most obvious in cats but present in most mammals, is almost completely lost in man,[36] since his natural posture is not pronograde. The "moro reflex" of newborn infants has been interpreted as a trace of an old clinging response.[37] One reflex that has gained in importance with the erect posture, however, has developed rather than declined: the wink of the eyelid. But it may also have undergone some corticalization because we can withhold the act for a short time, so that it is reflexive, yet to a degree voluntary. I do not know whether any other creature can do so, nor can I imagine any way of motivating such an act in an animal by way of experiment. Our breathing is a similarly automatic function, depending on muscular reflex action, yet under short-term voluntary control.[38]

Even the universally accepted "sex instinct" in man has suffered some deviation from the general pattern of the higher vertebrates, in being no longer seasonal except for a trivial rise of libido in spring that is only statistically demonstrable. There are good reasons for the frequent claim of biologically oriented psychologists that the sexual rhythm is the real pacemaker of animal emotions, wherefore the general temperamental responses of beasts and birds depend to some extent on the time of year.[39]

[36]Hans Hoff, in "Die zentrale Abstimmung der Sehsphäre" (1930), p. 35, remarked not only the loss of this reflex in man but also its reason, i.e., its eclipse by the supervention of cortical functions, saying: "Diese Reflexe sind freilich beim Menschen nur mehr in Rudimenten angedeutet, sie werden überdeckt durch andere, dem Kortex unterstehende Mechanismen."

[37]See the long discussion by H. F. R. Prechtl, "Problems of Behavioral Studies in the Newborn Infant" (1965), pp. 91 ff.

[38]Its highest degree of corticalization seems to have occurred in sea mammals, which cease to breathe when unconscious, as if breathing, in them, were essentially voluntary. See above, Vol. II, p. 36, esp. n. 57. The brief quotation there adduced goes on: "Anesthetizing drugs which primarily affect the cortex but not the lower centers will not work in such instances. By stopping the voluntary cortical processes, they interfere with breathing and produce death by suffocation" (W. N. Kellogg, *Porpoises and Sonar* [1961], p. 82).

[39]Irenäus Eibl-Eibesfeldt, who raised and studied the European red squirrel, reported that tame individuals will sometimes attack their keeper, "wobei ein jahreszeitliches Schwanken der Aggression deutlich wird. . . . Man beobachtet im Frühjahr oft Wutverhalten ohne erkennbaren äusseren Anlass: das ruhig dasitzende Eichhörnchen legt plötzlich die Ohren zurück und wetzt die Nagezähne" ("Angeborenes und Erworbenes im Verhalten einiger Säuger" [1963], pp. 726–27).
There are other examples of seasonal impulses, especially in birds, in Vol. II; e.g., pp. 97–98.

In man the vernal rise and culmination of this basic excitability is all but lost; he is ready for sexual activity at every season. The result is that his sex experiences are distributed and transformed into a wave pattern instead of a cycle, and as the effects of the endocrine stimulation very commonly outlast their stimuli,[40] his erotic tensions fuse into a fluctuating but unbroken continuum supporting a more or less coherent emotional life. This short pulse of intensified vital feeling, and perhaps of all feeling, by the organic pacemaker may have been an important factor in sustaining the stimulation of felt cerebral acts to the point of making many of them terminate in symbolic expression.

The most radical change, however, which must have started with the very beginning of humanization and is generally effective today, is the loss of the relationship among animals that is properly called "empathy," the intense degree of suggestion that transmits the feeling of one creature directly to another so it appears to the latter as its own.[41] We experience it ourselves upon occasion, but the physiological way it seems to work in animals, at the impulse level, is rare with us.[42] Our usual response to

[40]W. von Buddenbrock, in *Vergleichende Physiologie*, Vol. I (1952), p. 480, writes: "Die Reizung eines Sinnesorgans bewirkt unmittelbar, dass nicht nur in den afferenten Nerven, sondern auch in grossen Teilen des Zentralnervensystems vermehrte Entladungen auftreten. . . . von grösster Wichtigkeit ist nun aber, dass diese Entladungen den Sinnesreiz wesentlich überdauern können. Prosser zeigte, dass eine nur kurze Belichtung der Augen bei einem Präparat, das nur noch eine schwache Aktivität erkennen lässt, eine Steigerung derselben bewirkt, die eine volle Stunde nach Aufhören der Belichtung nachwirkt." Cf. also above, Vol. I, p. 32, n. 50, on G. H. Parker's work.
[41]For a definition and general discussion of empathy see Vol. II, p. 129, and, for examples, Chapter 15, *passim*.
W. Malgaud, in *De l'action à la pensée* (1935), pp. 18–19, has made an excellent attempt to render the operation of empathy in the guidance of a hunter by its prey, where the hunter's feeling remains superficial enough (probably due to sufficient species difference) to evade identification with the victim: "Tâchons de nous représenter comment l'épervier voit sa proie à ras du sol. . . . Le paysage, vu de haut, est dans son ensemble immobile. . . . un petit oiseau voletant tracera une sorte de zig-zag sur un fond uniforme. . . . le mouvement vu provoque un mouvement exécuté. . . . Le moment décisif du processus est celui où le mouvement en zig-zag s'inscrit dans le corps de l'oiseau de proie et s'accompagne d'un sentiment favorable. . . .
"Par un processus dont le détail nous échappe, un lien direct s'établit entre la figure d'excitation de réaction, de sorte que la seule vue de la proie détermine la plongée. L'important, c'est que nous éliminons toute connaissance véritable. La figure d'excitation n'a rien d'une image; elle est moins encore la représentation d'une chose avec un sens."
[42]I have once had an experience of unmistakable direct empathy: hurrying to take an opportune seat in a subway train, I felt my right eye suddenly watering, itching, then hurting. After applying a handkerchief to it, I looked about me. Across the aisle, facing me, sat a man whose left eye—vis-à-vis my right one—was horribly sore, running, obviously blinded and inflamed. I had not been conscious of the sight when my physical reaction set in; after a few minutes the effect abated.

indications of another person's sensory or emotive feeling is to imagine his experience and have a reaction of our own to the imagined feeling we attribute to him. That indirect reaction is not empathy, but sympathy, which has become the normal replacement for empathy in human life.

The word "sympathy" immediately suggests pity, understanding, and well-wishing; but in fact the worst instances of sadistic behavior—deliberate cruelty, torture—which are practiced only by human beings, [43] depend on a constitutional element of sympathy in ordinary social awareness. If the tormentor could not imagine his victim's pain, he would find no satisfaction in inflicting it. In animals, and unusually in men, a sudden empathetic seizure can stop an aggressive impulse, but there is nothing whereby the agent can purposely evoke it or hold it, nor can he evade it when it spontaneously occurs. Sympathy may be both evoked and by-passed; it normally varies directly with imagination, though it can, in emotionally responsive persons, overwhelm and block the act of imagining beyond a point. At that point it may possibly be touching off an atavistic moment of empathy.

The shift from the direct, physiological contagion of feeling to the conceptual form, sympathy, is slow and irregular, like most evolutionary advances, and the varying rates at which its elements progress set up some extreme tensions in human life. [44] Every society rests on at least a minimum of fellow-feeling; but in the course of our mental evolution the growth of sympathy has not kept pace with the loss of the animal reaction, empathy. So, although the exchange is clearly an essential step in the process of humanization, it also opened the way to mankind's most shockingly "inhuman" but apparently natural practice, cannibalism. Among the higher animals few, if any, of the carnivores—bears and wolves, lions and other great cats—habitually prey on their own kind. What restrains them? Hardly an accepted tradition of respecting signals of surrender, as Konrad Lorenz and Robert Ardrey would have us believe,

[43]The oft-mentioned "torture" of a mouse by a cat is not deliberate infliction of terror and pain, but incidental to the cat's play, the repeated enactment of the impulse to catch. The prey is usually too different from the hunter to evoke empathy, and the cat operates without any idea of the mouse's feeling available to engender sympathy.

[44]The influence of rates of change rather than the results of the changes *per se* has been pointed out by Seymour Parker in an article, "Ethnic Identity and Acculturation in Two Eskimo Villages" (1964). "Serious social problems," he says, "may result if innovations in the educational system inculcate widespread aspirations which have but a small chance of being fulfilled in the existing economic structure. The fault may not lie in the nature of the educational innovations themselves, but in an uneven relationship between them and other areas of social life. It is likely that differences in the rates of change of elements in the social system are more crucial in social and personal disorganization than are the absolute rates of change."

nor, as Wolfdietrich Kühme proposes, the realization that group life is safer and better than life in separate units,[45] but very likely a ready empathetic response, so common and effective that it takes no principle, moral or other, to safeguard the members of a species against each other's appetites under ordinary conditions.[46] Cannibalism, such as is widely known in savage societies where civilized conquerors have not suppressed it, is more natural to mankind than to most wild beasts.[47] The reason, I think, is that men have lost their prompt empathetic reactions, while their more complex cerebral functions are slow to engender new sensibilities to replace the former instinctive inhibition. With characteristic asymmetry, the development of such feelings on a higher cultural level is complete enough to make the eating of human flesh an impossibility to civilized people, while for tribesmen deep in the bush the loss of the older empathetic function is still the dominant change that outweighs any newly stirring revulsion. The incidence of cannibalism may thus be seen as a perfectly logical transitional stage in the evolution of man. What appears to the eye of a moralist like a terrible reversion to bestiality is really part and parcel of an elementary, exceedingly slow, advance.

Even the lowest savages, however, seem to feel the need of some balancing restraint upon the potential overgrowth of the cerebral organ when it reaches the stage of envisagement, fantasy, and speech, as it has done in every human stock. That need is met by ritual, especially sacrifice, apparently with a basic intuition that to keep the organic balance of mankind amid the vast opportunities for mental action requires some concession to the natural forces surrounding and upholding it. The ritualization of common activities such as eating, hunting or fishing, and gardening or gathering is probably a spontaneous reaction to the earliest conception of non-human powers as elements in the circumambient world, to be met with recognition, bids for favor, or defense—mental, magic defense—against their threats. Ritual is older than religion; it is the scaffolding in which all religious thought has taken shape. In its practice

[45]In "Freilandstudien zur Soziologie des Hyänenhundes (Lycaon pictus lupinus Thomas 1902)" (1965), p. 495, he writes: "Zum Problem wird das Zusammenleben von Artgenossen . . . bei den in Rudeln lebenden Fleischfressern, die einen essbaren oder zumindesten konkurrierenden Artgenossen leben lassen, weil man zu mehreren doch letztlich eher überlebt als allein."

[46]Some adult males in canine and feline species sometimes eat their newborn young; the difference of form and movement (and perhaps odor?) between the full-grown sire and a blind puppy or kitten may well be too great to let the young one evoke empathy in him.

[47]Many animals, especially males, do kill their own kind in fighting; rage may easily supervene over the normal emotional safeguard, especially where a contagion of feeling could only increase each antagonist's angry excitement. But they do not eat the victim, which for them is just completely subdued, not felled as prey.

the symbols of power are created. So without plan or deliberate intent society becomes culturally organized in a sacred round, its recurrent cycles punctuated by seasonal public rites, while on a smaller scale each individual life goes through its own "rites of passage," from its admission to the social order (usually with name-giving) to the closing ceremonial acts which each person's fellows perform for him.

It is those last rites that undergo a grave change of meaning when people are inescapably faced with the enigma of the final "passage" from the familiar scene of daily life to the inconceivable state of being dead. Birth, manhood, and rank have much the same significance in savage life as in modern civilization; our gestures toward them change in style, but not greatly in sense. But when the realization of death as the full stop not only of the dead person's activity but of all further potentiality breaks through the unconscious barriers—the "ritual ignorance," the dreams of "standing alive," the repression of interest in such matters—it strikes with terrible force into the primitive religious consciousness. It may take several centuries before all the members of a society feel the impact, but one by one they do, and one by one all cultural groups succumb to it, though some as yet have scarcely met it, some are still resisting it, while the civilized nations have already dealt fairly successfully with the emotional crisis and found at least a *modus vivendi* in a new, religiously supported ethnic balance.

The effect on mankind as a whole, however, has been not only a pervasive deepening of thought and subjective feeling, but also a quite unrecognized change of fundamental values; for instead of seeking indefinite length of life, we tend to seek a maximum of activity and experience in the short span which, we know, is all we can hope for, even if we reach a relatively ripe age. The brevity of that greatest human act, the passage from birth to death, makes any personal agent seem incomparably small within the stream of the ancestral stock, constantly proliferating into new death-bound individuals, in its immediate temporal dimension; and when the source of that stream is conceived as a godhead to which all power of animate and inanimate nature has been delegated, the contrast between human and superhuman potency becomes overwhelming. There no longer seems any danger of man's rivaling God's supremacy. The balance between mental individuation and vital dependence has, in fact, shifted in the direction of the latter, so the strongest minds feel quite safe and free to put out their utmost ability in defiance of death and fill a precarious lifetime with all the personal experience they can crowd into it. Gradually, quite unconsciously, the weaker souls follow the pioneers, until the daily anxiety to make sacrificial atonement for human arrogance is assimilated to the general religious background and given into the care of the priesthood.

And yet, wherever the knowledge of the tragic form of life has superseded the hope of its indefinite endurance, as it has for most of the earth's population, the shock of that truth precipitated a new and great preoccupation with the idea of death, for most people are simply unable to accept it. Philosophers and theologians, saints and bold heretics of every religious tradition have battled with the "problem of death," the problem being how to convince oneself of its unreality or, at least, its unimportance.

One of the earliest steps in such an intellectual venture is, of course, to present the difficult conception of inevitability in an imaginable symbol. In the meteoric rise of Greek thought one can often trace the formulation of ideas that other peoples have taken millennia rather than centuries to develop, so that their primitive phases in those cultures antedate any literary remains. In Greece we find the record of that process in the epic age, with abstract concepts still taking shape in the mythic mode but on the verge of the discursive. The symbol of inevitability is *Moira*, Fate.

The solemn image of *Moira* expresses a fairly intellectualized emotional feeling, the haunting sense of something approaching which is bound to happen to a person—in its oldest versions, typically to a family—in one way or another, let the human sufferers do what they will to avoid it.[48] In the growth of Greek *Weltanschauung* it was a late idea, too late to receive the true mythical treatment that spontaneously made gods out of the more primitive objects of fear or desire: love, strife, wisdom, victory, and, above all, power. The three women, the Moirai, spinning and determining and cutting the thread of each human life, present the furthest elaboration the mythical conception of Fate achieved. They are shadowy figures forever carrying out their symbolic acts; they have no

---

[48]W. C. Greene states that "there stands behind the gods a shadowy reality, a fixed order rather than a power, a divine conscience, at times gathering moral grandeur, at times dreadful and oppressive to man, the reality known as *Moira*. . . . The exact color of the word *moira* depends, of course, on its context in each case; sometimes neutral, sometimes suggesting what must be and therefore should be, it often tends, particularly when it refers to the one lot that all must accept, the μοῖρα θανάτου, to acquire, like *daimon*, an unfavorable meaning, and is given uncomplimentary epithets. . . . Homer recognizes no essential conflict . . . between the power of Fate as the will of Zeus (and other gods), between the remote Power and the immediate agency. . . . But Eustatheus, twelfth century commentator on Homer, oversimplifies the matter when he states that the will of Zeus and destiny are synonymous. Not only is Poseidon subject to *moira* (Od. 9, 528–535), but even Zeus is powerless to avert the death of his own son Sarpedon, though he apparently can postpone the day of his doom" (*Moira: Fate, Good and Evil in Greek Thought* [1944], p. 15). Here, obviously, *moira* is the final ineluctability of death.

adventures and amours like the gods, Olympian or lesser and local, and make the impression that their inventors themselves regarded them somewhat as allegorical poetic figments, human circumstances conceived in the still-current form of supernatural agents.[49] The same may be true of the Scandinavian Norns, that suggest a common origin with the classic Fates, being a similar triad of old women, sitting under Ygdrasil, the World Ash, and performing the same functions of spinning, determining, and ending human lives. Only in more easterly regions of the ancient world—in the Arabian deserts traversed by nomadic herdsmen and in the cities of Assyria and Babylonia—the concept of fate was developed out of deeper popular feeling. Such feeling evidently lacked a ready symbol to serve the common mind, which could not grasp mystic divinities and astrological calculations but required a plainer commandment of right and wrong and forgiveness of error and sin. Submission to the will of Allah set just such a simple standard. There is really very little in the Koran to support the thoroughgoing fatalism it inspired; the will of God was not absolutely unalterable by prayer or plea; but it offered a mold for the sense of inevitability which seems to have been intense—perhaps new, and therefore preoccupying—in seventh-century Arabian thought.[50]

The interesting thing about popular fatalism is that it is rarely entertained with relation to everyday acts and events, but centers on the anticipation of death.[51] That shows the intuition underlying the myth:

[49]H. J. Rose, in his brief article in the *Encyclopaedia Britannica* for "Fate," writes: "The idea of fate as an impersonal force that absolutely predetermines all events was, to the ancient world [meaning the Mediterranean world] as it is to the modern, a philosophical or theological conception rather than a popular notion. . . . The Moirai were conceived as very old women (though art does not represent them so). From the time of Hesiod onward they were even given individual names—Clotho (Spinner), Lachesis (Allotter) and Atropos (Inflexible). . . . But fundamentally the Moirai belonged to folk belief; their primary function was to assist at a birth and then and there to determine the career of the child, as the Moires still do in modern Greece."

[50]Resorting once more to the authority of *Britannica* (1960 ed.), under the (unsigned) entry "Fatalism," we read: "Primitive Islam taught that everything is ruled by the decree of almighty God; but influence from pre-Islamic fatalism in Arabia and fatalistic doctrines in Iranian religion (especially Zervanism) soon changed this tenet into belief in an inexorable fate (kismet, *nasib*), and submission to the will of God became resignation to fate's decree."

[51]The Koran itself is full of admonitions and warnings of hellfire addressed to those leading sinful lives, which would make no sense if men could not alter their ways at will. See, for instance, the chapter on emulous desire: "The emulous desire of multiplying *riches and children* employeth you, until ye visit the graves. By no means *should ye thus employ your time:* hereafter ye shall know *your folly.* . . . if ye knew *the consequence hereof* with certain knowledge, *ye would not act thus.* Verily ye shall see hell. . . . Then shall ye be examined on that day, concerning the pleasures *with which ye have amused*

the perception of life as one potential act, one person's potentiality, to be realized as it may in the span that Fate—the inevitable coming of death—permits.

A trauma to a special organ, however, while it may briefly confuse or even interrupt its operation, typically produces a concentration of energy in it which presently leads to abnormal growth, elaboration, or—most immediately—a burst of its functional activity. The mental organ naturally responds to an abnormal strain with acts of imagination and emotion and, at a level where ideas can disturb it, with cogitation. So the understanding of mortality, which comes as a blow to the mind in its phyletic progress, starts an epoch of heightened mental action and drives it to more intellectual advance and more individuation than ever. That has happened in most societies where the realization of personal mortality has dawned; and, reflecting the nature of its motivation, the new preoccupation is with a vision of life not as an indefinite length of days in the world of the living or in a similar world of the ancestral spirits (with spirit-bones and beards and tempers), but as a brief phase in an ascent of the mind to a higher sort of life without death. What aids the conception of such a life is the relatively huge impetus the forebrain has received, the furious activity beyond that of the somatic functions whereby the mind is so abetted and encouraged that it is apt to be still unexhausted when the rest of the life is finished; consequently most people feel the tension between their love of life and their loss of strength to live. The body threatens to be through before the spirit is through. Then the relations of death and life become urgent and central. The greatest thinkers, founding their speculations on the mythic premises of the religious traditions current in their day, elaborated theological and eschatological doctrines until fantasy and logic together wrought the conception of earthly life as an episodic ordeal (somewhat like an initiation) to prepare the human soul for a projected endless existence after death.

But here another imbalance between the powers of life and death made itself felt, especially in the society that seems to have gone furthest in the contemplation of sin and the cultivation of guilt feeling, the Jews. Almost

---

yourselves in this life" (George Sale, trans., "The Emulous Desire of Multiplying," *The Korân*, chap. 102, p. 589). The same limitation of fate to a few great contingencies (that we would call "fateful") and to the certainty of death, is noted by A. W. H. Adkins in *Merit and Responsibility* (1960), who says, speaking of fifth-century Athens: "In the face of death, man's precautions are futile; accordingly, it must be in the hands of the gods. A fatalistic attitude to the whole of life, however, does not result from this. Death is, as in Homer, still expressly contrasted with events which *are* controllable. As Collinus says, 'You will die when the *moirai* spin death for you; but a man should march straight forward brandishing his spear'" (p. 119).

every culture, savage or civilized, has some sacrificial rites to pay for its transgressions; but the crushing sense of sin, of congenital sin before any committed wrong, the notion of being conceived in sin and born in pain to a life of deserved punishment, was built up by the prophets of Israel and inherited by Christianity, where it was highly elaborated. This concept of man's utter worthlessness makes death more terrible than bodily disintegration, for it spells a death of the soul. Death and sin, especially sexual sin, are always closely associated; to be "sunk in sin" is, above all, to have forfeited any further life, even without the addition of hell fire. Clearly, no exercise of justice alone could level such a moral disequilibrium. [52]

In this impasse a new god image, derived from a worldly source familiar to all Mediterranean and Near Eastern peoples, offered itself to the religious imagination: the image of Yahweh enthroned in glory, outshining all the splendors of Solomon or Pharaoh or Caesar—the image of God the King. An absolute monarch might mete out justice but he might also be merciful; and the Christian's hope henceforth was for mercy, divine grace.

Yet the idea of living entirely by undeserved mercy did not restore the balance between sin and atonement; no human devotion or sacrifice, even the yielding of life itself, could pay for everlasting pardon and life beyond the grave. It would require the sacrifice of a god to buy such salvation. So the God of the Christians came to earth and gave his life as a sacrifice for their ritual conquest of sin and death.

In the subcontinent of India, meanwhile, the problem of accepting the brevity of life has found another solution, which requires no superhuman, single sacrifice to balance the measure of man's depravity. The ancient doctrine of the soul's cyclic return in successive incarnations makes human life a much longer ordeal than the short act between a person's birth and death; each episode of incarnate being prepares the next, so it is possible to rise, in a spiral of recurrences, on a somewhat (if only slightly) higher plane of beginning with each return. Because the soul keeps its identity not only from birth to death but from death to birth, it has eons rather than years to achieve its purification. Also, it is not

[52]It may cause one to wonder why natural disasters and pestilence are viewed even in high religions as punishments when no heinous sins have been lately or frequently committed, and why the idea of having deserved God's anger should be reassuring to people instead of crushing. In the first place, of course, it exonerates their God from any possible attribution of evil; but in the second place it feels like a restoration of balance if one assumes that it is "the wages of sin." Instead of seeming to break Abraham's covenant, self-accusation can make plague, flood, and earthquake seem to reaffirm it, as all punishment is designed to do; sometimes the sin has to be invented.

laden with Adam's sin but only with the dross of its own delusions, its carnal interests, the "veil of Maya," or unreality, that distorts its spiritual vision.[53] And above all, it has a different aim from the Judeo-Christian and Judeo-Mohammedan soul: its purpose is not to serve God, but to attain a complete liberation of the mind from the body and let it merge with the divine mind to embrace all understanding of nature, seeing it as an emanation of the spirit, Brahma.[54] According to the strictest Buddhist teaching, only Gautama has reached that highest degree—Nirvana—so far.

There may be other ways of restoring the balance between the mind's individuation and the earthbound hold of its roots in animal nature, the enormous potential of mental life and its tiny allowance of time for realization. The great religions are our present promises of a more proportionate future. In the centuries and millennia during which those promises were given and reiterated until they built a bulwark against death, a change overtook humanity's symbols of its highest value: the old symbols of power yielded their paramount place to life symbols. Even before abstract thought reached the stage of contemplation where people could envisage either an eternal life after death or a sovereign god, their life symbols acquired the status of supreme significance.[55]

The great importance and formal role of gifts in most precivilized

[53]India is vast, and many of its people are much more given to religious speculation, and freer to pursue it, than "Western" thinkers; consequently, there are countless schools and sects that would disagree with one aspect or another of any general statement of "Indian" philosophy that can be offered. Yet Indian thought has its historical Brahmanic background, as ours has its basic, often tacit assumption of a single (even if triune) personal deity. As one Indian philosopher, I. C. Sharma, has stated, "The two stages of self-realization, Moksa, *i.e.*, the Jivanmukti, or the liberation attained while living, and the Vidhahamukti, or the final release after physical death, have been recognized by Nyaya, Vatsesika, Samkhya, Yoga, Mimamsa, Vedanta, Jainism, Buddhism and even by the Bhagavatgita. Thus Upanishadic thought is the very rock and foundation of the metaphysical as well as the ethical concepts of all the systems of Indian philosophy" (*Ethical Philosophies of India* [1965], p. 102).

[54]Cf. James, *Sacrifice and Sacrament*, p. 50: "The Western affirmation of the individual personality stands in striking contrast to the oriental quest for perfection in uniting the self with the Absolute, for losing the Atman in Brahman as a river loses itself in the sea.

"A theistic interpretation in terms of the concept of a personal Deity at once transcendent and immanent results in a very different situation. . . . when Deity is thought of as a Person disclosing himself and dispensing his divine power to persons for specific purposes, the relationship between God and man and the universe must be maintained."

[55]Ian Oswald, in *Sleeping and Waking. Physiology and Psychology* (1962), p. 160, speaking of what stimuli will or will not arouse a sleeper, makes quite clear, by implication, that the evaluation of signs occurs at the impulse level of physical acts, below the limen of conscious judgment. The same condition appears to hold for symbolic values of objects, rites, and even imagery; their import is felt as sacredness to a distinct degree before it is intellectually understood.

societies rests on this preconscious evaluation. Especially a gift of food is received as a gift of life; the Navaho Indians consciously recognize their essential food, corn, as a life symbol, and its importance is stressed in the myths of its origin. These native Americans are among the world's most active symbol-makers; every color, every animal, as well as clouds, waters, mountains, and each point of the compass, all have a multiplicity of symbolic values in myth and ritual and in the Navaho's special art, the sand painting. Gladys Reichard has recounted one of these myths in her searching study of the Navahos' elaborate religious symbolism, where she says: "The Navaho have a sentimental attitude toward plants, which they treat with incredible respect. . . . However, in contrast to the numerous etiologies of corn, accounts of the origin of particular plants are few. In some myths corn is considered primeval, for First Man had some in the first world. Other myths account for it as the gift of a god or a neighboring people. Whatever its origin, its value is constantly emphasized. According to one myth, Talking God gave corn to Whiteshell Woman and her sister, Turquoise Woman, saying, 'There is no better thing than this in the world, for it is the gift of life.' Later, when he visited them again and they told him they still had it, he said, 'That is good, for corn is your symbol of fertility and life.' "[56]

Jane R. Hanks found the same attitude toward gifts in Thailand, and the same significance of food as a life symbol. "The idea," she says, "that to nourish is to give life has been socially translated to a general feeling that a gift of food is especially acceptable, important, and appropriate. . . . A reputation for generosity with well-cooked foods is an integral part of leadership. Buddhist precepts have reinforced the importance of food-giving."[57] There are other life symbols which tend to displace—or have displaced—the older images of power. The pillar of cloud by day and fire by night which led the Israelites through the wilderness was the visible power of Yahweh; but the blood of sacrificial victims that was poured out in front of the altar was a symbol of life, and, like every sacred symbol, not only meant but was life itself. Indeed, the Jewish blood rite, which Roland De Vaux finds peculiar to Israel among the nations of the world they knew,[58] contained one ritual act which might be regarded as transitional between the worship of power and of life: when the blood of

---

[56]*Navaho Religion: A Study in Symbolism* (1950), Vol. I, p. 23. In Vol. II, a concordance to Vol. I, the author notes: "there is probably no rite or ceremony in which corn does not function in some form or other" (p. 540).

[57]"Reflections on the Ontology of Rice" (1960), p. 300.

[58]*Studies in Old Testament Sacrifice* (1964), p. 42. De Vaux restates the principle which the Pentateuch expresses repeatedly: "the blood contains the life; in fact it is itself the life. That is why man has no right to consume the blood." And in a later passage (p. 93) he refers to Leviticus 17:11 as his authority.

the sacrificed animal was poured out before the altar, the priest was enjoined by the scripture to take some of it on his finger and daub it on the horns of the altar, which were the symbols of God's power. Here the two values, power and life, are almost equal; but it was the blood rite that went on to make cultural history, for the concept of atonement by blood sacrifice underlay the subsequent Graeco-Judaic development of the Christian myth.

A much more spectacular record of the same shift from the ideal of sheer power to that of intensified life may be seen in sculpture and architecture, a record that stands for hundreds or thousands of years. The form of the pyramids in Egypt has long been recognized as a phallic symbol, and the phallus is a very ancient image of power. A Pharaoh's tomb is a huge edifice bespeaking the power which he wielded on earth and has taken with him to another world, pictorially conceived yet accepted as reality. The chamber in which his body was preserved held the despotic force that imbued the pyramid, pervading it from within. The stark lines of the monument declare nothing but royal power, obstinately defying time and transience (Fig. 22–1). This is the impression the pyra-

Figure 22–1. Pyramid and Mortuary Temple of Chephren, Giza
the stark lines of the monument declare nothing but royal power
(From I. E. S. Edwards, *The Pyramids of Egypt* [Baltimore: Penguin Books, 1967].)

Figure 22–2. Sāñcī, Stupa I, Third to First Century B.C.
a simple, austere mound topped by a sculptured emblem of royal rule
(From Ananda K. Coomaraswamy, *History of Indian and Indonesian Art* [Leipzig: Karl W. Hiersemann, 1927].)

mid rising out of the sand made before its surroundings were excavated; the whole pyramid city in its day must have had much the same effect.

In India, the Buddhist temple architecture known as the stupa was at first a simple, austere mound topped by a sculptured emblem of royal rule (Fig. 22–2), in that part of the world an umbrella. The original stupa may or may not have had the same connotation as the Egyptian pyramid, but its form does not immediately suggest command or aggression; it figures somewhat as a life symbol from its very beginning. Like all indigenous Indian architecture, it seems to emerge and grow from the ground itself rather than to have been placed on it; the great mound resembles a breast of the earth, a symbol of life-giving, more than an image of human power and arrogance. It belongs, of course, to a much later civilization, which had undoubtedly long passed the crucial confrontation with the fact of mortality.

The Buddhist temple that derived from the mound, however, and is still called a stupa, itself took on the form of the lingam, the sacred phallic icon that was housed in it and was carried in procession on festive occasions (Fig. 22–3); its shape is more realistic than the geometrically simplified pyramid, and all its modifications tended to make it a life symbol, with every suggestion of procreation: generation, progeny, and growth. The great temple in the Bhubaneswar complex is a perfect example of the lingam form built up as an edifice; it is dedicated to Siva, one of whose names is Lingaraja, which is also the name of the temple (Fig. 22–4). On its surface, little replicas of itself are carried, like the sprouts on a cactus, and small shrines of similar form crowd around it. Despite its height and the obviousness of its phallic character it has little or no appearance of a power symbol, but is like an architectural extension of Indian sculpture. Even its placement among a host of little stupas and other shrines enhances its organismic form.

The most perfect exhibit of the passage from the ideal of infinite power to that of endless life, however, takes us again into the realm of ritual centering on an image which represents that highest value. Jeanne Cusinier, in her book on pre-Islamic and pre-Christian beliefs which she found still current in southeast Asia (Malay and Indochina), notes how the victim, originally a buffalo—a common symbol of sheer power—was supplanted by a bull (still the same), then a goat, then a fowl, and finally by an egg, "because of the germ of life which this contained."[59] In fact, the author of *Sumangat* holds that the magic healing rites found in this part of the world as in almost every other are never limited to that function, but are always rites of homage to Life as such, and represent the highest forms of the cult. The souls of living persons are not really their chief recipients; but "through these they are addressed to everything that lives, to everything that creates, upholds and encompasses Life, to the principle itself, moving, fragile and imperishable, of existence. . . . It is not only a cult of living souls, but a cult of Life" (p. 250).

Figure 22–3. Lingam
the lingam, the sacred phallic icon
(From Ananda K. Coomaraswamy, *History of Indian and Indonesian Art* [Leipzig: Karl W. Hiersemann, 1927].)

Wherever the balance between man and the greater powers that sur-

[59]*Sumangat: L'âme et son cult en Indochine et Indonésie* (1951), p. 221.

Figure 22–4. Lingaraja
a perfect example of the lingam form built up as an edifice
(From Ananda K. Coomaraswamy, *History of Indian and Indonesian Art* [Leipzig: Karl W. Hiersemann, 1927].)

round him has been established by some fundamental religious expression, as it has largely been today, it fills the background rather than the foreground of conscious thought.

But no balance holds itself passively for very long in the course of evolution. A state of equilibrium in nature generally indicates a fulcrum between two antagonistic forces, as depicted in the central panel of the Indian sculpture shown above, which reflects the crowding, teeming, ever-burgeoning life from which the eternal conflicts spring (Fig. 22–5).[60]

[60]A note referring to the central horizontal panel shown in this figure states that "gods (*right*) and demons (*left*) have wound the snake (Shesh) round the mountain so that they may churn the sea of milk and obtain the drink that bestows immortality" (Odette Monod-Bruhl and Sylvain Lévi, *Indian Temples* [1952], p. 10).

Figure 22–5. Madura, Detail of the Great Temple
Indian sculpture, which reflects the crowding, teeming, ever-burgeoning of that populous country
(From Odette Monod-Bruhl and Sylvain Lévi, *Indian Temples*, 2d. ed.; orig. English ed., 1937. Translated by Roy Hawkins [London: Oxford University Press, 1952].)

Even though we may be in the midst of an eon of cerebral elaboration rather than radical mutation, intellectual drives and cultural checks are always shifting the ethnic balance, and its present direction seems to be toward internalization, i.e., toward a centering of the fulcrum of social equilibrium not between men and Supernaturals, but in society itself. We may be at the very bottom of a new ladder of mental and moral ascent, in a human world stunned by civilization, and in a moment of pause in its otherworldly concerns, meeting the challenge of its own technical and economic construction of a world-wide civilized society.

23

The Breaking

AS THE development of religious and moral codes records the evolution of subjective new experience, the overt expression of that same process is a long, spectacular achievement: the rise of civilization. That aspect of man's mental advance has inscribed itself objectively on the face of the earth, in spite of the obliterating forces of time which have caused many of its effects to return to the dust again. There is still enough cumulative progress to mark its course, even to spelling out some of the acts, prehistoric, ancient, or recent in history, which turned forested mountainsides into barren rock or won fertile lands from the sea that used to cover them, separated continents by cutting canals through the isthmuses that joined them, built lakes and harnessed the dammed-up power of their waters. All these grand scars on the earth, however, tell only indirectly the newest chapter in the story of man, the emergence and persistent growth of civilization; for the story itself is the life history of the mind, and the new chapter began only a few thousand years ago.

The most spectacular aspect of the new age is the rise of cities in several far-separated parts of the world, at shortening intervals and, once started, in rapidly increasing numbers; and the surest sign that this phenomenon marks an evolutionary step in human history is that various apparently independent occurrences have different motivations, yet converge in their consummations. Cities arise under widely varying conditions. The oldest sites so far found by present-day archeologists are still the ruins, sometimes deeply buried, in Mesopotamia,[1] or even further east, in

---

[1] Paul Lampl, in *Cities and Planning in the Ancient Near East*, says (p. 34): "The recent excavations of Jericho have uncovered the earliest urban settlement in the history of mankind discovered so far, dated by the carbon-14 method to the Eighth Millennium B.C. The town designated as 'Pre-Pottery Neolithic A' developed over a mound of occupational debris more than 4 m. in height covering an area of not less than 4 hectares. It was fortified by a strong stone wall. Traces of curvilinear houses of the period have been found.

"In the Seventh Millennium B.C. newcomers with a fully developed type of architecture—which implies an urban development somewhere else as yet unknown—built a new town on the site, 'Pre-Pottery Neolithic B' with rectilinear houses consisting of several rather large rooms arranged around courtyards, and shrines."

Figure 23–1. The Oldest Ruins of Jericho ("Neolithic A")
The oldest sites so far found . . . are still the ruins of Mesopotamia, or even further east, in central Asia
(From Kathleen M. Kenyon, Digging Up Jericho [New York: Praeger Books, 1957].)

central Asia (Fig. 23–1).[2] No one knows what caused the ferment in one people after another, who had apparently lived for thousands if not hundreds of thousands of years in family groups formed by the occurrence of births and deaths in natural lines of descent, which automatically expanded into village settlements as overlapping generations built up groups of related families. Uncounted millennia seem to have witnessed only increasing complexities of tribal organization, developing rules of exogamy or endogamy, formal agnatic and affinic relations, taboos a-plenty and peculiar liberties, totemic divisions and sometimes a separation into

[2]Edith Ennen places it in Anau, on rather interesting grounds, as she says: "Die älteste stadtartige Anlage fand Menghin in Zentralasien, in der ersten Kultur von Anau bei Merv in Transkaspien. Die Annahme, dass wir in der Gegend von Anau die überhaupt älteste Stadtkultur der Erde zu suchen haben, verdichtet sich. Von besonderem Gewicht ist dabei wohl die Tatsache, dass die altsumerische wie die altindische Astronomie die Dauer des längsten Tages nicht nach ihrer eigenen sudlicheren Breite berechnen, sondern in [sic; ihr?] etwa den 53. Breitegrad zugrundelegen, was auf den Raum von Anau passt; die Berechnung müsste also dort konzipiert sein" (*Frühgeschichte der europäischen Stadt* [1953], p. 117).

moieties that were not totemic.[3] But there came definite times—though very different times in different parts of the world—when there was, apparently, a growing tendency for persons of unusual courage and energy to arise out of each habit-bound general population, and go venturing beyond the familiar foraging grounds, perhaps ostensibly in search of food, but really from a deeper impulse in search of excitement, discovery, adventure—in short, of greater potentiality for action than their known world offered. Such people are "born leaders"; and where a leader appeared, it was easy enough to find followers in a society that was still prone to act in concert if anyone suggested and led the move. Perhaps just a modicum of the restlessness that possessed the leader stirred in the average man, too; in any event, there arose a wish and readiness among men to go afield on expeditions.

That common readiness and the rise of forceful personalities prepared the first break in the tribal pattern of human society, though it must have gone quite unnoticed by the people who enacted it. There had surely been leaders in village affairs before—men who spontaneously organized and led the occasional or perhaps frequent migrations of the hordes when hunger, land desiccation, enemies, fire or flood, or even regular seasonal changes of conditions that closed one wild habitat and opened another drove them from their homes.[4] Migration in itself need not break up the

---

[3]This subject, to my mind, has never been adequately handled, and its treatment would require a monograph rather than a note. The divisions of local populations into moieties seems to be largely of prehistoric origins. It is found in Asia, in South and Central America, Australia, and Africa. J. Bram, commenting on its existence in the Andes (*An Analysis of Inca Militarism* [1966]), says: "R. Latcham, who studied a mass of material containing references to the dual divisions in the Andean area, admits that he has not been able to discover that the moieties were at any time exogamic; he states that, in general, "the original functions of the divisions had been forgotten at the time of the Conquest" (p. 26). The most thorough study I have seen is Hans Scharer's *Ngaju Religion* (1963), dealing with a South Borneo people whose whole cosmos is divided into "Hornbill" and "Watersnake"; but Scharer, being a missionary, may be reading somewhat too advanced ideas into his findings.

Clyde Kluckhohn, in his article "Navaho Categories," notes the tendency of mythical figures toward what anthropologists have often called "pairing," and remarks: "The most pronounced tendency is pairing by sex: Rock Crystal Boy, Rock Crystal Girl; Whiteshell Boy, Whiteshell Girl; Dawn Boy, Dawn Girl," etc. (p. 80).

[4]See e.g., Godfrey Lienhardt's account, in "The Western Dinka" (1958), pp. 97 ff., of the seasonal migrations of the many Dinka tribes who have to move between land which is arable in the wet season and such as supports pasturage in the dry months. Such dependence on the seasons holds in the frozen zones as in the tropics, and the adjustment to it makes no difference in the tribal order of society; compare Asen Balikci's statement in his "Shamanistic Behavior among the Netsilik Eskimos" (1967), p. 192: "Around Pelly Bay lived 54 people at the time [of Rasmussen's visit in 1923]. This group, the Arviligjuar-

familial pattern of primitive society; the villagers simply move their households, taking babies, dogs, and even their home fires with them.[5] That does not disturb the social order. The elders of the clan are in authority, and allegiances and duties suffer no change by such migrations; nor do they when people who live by hunting and gathering wild foods abandon exhausted sites and move to new or recovered ones. In case of hostile attack by man or beast or monster, every man is a warrior without need of direction to defend his own, and an avenger of every fallen brother-in-arms or noncombatant victim; but when the fray is over he still holds his family status, even if he has distinguished or disgraced himself so as to lift or lower his unofficial personal dignity.

Expeditions, however, are a different matter; for instead of being decided and directed by the elders of a community, they are conceived and led by young pioneers. Once the raiding party or week-long elephant hunt is away from the village it is away from councils and priests, and makes its own arrangements around a charismatic leader whose directives are voluntarily followed. Sometimes his authority becomes vested in his leadership, and chieftaincy is born in his society without regard to age. That new function may be temporary, tied to the occasion,[6] or reach beyond it as a permanent status.

---

muit, in traditional times moved annually along a two phase migration circuit revealing a winter marine and summer land adaptation. In winter a large sealing camp was set on the flat ice in the middle of the bay, the men collectively hunting seals at the breathing holes. In spring, sealing was conducted from the shore camp with the help of women and children."

[5]Alan Moorehead, in *The Fatal Impact: An Account of the Invasion of the South Pacific 1769–1849* (1966), says of the South Sea Islanders and the native Australians (p. 126): "On their journeys, and they were forever on the move, they carried a fire-stick, a dead branch with a burning end that was waved about to keep it alight, and on making camp their first thought was to start a cooking fire."

Victor W. Turner, in *The Drums of Affliction*, p. 10, speaking of a South African tribe, said: "Among the Ndembu individuals and families have high rates of mobility. Men, of their own choice, and women, through marriage, divorce, widowhood, and remarriage . . . are constantly moving from one village to another. . . . The villages, too, move about and not infrequently tend to split in the course of time into several fragments. Individuals continually circulate through these moving villages."

[6]The extreme of individual pride and independence is presented in Walter B. Miller's "Two Concepts of Authority" (1955), wherein the author contrasts the European's respect for vested or delegated authority as impersonal and binding with the American Indian's intolerance of any tone of command no matter who employs it. In the Fox tribe, which he selected as important and representative, authority was vested in the war chief only for the duration of a fight, and was expressed in the form of suggestion, never in the imperative mood. There was a "village chief" whose role incumbency was constant; but his authority went no further than "to act as arbiter and peacemaker in the event of dissension in council meetings" (p. 283). As for the leader of a ceremony, "like the war chief, his

The Breaking

The latter tendency became paramount when men began to move on the waters. Many historians and prehistorians have recognized the crucial impact of seafaring on tribal society, notably Gustave Glotz, as early, as 1904. Glotz made a fair reconstruction of the archaic conditions which sent active young men out on the sea, when the restraints of low birth, being late in a sequence of many brothers, lack of land and means, or sometimes even exile because of a blood feud deprived them of a normal chance and sphere of action. "Those who despaired of bettering their lot by becoming land owners soon got up the courage to brave the open spaces. Sea-faring, the readiest way for individuals to acquire riches, could not exist without affecting the personal relations within the descent groups (γένη).

"This was still in the time when land and cattle were collectively owned by families. . . . Commerce was possible only with people from far away. . . . For a long time trade was no more than a pretext for brigandry and piracy. . . .

"Thus piracy, in that remotest age, together with war, made the fiercest attack on the immutability of family holdings. It enriched some and impoverished others. But it did more than change the material situation of the γένη; it changed their very composition. Those bands of merchant-pirates were formed outside and at the expense of the regularly constituted families. . . . Those ships borne on the foaming seas were little floating republics, and also colonies which moved at the pleasure of the winds or with the chances of staging attacks; at the same time they were despoiling the established societies of their men and throwing their structure into disorder. There are some bonds which, once broken, can never be restored. When the leader of a band has made a fine fortune, though he be a bastard or even worse, that outcast becomes a 'respectable' personage (αἰδοῖος), and the place he holds in society is not at all that which his standing in his γένος would assign to him."[7]

In time, these marauders set up permanent colonies on land, around harbors where they were wont to cast anchor. This soon changed their attitude toward piracy.[8] They tried, naturally enough, to organize their

---

authority functions were limited to the duration of the ritual itself and did not extend beyond the area of ceremonial activity" (p. 284).

[7]*La solidarité de la famille dans le droit criminel de la Grèce* (1904), pp. 7–9.

[8]*Ibid.*, p. 9: "La colonisation fit à peu près disparaître la piraterie en la remplaçant. Elle eut les mêmes causes et les mêmes effets. 'L'étroitesse du sol, ' . . . l'inégalité matérielle dont souffraient les fils illégitimes et l'inégalité morale dont souffraient les puinés, la révolte contre des chefs sots, méchants, infirmes, despotiques, ou simplement l'impatience de toute autorité imposée."

communities on the model of the villages they had left, but that organization could not be achieved under the new conditions. Their new settlements were cut out of whole cloth, so to speak, not grown from any
family cores; they were founded as cities, not villages. The seafarers had
picked up companions from many places who had the same motives as
the original members for leaving their homes, so the colonists had no
common ancestors or clan allegiances. In such a society there was no
γένος with its natural council of elders.[9] The obvious design for their
social structure was that which had developed at sea, where it was the
only possible one—the captain with his crew: one commander, and his
men bound to absolute obedience. This, in turn, led naturally to the rise
of royalty and the founding of kingdoms, each centering in a city and
extending as far as the terrain was controllable and defensible.[10] Here the
new pattern of life was at least temporarily free to develop.

We know little about that early phase of human settlements around the
Mediterranean because it reaches so far back in history that the beginnings of Greek, Italian, and more westerly cultures, as they must have
been under savage conditions before invasion or infiltration by peoples
from the east, are hard to establish on any better grounds than anthropologically plausible surmise. But in another part of the world, where
natural conditions were harsher, the age of seafaring, exploration, and
venture beyond the confines of clan-engendered villages fell into a time
when civilization was already long established in the Roman Empire, so
we have documentary evidence of their progress. The Viking age in
northern Europe illustrates, step by step (with occasional backward and
sideways as well as forward ones), the course of the change from tribal
society to civilization; and there we can see most plainly the forceful
influence of maritime organization on the companies that landed on
foreign shores and built their settlements according to their own simple
societal framework. Bertha Phillpotts's well-authenticated account of this
early adaptation of shipboard relationships to the new city on land shows

---

[9]Ibid., pp. 9–10: "Comment parler, dans ces cités créées de toutes pièces, de γέυn
autochthones et autonomes? Comment imaginer, dans ces pays neufs, des domaines
constitués par un ancêtre légendaire? . . . Leurs compagnons, hommes de toutes prove-
nance[s], s'étaient laissé entrainer par le désir d'une terre à eux: qui leur eût opposé les
règles d'un système fondé sur l'exclusion des étrangers et le privilège de l'aristocratie
terrienne?"

[10]In a footnote Glotz quotes Fustel de Coulanges: "La royauté s'est établi tout
naturellement. . . . Elle ne fut pas imaginée par l'ambition de quelques-uns; elle naguit
d'une nécessité qui était manifeste aux yeux de tous. Pendant de longs siècles elle fut
paisible, honorée, obéie. Les rois n'avais pas besoin de la force matérielle . . . , leur
autorité était sainte et inviolable" (ibid., p. 11).

the natural development of monarchy from the position of the captain among his men, as she says: "We must note how very few traces of a hereditary class of nobles there are in the earlier period of the Viking Age, and indeed in the literary traditions from the Age of National Migrations. Kings there are in bewildering plenty, and it is they who lead migrations and Viking expeditions of every kind. Such nobles as there are seem to be officials of the king. Round him are gathered an aristocracy of fighting men, often, it would seem, foreigners, to the wealth of whose equipment archeological finds testify."[11]

The great break with the kinship pattern of society which came with the increasing desire of men to rove, discover, win, and possess[12] was made in principle and practice by the change from the ancient authority of elders to leadership by young and adventurous men. Leadership, of course, is required for every great and permanent migration; but how much faster clan rule and clan solidarity, such as the joint responsibility of a man's kin for the wergild exacted as indemnity for a slaying, were abandoned in consequence of seaborne expeditions than of overland treks is illustrated by a later passage in Phillpotts's *Kindred and Clan* contrasting the effects of the two modes of travel: "The laws of the Swedish kingdom in Russia, won by naval expeditions, show but a feeble conception of kinship: the slayer alone pays for his deed, and the right of vengeance is limited to brother, father, son and nephew. On the other hand, West Gothic custumals in Spain show division of wergild between kinsmen, definitely organized blood-feuds between kindreds, and oathhelpers of the kindred. . . . The West Goths travelled a long way, but they travelled by land" (p. 264).

This was an active time of city-building in Scandinavian history,[13] first

---

[11]*Kindred and Clan in the Middle Ages and After: A Study of the Teutonic Races*, p. 253.

[12]Edith Ennen, in *Frühgeschichte der europäischen Stadt*, though elsewhere she stresses the tendency of Germanic peoples to cling to the kindred pattern and apparently finds it a virtue, nevertheless speaks with enthusiasm of the individualistic captains royal, the Vikings who were driven much less by necessity than by ambition to roam the seas: "Kriegerische und handlerische Unternehmungen sind die wesentlichsten und gebräuchlichsten Mittel, gewissen Schichten eine höhere Lebenshaltung zu ermöglichen. Darum nämlich geht as. . . . Weniger Landnot, als das Streben nach einem Herrenleben, nach Ruhm, Entdeckungen, Abenteuern, nach Beute, Handelsgewinn, Tributen, nach besserem Land, als man besass, trieb die Wikinger in die Weite" (p. 51).

[13]Cf. Gwyn Jones, *A History of the Vikings* (1968), p. 166: "The Viking Age was a period remarkable for the rise, development and sometimes decline, of towns and market-places. The Norseman abroad, whether as invader, settler, or merchant, needed havens and bases. Sometimes he took into his use towns already in existence, sometimes he established them for his convenience, from Limerick on the Shannon to Kiev on the Dnieper."

on all the northern coasts the Vikings touched,[14] then up the Russian rivers and the incredible land journeys over the divides between watersheds, from the streams which debouched into the Baltic to the headwaters of the Dnieper, the Don, and the Volga, to build new riverboats that reached and plied the southern inland seas even to Byzantium. The thousands of miles the adventurers traversed, especially in the northern parts, felt the impact of their city organization, sometimes on tribal villages, which it swallowed, sometimes in sheer wilderness—cities built by acknowledged leaders with followers, not seats of elders and children's children. Small settlements indeed, but founded and ruled on a civic pattern. Kiev and Novgorod were Viking trade centers. Those and a far-flung chain of other permanent establishments closed the ring of urban stations around the theater of European culture, destined to become the hub of the modern world.

But in Byzantium the Nordic warriors and traders found a new and fabulous sort of city, ancient in comparison to their oldest wicks and emporia, and of dazzling splendor: an imperial city on its steep hills above the Golden Horn such as they had never seen. They had had sight or at least report of Rome and the Roman provincial cities of the Riviera and the Rhone Valley, which were rapidly achieving their commercial independence from the weakening mother capital in Italy.[15] Byzantium, for all its westward trade through Venice and the Sicilian kingdom, belonged to another culture. It represented the closing phase of the oldest civilization we know from archeological researches, that which began in

[14]*Ibid.*, p. 267: "By the end of the Viking Age Norway had seen the birth of Trondheim, Nidaros, Bergen, and Oslo; Sweden knew Skara, Lund, and Sigtuna; Denmark had well-established centres of population at Ribe, Viborg, Arhus and Alborg, Odense and Roskilde, some of them centres of mercantile and religious life, some royal creations."

[15]Her weakening was a natural economic result of the spread of Roman civilization with its political dominance, as Rostovtzeff pointed out in a passage from *Rome* (1960) anthologized by T. S. Baker in *The Urbanization of Man* (1972): "Districts which had formerly depended upon imports from the large manufacturing centers now began to take a share in production. Hence, the large centers lost their economic positions and grew impoverished.

"The provinces had started production to satisfy their own needs, and mass-production at low prices. Thus, the finer and dearer article was driven out of the markets; and the factories and workshops of the purely industrial countries, which found a ready sale in earlier times, now stood idle.

"As the provinces became more self-sufficient their need of importation decreased, and the market of every town and village was stocked with local products" (pp. 194–96).

We have a similar problem today, when the colonial lands "opened" by the European powers to create sources of raw materials and markets for their goods have become "developing nations" which will soon use their materials to manufacture their own atomic lethal devices and supply their own markets with consumer products.

The Breaking

Mesopotamia some time before the dynastic period of Egypt. Those Near Eastern cities had a different history from the urban centers of medieval Europe, which were walled towns, sometimes of Roman colonial origin but dominated, after the loss of that linkage, by feudal lords, ecclesiastic or lay, and animated by trade and industry. The ancient cities of Mesopotamia were not originally designed as trade centers, but were founded with a grander motivation, as seats of power raised by royal conquerors for their own glorification. These proud cities each centered in a high temenos, the paved area around a monumental power symbol, the ziggurat, a towering step-pyramid; the temenos was flanked by one or more temples, some service buildings, and the key structure of the realm, the king's palace, adapted above all to pomp and ceremony. Paul Lampl, in *Cities and Planning in the Ancient Near East*, said: "The glory, power and wealth of the Achaeminid great Kings found tangible expression in ceremonial palaces. It was to their construction and decoration that the kings directed their main architectural and artistic ambitions" (p. 18). In earlier passages he cited examples of such cities founded by kings: "Metropolitan Nineveh, covering an area of 728.7 hectares with a probable population of over 170,000, was the creation of Sennacherib (704–681 B.C.)"; and of Babylon he says, "Time and again it was ruthlessly destroyed by invaders, most thoroughly by Sennacherib; it was often rebuilt and its temples restored because of its importance as a religious center. The city as excavated is mainly the creation of Nebuchadnessar II (604–561 B.C.)" (p. 17).

The wealth of their kings was derived originally from conquest and tribute more than from trade, for war and plunder were the basis of their ascendancy. Each city was served by its surrounding villages and so constituted a city-state; and its resources came from conquered princes and the slave labor of their captured rural populations. How did these kings rise to their royal estate? The cities they founded were chiefly in the great river valleys of the Nile, the Euphrates and the Tigris, yet none of them were built by seafarers. The time of their origin antedates by many centuries the age of ships and maritime adventure,[16] such as seems to have made kings and henchmen out of the Norse captains and crews. Yet somehow the old tribal pattern had broken long ago in the Near East and given rise to an organization of rulers and subjects, which became pro-

---

[16]No one knows how many centuries. The oldest ruins of Jericho go back to the eighth millennium B.C. (Lampl, *Cities and Planning in the Ancient Near East*, p. 34). M. I. Rostovtzeff, in *Caravan Cities* (1932), p. 13, said: "In these early days the land routes were much more used than the sea. The sea was as yet neither favored nor trusted and was used only when absolutely necessary."

gressively intensified in Mesopotamia to a much higher degree of despotism and thralldom than western Europe ever knew.

In Asia, perhaps, some of the tribes in the south-western part of that great continent fell under a natural influence not unlike that of the sea. If there were primitive men living in coastal and riverine jungles (like the Andaman Islanders of today) in southern India and spreading west and northwestward throughout long ages by population increase, they would gradually encounter a terrain which has some of the vastness and emptiness of the open sea—the desert. The first settlers in Mesopotamia had found a paradise for their tribal villages, but to north and south and endlessly westward and behind every mountain range eastward lay that great emptiness. Like the ocean, it could be braved only by organized expeditions, which gave rise to kingly leadership much as the life of mariners did. Perhaps it was the deeply, unconsciously accepted influence of the yellow sand as much as the potentialities of the green river valleys that made Mesopotamia and Egypt, the two horns of the "fertile crescent," the first keepers of civilization.

In Egypt, the self-exaltation of a single line of individuals, the Pharaohs, reached an apotheosis quite beyond the superficial emperor-worship which later was demanded by the Roman Caesars. It seems to have arisen gradually from the tribal stage rather than to have been imposed by a superior power. The peculiar nature of that country caused human life not only to be fixed in a definite zone by the conformation of the Nile Valley, the waterless wastes hedging it in and the broad, shifting delta, but also held it to a time schedule and rhythm of activities by the annual flood. This inescapable round seems to have molded the native population in a highly uniform pattern and slowed the phylogenetic process of individuation, so that most people had not felt the drive to self-assertion against their ancient tribal stock when the first dynasty was founded, or it could never have reached such divine proportions; the Pharaoh must still have been a welcome symbol of human power and of the continuity of Egyptian life. Civilization arose in Egypt under unique circumstances and consequently in a unique way; the terrain and its possibilities were so familiar that a high material technology developed without any great intellectual advance until the precocious, and therefore unstable, philosophic "breakthrough" of the philosopher-king Akhenaton. It has often been remarked that the Egyptians have given the world much knowledge of physics and practical mathematics, means of computation, insight into principles of balance, leverage, and mechanical advantage, and systematic astronomy (with the usual supercargo of astrology thrown in), but no comparable theoretical treatises on moral or eschatological subjects, no great poetry or skeptical criticism or interpretation of natural events beyond the naive assumptions of the world-wide magical medicine which sometimes hits upon a genuine medical practice.

Yet their culture, all concentrated in the Pharaoh symbol, carried on their mental individuation also primarily in the exalted royal personage, through one dynasty after another, far above the common people or even the priesthood, to the point of overcoming tribal government by force of the new stratification of society into slaves, common people, conscripted soldiers, officials, priests, and the Pharaoh with his queen and their retinues. The very family stocks of the rulers seem to have tended away from the typical Egyptian mentality and occupied a sacred interspace between men and gods, where the monarch was in direct contact with the latter, still including the peculiarly primitive, lion-headed, ibis-headed, or jackal-headed deities. In actuality as well as *ex officio*, i.e., symbolically, the Pharaohs appeared like a race apart. The Egyptians either went through a different process of individuation from that of other people or else, perhaps, the uniformity of their lives imposed by their environment held that process back and elaborated an early stage which never developed as fully anywhere else, the "god-man" that personally lived what he was set up to express, the awesome representative Individual. A sign of this significance of the Pharaoh for his people is the special law for his family permitting brother-and-sister marriage, which in almost all tribes and nations is under one of the most elementary taboos; the motivation of the moral protest usually evoked by sibling incest is the fear of the concentration of family power, family interest, and increased talents, especially magical, which would be abetted in such an inbred single line to the degree of making an organism within the social organism a state within the state. In the case of a pharaonic dynasty this danger did not threaten; the more pure and authentic the origin of that divine Being, the more potent was his presence.

These supersocietal families of Egypt did, in truth, produce some of the greatest individuals in its history: Akhenaton, Hatchepsut, Ptolemy I, Ptolemy II (Philadelphus), Cleopatra. The old explanation of the incest taboo, that inbreeding soon leads to degeneration, is certainly not borne out by observation where the human stock is superior. But the great forced creation seems to have been at the expense of the general public's progress in a changing world;[17] when the autocratic-theocratic rule of the

---

[17]Boris de Rachewiltz, in *An Introduction to Egyptian Art* (1966), wrote: "To have one's own image in the form of colossal statues, a veritable elephantiasis of stone, denotes a megalomaniac affirmation of the king's individuality at the time when the spiritual background was in decline. By their physical size alone these statues reduced the citizens

Pharaohs weakened, Egypt faltered and failed, and waves of politically advanced powers—Persian, Hellenic, Roman—extinguished her greatness. The semi-individuated phase of her people in her unique enclave between the deserts, under a symbolic absolute king, had lasted too long.

Yet, of course, the Egyptians, in their three thousand years of continuous though shifting prosperity, and despite occasional major crises, had reached the stage of city-building. Their cities, however, were of neither the eastern nor the European kind. Two kinds of urban settlement were, indeed, unique Egyptian foundations: the pure temple city, of which Karnak was a grandiose example,[18] and the "pyramid cities" that arose with the building of those huge monuments. They were sacred cities of the dead, erected round the sites of pyramids in process of their building, and afterwards maintained to house the thousands of people engaged in their upkeep, safeguarding, and the constant religious services of homage to the gods and to the deified Pharaohs whose death chambers were hidden, each in the most inaccessible center of his tremendous phallic power symbol, the pyramid.[19]

Between the spectacular cultures which had sprung up separately at the two ends of the "fertile crescent" lay the deserts of the Levant and northern Arabia, traversed by treasure-laden caravans; and, naturally, cities grew up at the oases which punctuated the long journey and made the Bedouin commerce possible.[20] But the older ones had not originated as caravanseries; they had long been human settlements, agricultural villages of the owners of the oases, who irrigated and cultivated the rich

---

to subjection to an extent which could no longer be imposed by the respect inherent in the idea of 'sacred' kingship" (p. 168).

[18]Ibid., p. 170: "the 'temple city' par excellence in Egypt is undoubtedly Karnak, in the neighborhood of Thebes. . . . The temple zone was transformed into a veritable mosaic of buildings, grafted one upon the other, and as a result of the continual alterations the ponderous stone architecture became strangely fluid." And, quoting the maxim of King Khety, "Erect monuments to the gods, that the name of the builder may live again," he comments: "Karnak is in reality a royal self-glorification, despite the fact that it is dedicated to Amun" (p. 171).

[19]Cf. Lampl, Cities and Planning in the Ancient Near East, p. 25: "One type of 'city' is a purely ancient Egyptian phenomenon: the so-called pyramid cities, prevalent during the Old and Middle Kingdom, were created by royal charter to house the workmen and masons constructing the pyramids and—after their completion—the priests performing the royal funerary services, as well as tenant farmers and laborers who worked the land set aside for the purpose of producing revenue for the continued maintenance of the monument and its ritual duties. The citizens of these towns were exempted by royal decree from any other compulsory labor."

[20]Among the cities flourishing through caravan commerce Lampl mentions Aleppo, Tell Atchana, Hamath, Qatna, and Damascus, and on the coast Tyre, Sidon, and Byblos (ibid., p. 33).

supporting soil where the water brought it to life. Certainly a community like Petra, with close-ranged dwellings and numberless tombs hewn out of the steep, solid walls of narrow canyons, did not start as a cross-road station or a transient restingplace (Fig. 23–2), although it emerged as such when it expanded beyond the opening of the gorges into the lake-fed

Figure 23–2. Entrance to Petra

certainly . . . Petra, with close-ranged dwellings and numberless tombs hewn out of the steep, solid walls of narrow canyons, did not start as a cross-road station

(© J. Allan Cash; courtesy of Raphol Photo Researchers.)

[167]

plain below.[21] Dura, on the Euphrates, was originally (and always primarily) a fortress, though it became an important starting point of expeditions.[22] As for Palmyra, which Rostovtzeff called "the most typical caravan city of antiquity" (p. 126), it began, according to his own testimony, as a somewhat unpromising site for a great city. "This village," he said, "which the Bible calls Tadmor, but which was later named Palmyra, served as a centre for the tribe which owned the oasis. Yet a tribal centre, [sulphur] springs, and an oasis do not alone transform a village into a caravan city; for this purpose facilities for the exchange of goods and comfortable rest-houses are necessary. Tadmor was not a caravan city and it lacked the requirements essential to such."[23] But history takes some odd and unexpected turns; the long international tensions between Parthia and Rome, and the Persian conquest of Egypt, sent the main caravan routes from Dura through Palmyra and made her one of the world's greatest caravanseries.

That the Near East had an ancient high culture is well known, but it is hard to realize what a full-fledged civilization—literate, urban, economic—had risen on that indigenous culture some five thousand years ago. Rostovtzeff has given a description of it based mainly on a modern archeological find of clay tablets, of which he says: "The Cappadocian documents have brought to light numerous facts of interest regarding the organization and development of caravan trade. . . . most of the documents formed the archives of important trading and banking houses. These firms equipped and financed the large caravans, generally composed of donkeys, which travelled south and south-west. The tablets tell us of the complicated business enterprises of the period and of the fully developed legal and civil procedure of the time" (p. 10). Still more astounding is the further statement: "One of the greatest achievements of the Sumero-Babylonian culture in the realm of trade took place at this time, . . . the later part of the third millennium B.C. This was the introduction of a metal unit of exchange which was partly created by, and partly responsible for, an amazing development in the standard of indi-

[21]See Rostovtzeff, *Caravan Cities*, chap. 2, *passim*.
[22]"Originally Dura was probably little more than a Seleucid, and later a Parthian, frontier fort, a fact which must account for her military features, her great walls, and her citadel. With Palmyra's foundation Dura grew from a mere fort into the point of departure of the main caravan route from the Euphrates to Palmyra. . . . The garrison of Dura was responsible for the safety of the roads leading to the west, south, and east across the Euphrates. . . .
"As a result of this Dura's wealth increased. . . . A study of the ruins shows that in the first century A.D. Dura must have been a large and rich town" (*ibid.*, p. 105).
[23]*Ibid.*, p. 93.

The Breaking

vidual life and an ever-growing complexity in the life of civilized humanity. This metal unit was the direct predecessor of coined currency, which made its first appearance two thousand years later, in the seventh century B.C., in Asia Minor and in Greece. The early unit was based upon the silver 'mina,' with its subdivision into 'shekels.' This innovation was partly the work of private merchants (the earliest banker-tradesmen in history), partly that of the state" (p. 11).

The wealth and splendor of Palmyra around the beginning of our era must have been dazzling; at its height it outshone all other caravan cities of the Near East. Here was a different sort of trade from anything that went on in the fairs and emporia of Roman and medieval Europe north of the Alps. The shores of Anatolia and the Levant were the western limits of a vast Asiatic commerce that penetrated not only the subcontinent of India but even China, the Spice Islands (Indonesia), and Ceylon.[24] Unmistakably Far Eastern fabrics, jewelry, gold and glass vessels, and especially spices and incense were carried across the steppes and deserts of Asia to Phoenicia and from there to her north African colonies, to Byzantium, Athens, and Venice, to be thinly disseminated through European markets, as long as no one asked what sinful Christians had dealt with the infidel to acquire them.[25]

With such conditions of trade and genuine high finance, such mobility and competition, the rise of civilization was spectacular, especially in the cities; besides material wealth, knowledge and invention and tales of wonder traveled with the caravans from one royal capital to another. So did great complexes of thought, mythological ideas, and a cumulative medley of rites—in other words, religions—that gathered like storms and clashed. Then city after marvelous city collapsed in flames. But not only militant Moslems and Christians destroyed the products of civilization; war was an endemic scourge throughout the civilized world. Kings and adventurers did their share of destroying what their predecessors—often recent ones—had created.

[24]*Ibid.*, p. 19: "Literary references tell of constant commercial intercourse between Persia and the Farther East, India and China. . . .

"Even more extensive was Persia's trade with the west, her intercourse with the city-states of the Greek mainland, with the Black Sea coast, with Italy and Sicily, and the Phoenician colonies in northern Africa, and through these channels with the tribes of south-western and northern Europe. It was chiefly the products of caravan trade that were exported to these countries, notably the various kinds of incense essential for religious observances."

[25]Henri Pirenne, in *Mediaeval Cities* (1925), p. 87, made Venice the culprit in this unholy transaction, saying: "No scruple had any weight with the Venetians. Their religion was a religion of businessmen. It mattered little to them that the Moslems were the enemies of Christ, if business with them was profitable."

Such wanton destructiveness was much more common in Asia than in Europe, and historians have raised the question of a reason for the difference. So Ahmed Ali, in his valuable dissertation, *Historical Aspects of Town Planning in Pakistan and India* (1971), quotes H. V. Lancaster's observation: "'To begin with, while many Indian cities vie in antiquity with those of Europe, it may be noted that the existing city in Europe is on the average more stable than that in India. Though some have declined, there are but few deserted cities such as are not infrequent in the east. Despite wars and catastrophies almost all the places that show prominently in the history of the last 2000 years are going 'concerns' of today. While what is the case when we review Indian history for 2000 years? Some of the glorious cities of the past exist but in name, others are inhabited by goats and bats. There must be a reason for this—even if one fails to find it, it seems worth seeking. Dynasties have risen and fallen in Europe as in India. The cities of Europe have stayed, in India they have gone with the dynasty'" (p. 15).

Dr. Ali's monograph does not solve this puzzle, but rather supplies the facts suggestive of its possible solution. The source of the difference is, I think, the earlier difference in the motivations whereby Western and Eastern cities, respectively, were established. In Europe they were chiefly of Roman origin and administrative function, and as long as they implemented political control of the countryside they could change hands, from emperors to popes, to princes and kings, and more locally from governors to bishops, to feudal lords, to burgomasters and aldermen. Under the Pax Romana the cities of early western Europe did not have to fight each other. Their fortifications were against Vikings and Mediterranean pirates, hordes of Huns, Goths, and other unconquered migrant tribes, not rival Roman provincial towns. Even when the disasters of war swept through them, the breaches in their walls were mended, their temples cleansed of fire damage and ashes, houses gradually rebuilt, and the life of the town continued; for the constant aim of Rome was to rule orderly people and to be the center of a balanced economic system, a single civilized world.

The splendid cities of the East were differently conceived; since they were the individual works and personal possessions of absolute monarchs asserting their supposedly unlimited power, symbols of self-exaltation, to overcome a rival for majesty and honor in the worldly contest meant, above all, to destroy his capital; and such destruction, having as much symbolic as political purpose, went beyond the needs of military victory. The city had to be totally annihilated, because that represented its founder's annihilation, the demolition of his name and fame. Paul Lampl observed how all through the Near East and beyond, through India, "the tragic role of the city in a continuous cycle of life and death, of construction and destruction, is a main theme in its portrayal. The city as a symbol of royal pride, as well as the actual seat of wealth and power, stands in the center of an unending struggle for and against political domination. In the annals of every land of the ancient Near East, kings and heads of state boast as much about the creation of their own cities as about the annihilation of conquered cities."[26] And in support of this statement he quotes the words in which Sargon II (722–705 B.C.) recorded his own achievements: "'With mighty battering rams I smashed the fortified walls and levelled them to the ground. The peoples and possessions I carried off; their cities I destroyed, I devastated, I burned with fire. . . . And at that time I built a city with the labor of the peoples of the lands which my hands had conquered, . . . according to the command of God and the prompting of my heart, and I called it 'Dur-Sharrukin.'"[27]

Not only in the Near East but throughout the Caucasus, Baktria, the great land of Persia, and all across India cities rose and fell in this same way. Here or there in India, where war was especially likely to sweep over them, they might be fortified or otherwise protected, but for the most part they relied on the power of their princes, who dictated their laws and safeguarded their lives. That power was exhibited and asserted in the splendor of their palaces, which defiantly challenged destruction and usually received it; their temples, whether built and covered with sculpture or carved out of solid rock like the cave temples of Elephanta, Ajunta, Elora, or Mahabilipurum, made no claim to any worldly power of the gods whose existence they celebrated, and have largely survived the long history of fire and sword. But if cities have ever risen around them, they have perished like the priests and cults that used them.

Finally, in China, the archeologist excavating ancient sites that speak of long occupation meets with a peculiar frustration: there seem to be no foundations, no urban ruins where a civilized traditional culture would lead him to expect them. So one researcher of ancient and medieval China declared, only twenty-odd years ago, "The origin of the Chinese city is still unknown. We know for certain that the last capital of the Shang dynasty, near An-yang, was a city. We can, with a certain amount of safety, assume that their earlier capitals were cities, too. We have,

[26]*Cities and Planning in the Ancient Near East*, p. 9.
[27]*Ibid.*, p. 10, quoted by Lampl from D. D. Luckenbill's transcript in "Ancient Records II, 6."

however, no textual testimony or archeological data to determine the character of earlier settlements.

"Only one fact seems to be clear: the 'local cultures,' which became the 'Chinese high culture,' did not have cities at all. Thus, we may say that the emergence of the Chinese city marked the birth of Chinese high culture."[28]

Even an archaic sort of dynastic rule could hardly have arisen without a seat of authority, the equivalent of a capital from which the ruler issued his decrees; and he would certainly be surrounded by his own descent-group, i.e., the royal clan, as well as by an army, or earlier a horde, of defenders; also there must have been servants (hirelings or slaves) and a food-producing peasantry. Here are all the makings of a city; the exalted position of the king is enough to make a classification of the society he rules into noble and common people; among the former, degrees of nearness to him determine degrees of privilege, while the latter, the commonality, fall into social strata according to the functions assigned to them.

Yet the modern diggers for palace foundations, floors and steps, vaults and pilasters, find no signs of any royal establishment, nor of temples, nor of ancestral halls such as all Chinese families have owned since time immemorial and very probably had at the very beginning of kingly power, statehood and urbanism. So it does appear that "the 'local cultures' . . . did not have cities at all."

From another source, however, we may gain another picture of the Chinese city, which shows it not as an edifice or collection of such, nor even as a place; in his book *Early Chinese Civilization: Anthropological Perspectives* (1976), K. C. Chang has drawn that picture by methods apparently more approved by American scholars than by his own colleagues.[29] His reconstruction of the earliest urban establishments reveals not only a new type but, to most Western people (and today to his own compatriots, too), a new conception of "city," namely, as a group of people organized by fixed relations to each other apart from common descent or marital connections—functional relations, over and above familial ties or age groups, i.e., apart from clan structure; though the latter may persist with regard to marriage regulations, mourning ceremonies, ancestor veneration, and other close-linking substructures of social life. The physical frame of the city seems to have been no more

[28]Wolfram Eberhard, "Data on the Structure of the Chinese City in the Pre-Industrial Period" (1956), p. 256.
[29]In the Preface (p. v) Dr. Chang records the indignation of one of his former teachers, now his colleague and critic, at his trespassing on "research spheres" not his own.

than clay-and-wattle, chiefly one-storey, houses, with roofs of thatch and floors of pounded earth. It certainly is a surprising novelty to read of a capital city: "The Shang had stones and knew how to work them. . . . Nevertheless, they built not only their houses but also their palaces and ancestral halls of nothing more durable than clay, not in the form of adobe or brick but in wattle-and-daub standing on foundations of pounded layer upon layer of pure loess . . . and their roofs were probably covered with nothing more elaborate than thatch. The royal tombs were formed of earthen pits and ramps, in which a wooden chamber was built to contain the coffin. . . . In short, the Shang made no apparent effort to create monumental architecture to impress or to immortalize, in the way Lewis Mumford has described for Babylonia and Greece."[30]

Yet, says Dr. Chang, "In this setting, standing tall and conspicuous are the essential components of the first Chinese civilization, and of civilizations elsewhere: political kingship, a religious system and hierarchy that coupled with it, segmentary lineages, economic exploitation of many by a few, technological specialization, and sophisticated achievements in art, writing, and science" (p. 47).

Such a "capital" made no pretension to grandeur or symbolic display of might, and therefore (like the cave temples of India) did not evoke any strong impulse in enemy kings or armies to tear it down; Dr. Chang, after listing the urban traits of the population in these un-urban-looking settlements, continues: "All of these we see in the earliest cities of China: Yen-shih, Cheng-chou, and An-yang. These are all names of modern cities in Honan province, and we borrow them to designate the old city ruins found in their environs left by the Shang of about 1850–1100 B.C."[31]

The most extraordinary aspect of those ancient royal cities, however, is that they were not anchored in their locations on the earth. They could be moved, at the king's behest, from one place to another. These most radical ventures in urban renewal may account for the absence of monumental architecture; in Chinese terms, "The city was the institution, not the site, and its movements from site to site was [sic] obviously at the king's option. The layout and structuring of the new capital were designed to serve him as the center of attention. . . . In the Shang conception of the world, there were five cardinal directions: north, south, east, west and the 'central Shang,' the last being wherever the king and his court resided. This central city apparently exerted political control over

[30]*Ibid.*, p. 49. Reference is to Mumford's *The City in History* (1961).
[31]*Ibid.*, p. 47. By way of historical orientation, his text continues: "The Shang built one of the so-called Three Dynasties, Hsia, Shang, and Chou, the earliest in Chinese history. . . . Traditionally, the Hsia dynasty is placed between 2205 and 1766 B.C."

the other settlements through an effective mechanism of hierarchical government."[32]

No wonder it is hard to define the word "city," in view of the many forms its designatum may take. Urbanization is essentially a sign, a product, and at the same time an implement of cultural advance to civilized life.

But it is not the only crucial influence effecting the basic phenomenon, the change of social structure which has begotten the modern world. The breaking of the old order had many beginnings, some rising with or upon the rise of the city, some starting from elsewhere to meet it. So, for instance, what in each actual case was the character of the fighting force a city-state could send into the field depended largely on the type and degree of its organization; for with the growing power of kings there was a concomitant shift in military control and strategy as the combatants changed from warriors to soldiers. The formation of armies under a single command was a radical departure from the fighting of independent warriors who met their adversaries man to man by their own decision. The solid ranks of Assyrian heavily armed men, the Greek phalanx, the Roman legion mounted or afoot were soldiers, components of a war machine manipulated by the commanding generals.

This innovation, wherever it occurs, makes a revolution in the social significance of war. Organized warfare is part and parcel of civilized life, though it begins early on the road to that gradual attainment. In savage societies fighting is apt to be brief and relatively harmless to the tribe as a whole; indeed, the further one descends the cultural ladder, the briefer and less important become the armed encounters. Among true savages most fights are bursts of temper in people whose acts normally draw everybody else into any fray. Radcliffe-Brown, writing about the native Andaman Islanders, says: "Such a thing as fighting on a large scale seems to have been unknown amongst the Andamanese. In the early days of the [British] Penal Settlement of Fort Blair, the natives of the South Andaman combined in large numbers to make an attack on the Settlement; but this seems to have been an unusual course of action in order to meet what was to them an altogether unusual contingency, their territory having been invaded by a large force of foreigners. Their only fights amongst themselves seems to have been the brief and far from bloody skirmishes . . . where only a handful of warriors were engaged on each side and rarely more than one or two were killed. Of such a thing as a war in

---

[32]*Ibid.*, p. 51. Cf. p. 75, where Dr. Chang also proposed the noted connection between the movability of the city and its lack of impressive buildings.

which the whole of one tribe joined to fight with another tribe I could not find any evidence in what the natives were able to tell me of their former customs."[33]

The little Negritos of Malaysia, the Andamans, and the Philippines were low, indeed, in cultural attainment or demands; and scarcely higher, if at all, were the true "blackfellows" of Australia, about whom Moorehead reported: "Wars were usually caused because some tribe trespassed upon the hunting grounds of another, but there were long-standing feuds as well, traditional animosities, and perhaps too, they sometimes suffered from ennui and felt an instinctive urge for a sudden commotion."[34] To start the commotion—that is, to open the battle—there was much spontaneous dancing and mutual abuse between the eager opponents; "Then the first spear would be thrown and that would be the signal for a general assault which would continue perhaps for an hour or two. . . . Hatreds seldom continued for very long; it was not unusual, after the first fury had spent itself in a tribal war, for peace to be made and then both sides would make camp and carouse together."[35]

That sort of "war" is certainly a far call from what we understand by the word today; so far, indeed, that there are many intervening steps between the challenges and attacks of the forest hunters or Australian blackfellows and the horrors of our international wars once they cease to be "cold" (i.e., diplomatic), and reach the shooting phase. Even organized conflicts, staged at higher levels of precivilized life, may threaten no serious destruction to either of the parties involved, as, for instance, the custom of raiding neighboring villages for wives or, in more established societies, for cattle. The raid is a typically tribal phenomenon which may, under extenuating circumstances, even be viewed as pardonable, not only by uninvolved people but by those who, in self-defense, have to repulse it. So Jomo Kenyatta, in *Facing Mount Kenya*, said of his own people: "The fights which were carried on from time to time between various tribes, such as the Masai, the Gikuyu and the Wakamba, can hardly be called 'wars,' because all fights were in the nature of armed raids. For example, when cattle disease invaded the Masai country and reduced their livestock below minimum, the Masai, whose lives depended entirely on meat,

[33]*The Andaman Islanders*, pp. 86–87.
[34]*The Fatal Impact*, p. 127. Even in civilized societies the motivation of bellicose expeditions may be essentially like these of the savages, though in moralistic disguise. So C. D. Eckhardt, in the little selection anthologized by Baker in *The Urbanization of Man*, says with embarrassing candor: "European nobles and adventurers went on crusade in hopes of acquiring kingdoms and wealth, or for the mere love of war" ("The Influence of the Church on Medieval Culture," p. 253).
[35]*The Fatal Impact*, p. 127.

milk and blood of the animals, were forced by necessity to raid the stock of their neighbors or die of hunger and starvation. In order to save their livelihood, spies were sent out to investigate . . . in what district in the neighboring tribes the stocks were abundant and least protected.

"After the spies had reported a raid was at once organized. . . . The cattle pens were surrounded and a few of the herdsmen killed to avoid any cry that would give the signal to the warriors of the enemy's tribe. The cattle were . . . led away as quickly as possible in a zigzag way, and at the same time some of the warriors were left behind to cover the trail and also to await the enemy who might follow; so that while they were engaged in fighting, the cattle would reach the starving families in Masailand" (pp. 208–9).

These raids Kenyatta likened to robbery—"smash and grab," he called it—as it is met in "civilized" countries; but there is a great difference in the ways those two similar offenses are received in their respective cultures. The raid among tribesmen may incur retaliation, but not legal judgment and sentence, because there is no vested judiciary above the antagonists. Punishment is at the will of the injured party, namely, vengeance. Raiding, in tribal society, belongs with war, not crime; and war is deemed an honorable action.[36]

But with the rise of powerful commanders and their men, raids became more serious acts of war; not cattle pens but cities and towns were besieged and plundered. The advance of ship-building raised a particular problem for island and coastal settlements, the problem of piracy. In the Mediterranean there have repeatedly been long historic periods when the beautiful Aegean islands—the Cyclades, the Dodecanese—were rendered uninhabitable by the depredations of such seaborne marauders. The pirate ships appeared suddenly, made land in a precalculated favor-

---

[36]A contrast in dignity of the two actions is exemplified in an anecdote cited by H. R. E. Davidson in *The Viking Road to Byzantium* (1976), p. 28. Egil, the hero of "Egil's Saga," and his men (a dozen of his crew) were captured by a Kurland farmer whose farm they raided, and were tied up in an outbuilding. They escaped, and in doing so found and freed three previous captives. One of these led them through a storeroom where the farmer kept his wealth. Egil made off with a cask full of silver. "On the way back, Egil insisted on returning to the farm, saying that it was cowardly to rob the farmer without letting him know. He did so alone, found the Kurlanders feasting in the hall and serving lads carrying in trenchers from the cookhouse, where cauldrons hung over a great log fire. Egil seized a log . . . and thrust the burning end into the thatch. The men inside knew nothing until the roof was alight, and when they ran to the door Egil was waiting there to cut them down as they emerged. Finally the roof fell in, and Egil set off to rejoin the ship."

The story may be pure fiction, but even as such it bespeaks the Vikings' indignation at the mean act of stealing and their admiration of the daring raid.

able spot and moment, and could get away to unknowable distant spaces with the loot of a day or an hour.[37]

In the northern European seas a simpler vessel, for hardier men, opened the same opportunities, which always found heroes to take them. Though the Vikings were explorers and city-builders, they were above all fighters, plunderers, daredevils; there was always a large element to whom the pirate's life was the ideal life.[38] These people, too, made raiding their regular practice, not a rare act of desperation but their means of existence, and as such, of course, it could not endure indefinitely amid the cultural developments of Europe, which were on a rapid rise. As kingdoms rather than scattered city-states became established on the Continent, the robber-barons who sallied out of the castles which crowned the many hilltops, especially in central Europe, to waylay companies of merchants traveling on the roads below were gradually brought to justice (which meant, in their day, to the gallows) or discouraged to the point of disappearance by the presence of the trained soldiery of the realm. Their counterparts on the sea, the pirates, were harder to punish and tame; yet their activities seem to have been the first stimulus that carried military protection beyond the relatively pacified lands by prompting King Alfred to build his large fleet of fighting ships, the beginning of the famous later English seapower.[39]

[37]Colin Renfrew, in his beautiful book *The Emergence of Civilization* (1972) (subtitled *The Cyclades and the Aegean in the Third Millennium B.C.*), writes: "It is piracy . . . rather than warring between towns and cities, which can best explain the differences in the prehistoric Aegean growth patterns. The evidence of the fortifications indicates that this had already become a problem in the early bronze age, following the great expansion of settlement and population at that time. . . . The evidence from the Middle Ages, when an analogous situation held in the Aegean, makes this very clear. . . .

"During the Middle Ages, piracy was practiced not only upon passing merchant vessels, but upon any island settlements inadequately defended, nor was it merely the occupation of ruffians of no account, but of lords and barons. . . . [F. W.] Hasluck ["Depopulation in the Aegean Islands" (1910–11)] has documented the terrible mediaeval depopulation when slave raiders and pirates brought about the complete abandonment of several islands" (p. 263).

[38]See R. M. Dawkins, "Greeks and Northmen" (1936), p. 45: "The Northmen we see as men brave and loyal, but quarrelsome and acquisitive; men to whom warlike enterprise, preferably in small undertakings where their individuality was in no danger of being sunk, was the best thing that life had to offer." This judgment is corroborated by Gwyn Jones in *A History of the Vikings* (1968), pp. 166–67, where he says: "Over long periods the south-west coast of Norway, the Øresund passage, and the Baltic were infested with pirates. . . . Scores of references in the Icelandic sagas, and almost as many in Snorri's *Heimskringla*, relate to pirate haunts, ships' crews out viking in Skagerrak, Kattegat, and Baltic, raids on coastal and sometimes inland towns, and the taking of merchant ships.

[39]See A. W. Brøgger and Haakon Shetelig, *The Viking Ships: Their Ancestry and Evolution* (1951), p. 178: "With an eye to the future, King Alfred organized a more

So, with the advance of European cultures, the typical civilization of today arose, as the older civilization of the Near East had risen a thousand years before from the Mesopotamian and Mediterranean cultural heritages. But no one in Europe or Asia suspected what was going on in another part of the earth, an unknown and even unsuspected part—the Americas.

In that great Western world, an extraordinary thing occurred: an impressive civilization took shape without, apparently, any true humane culture underlying it. The most striking exhibit of that historical process is the Inca supremacy which arose in Peru; the most terrible, the Aztec war culture which, at its height, held Mesoamerica in thrall and terror.[40]

No one knows with any certainty where the early Americans originated. Despite some very old human remains and primitive stone tools, mankind does not appear to have had a prehuman stage in the New World. There may have been several independent migrations from Asia over the ice of the Bering Strait or the former land bridge as well as from Oceania, possibly even Australia, and perhaps some countermigrations;[41] but in the course of time most of the immigrants seem to have merged into a single, remarkably fused, yet widely dispersed new "archaic race,"[42] with its own skin color (leaving a few white- or olive-skinned

---

powerful sea-defense during the last war with the vikings. The chronicle relates that he built warships almost twice the size of the *aeses*, some with 60 oars and some with more, and they were faster, bigger and higher, and were neither of Frisian nor Danish design, but such as the King thought would best serve their purpose.

"Thus King Alfred had created a new type of vessel built for war at sea, in order to keep the vikings away from the coast. This fleet was the foundation of a sea power which was kept up by the later kings of England. By the middle of the next century it was stated that the fleet had 3600 ships and that it was ordered out each year for manoeuvres."

[40]The Mayas, largely concentrated in Yucatan, were long considered a peaceful element in the native population, but later research has reversed that belief. All the tribes who achieved a level of social organization that could be called "civilized" were fierce, aggressive people. Frederick Peterson, in *Ancient Mexico: An Introduction to the Pre-Hispanic Cultures* (1962), p. 63, says: "The Maya were once hailed as a peaceful people, set apart from the rest of Mesoamerica; but we now know that they were just as warlike as their neighbors."

[41]Peterson (*ibid.*, p. 20) said: "There may have been several migrations at different times in the remote past, each one of a different kind of people. Asia has now a great spread of racial types; but how many inhabited it in prehistoric days is uncertain, and we do not know which Asiatic groups contributed to form the American Indian."

Carleton Beals, in *Nomads and Empire Builders: Native Peoples and Cultures of South America* (1961), pp. 67 ff., gives a fair summary of present-day theories concerning Indian origins, too long to cite or give in excerpt here.

[42]Peterson further observes that in 1913 Franz Boas and Manuel Gamio, making a stratigraphical survey in the Valley of Mexico, found a great many clay figurines. Other, similar finds were made at about the same time, establishing not only a single, widespread

enclaves here and there), and a great assortment of languages with an even greater wealth of dialects. In a rugged land of mountains, sharply separated valleys, and great rivers, a rapid speciation of languages would be natural.

What does not seem natural is the almost universal practice of cannibalism among people who have built cities with temples and palaces, military roads, aqueducts, baths, walled plazas, and great flights of rock-hewn or rock-built stairs. These edifices were not the megalithic monuments which usually belong to a prehistoric phase of culture,[43] but planned and directed works. To find thriving cities like Cuzco in Peru or, in Mexico, Tenochtitlan with its markets, boat traffic, causeways, and temple-crowned pyramids,[44] inhabited by savages who were evidently their builders but who went naked except for belts and feather ornaments, sacrificed human beings on their altars and indulged in cannibalistic feasts is ethnologically bewildering, to say the least. Something unusual must have happened to their societies to engender such paradoxes.

It seems, on the face of it, that the earliest Americans, when they finally reached the countries in which they developed their astounding civilizations, had found ideal conditions to make their swift advance from the primitive hunting and foraging stage of savagedom to urban life and rule. They found fertile valleys where important vegetable species—corn, peppers, tomatoes, and potatoes—grew wild and responded to cultivation, where there were guinea pigs and larger game, vines and fibers that yielded cordage, and rivers which lent themselves to irrigation projects. Above all, the human newcomers found freedom to develop their natural talents, which in some departments were remarkable.

---

art style but also a basically uniform human type over a wide area. Peterson reports that "Herbert Spinden began to trace the geographical distribution of these figures over the Americas, and theorized that there was a single basic culture for all Mesoamerica and the Andean region, which he called Archaic" (*Ancient Mexico*, p. 32).

Victor W. von Hagen, too, maintains that the rise of all Indian cultures belongs strictly to America, and says categorically of the most disputed one, the Mayan: "The Mayas, as a culture, developed within the Americas; nothing came from without" (*The Ancient Sun Kingdoms of the Americas* [1961], p. 211).

[43]Many prehistorians have reasoned that a task force great enough to move the stones of most megalithic monuments must certainly have required a director who was obeyed by the individuals performing the work. But that is probably to misconstrue the consciousness of the actors, who did not feel themselves as individuals with their own ideas, but plunged into the work as one falls into a rhythm struck by a distant parade band even before being aware of having heard it. True savages are not aware of themselves, but of hauling the heaviest objects they can move; they are demonstrating their power. The structure they are erecting probably takes shape in their minds as it does so for their eyes.

[44]Peterson, *Ancient Mexico*, p. 104.

This very freedom, however, may have been a dangerous advantage; for it let any dominant hereditary trait of the forming population run to its full expansion without being limited and modified in normal cultural competition with peoples of other stock and mentality. Consequently an outstanding talent could—and did—throw their cultural advance out of balance, letting the exercise of that special gift become a prime value which entrained or else smothered all other interests.

The Amerindians[45] possessed a veritable genius for military organization and political mastery. Most of them must have reached the New World at a very early date in their history, for they were evidently completely savage, being at the stage of evolution which seems to be universally marked by successive forms of cannibalism, from simple manslaughter for meat to solemn religious ritual. Cannibalism is an early step in humanization; not the very first, which probably occurred with the beginning of speech, but perhaps the next, for it belongs to the breaking up of the empathetic bonds which unite wolves in packs and once united prehuman primates and held them safe against each other in a horde. The amazing thing is how long an evolutionary transition can take, how late it may have set in, and what atavisms can persist even for millennia, protected by religious dread and cherished as mysteries while a new imaginative activity, still deeply unconscious, is preparing a new feeling of human beings toward each other: sympathy.[46]

The transition, in the case of the long-established primitive life of American humanity, was very irregularly achieved due to the immigrants' peculiar phyletic history, which seems to go back to a time when successive droves of the Asiatic population, still in the semi-social condition known to anthropologists as the "band" state (i.e., before tribal organization), were pushed out of their homelands by changing natural conditions or possibly demographic pressure. That does not mean that all the earliest migrants were at the same cultural stage (or pre-cultural, if that is possible for genuine hominids) whenever and wherever they entered the New World. But after their entry their further history was extraordinary.

<hr/>

[45]This term, which has found acceptance by many anthropologists, seems to me a good designation to distinguish the American "Indian" from the inhabitants of India, especially since today the latter have come into their own again on the demographic map of the world. Webster's *New World Dictionary of the American Language* gives the word as "Amerind"; I prefer the more widely used "Amerindian" because of its obvious reference to the traditional "Indian."
[46]Cf. above, Vol. II, Chapter 14, *passim.*

The Breaking

One of its notable characteristics was certainly its headlong progress, another, however, its instability. Since, at the time of the Spanish invasion, the ruling power in South America—the Inca of Peru with their great conscript armies—numbered hundreds of thousands, the weakness of their proud, fortified, and sternly governed cities is as surprising as their indigenous rise in the isolation of the Andes plateau.

There had been civilizations in South America before the Inca Empire, along the northwestern coast and its populous river valleys, centering in cities with public squares and buildings, gates, markets, and defensive walls running from the shore up the hillsides; and not only on the coast, but also in the high sierra, from Quito in the north to Tiahuanaco south of Lake Titicaca, and on the shores and islands of the lake. Yet somehow those civilizations had broken down again; their great installations belonged to vanished ages. The tribes that inherited their ruins had apparently started anew from primitive life and made varying degrees of technological progress, as in spinning and knotting llama wool into nets and hammocks, some of them also weaving, all practicing pottery and other early arts; some had learned the use of gold for ornament and various metals for weaponry, i.e., for points and blades. The Chimu, the Nazca, and the Chanka—these last, the most serious military rivals of the Inca—had all made their contributions to Amerindian civilization, even urbanization, yet none of their political establishments had proved viable in the long run.

The Inca were not ideologically superior to the tribes they conquered. Their ethos always had a peculiar frangibility, extremes of royal pomp mingling with equally great extremes of wildness and backwardness. This is most evident in the contrast between their systematic urban administration, their bureaucracies and concepts of order and authority, and the very low level of their religious thinking, almost too low to be classed as thinking at all.

None of the politically important South American tribes had progressed even as far as a belief in anthropomorphic gods at the time when the military alliance was formed which later became the Inca state. The recipients of their worship and sacrifices were so-called "huacas," chiefly natural objects—fantastic rocks or lava formations, strange trees, even posts or columns, caverns, pools and hot springs. These were genuine fetishes, of magical rather than divine character (Fig. 23–3). They controlled the ruler's—and thereby the tribe's—luck from day to day, and had no relation to moral values, precepts, prohibitions, or the fate of souls after death. Such a wide gap between the different intellectual

[181]

Figure 23–3. Huaca
the recipients of their worship and sacrifices were so-called "huacas," chiefly
natural objects. . . . These were genuine fetishes, of magical rather than divine
character
(From Burr Cartwright Brundage, *Empire of the Inca* [Norman: University of Oklahoma Press, 1963].)

achievements of a generally homogeneous society makes one wonder what held back its religious development while its worldly advances progressed without obstacles by their own push and growth.

The trouble seems to have been deeply hidden (even from themselves) and subjective, and to have stemmed from that very freedom which permitted their phenomenal rise to power and dominion—a fatal by-product of their millennia of isolation. Apparently, in this human stock so long separated from the rest of mankind, there were tensions between the different rates of mental development which had become too great to be taken in stride much longer. The separation had been long enough to permit even some evolutionary processes to depart from the normal pattern and run their courses at an exaggerated pace while others were unhurried or actually dragged in their advance.[47] This happens to some

47Compare the discussion of this topic in Vol. II, pp. 340 ff., and especially the references to Tilly Edinger and to Ignace Meyerson on p. 341n.

[182]

extent in all complex organic developments, but as a rule the pressions of the given human situation obviate any extreme discrepancy before it can endanger the ethnic balance on a wide cross-section of hereditary lines. The history of the American savages is probably unparalleled in its lack of cultural influences or foreign models to call customs and traditional values in question. No one knows when they entered the phase of cannibalism, though in some cases it may have been in America, for it is said that the earliest Andean cultures had not practiced it—whether not yet or no longer is hard to tell, for they have all been known as man-eaters since.[48] It seems, in fact, that every human stock in the course of its humanization goes through that phase as the empathetic animal reactions of its members to each other weaken and the rudimentary intellectual function of sympathy for human beings as such, rooted in a subjectifying imagination, has not evolved far enough to replace them.[49] Cannibalism appears to have obtained at one time or another in every part of the world (which is a strong argument for the supposition that it is a step in man's general evolution), but the times of its occurrence and passing in particular localities vary widely, ranging from the beginnings of culture (probably not before that) to the recorded memory of the conquistadores and even to present-day scenes of horror.[50] E. M. Loeb has devised a map (Fig. 23–4) recording and distinguishing the known sites and relative times (i.e., prehistoric or historic) of anthropophagy and —in view of his own topic of interest—human sacrifice;[51] man-eating, whether for food, for incorporation of the victim's physical and magical powers, or for an enemy's final subjection and denigration, has been practiced at some

---

[48]Carleton Beals, citing José Imbelloni, says: "The earliest folk did not practice cannibalism or go in for war trophies, though Amazon forest gatherers soon resorted to cannibalism. There was no organized religion in the form of temples, priests, or idols; human sacrifices and ritual cycles were absent, though likely they had beliefs on the existence of the soul and life hereafter" (*Nomads and Empire Builders*, p. 85). The last supposition seems unlikely to me.

[49]See *ibid., passim*, esp. pp. 10, 95, 164, 180, 187.

[50]See, e.g., Jens Bjerre, *The Last Cannibals* (1957), p. 81, where he describes his visit (by very rare permission) to the Kukukuku on New Guinea. These savages are fierce little mountaineers, simply but effectively armed with spears and boomerangs. Bjerre was with two anthropologists and a couple of government agents. "Jack [one of these agents] told me," he wrote, "that, six months ago, two men had been eaten in a village, Jagentsaga, not far away; and that a month ago he had, by chance, found the hand of a man who had been eaten shortly beforehand. The rest of him had been hidden in the jungle. 'They know,' he said, 'that we will punish them for cannibalism, so they do everything to conceal it now. But it still occurs and probably will do so for a long time.'"

[51]His Yale thesis, published in *Memoirs of the American Anthropological Association*, is entitled "The Blood Sacrifice Complex." References here are to the 1964 reprint of the *Memoirs*.

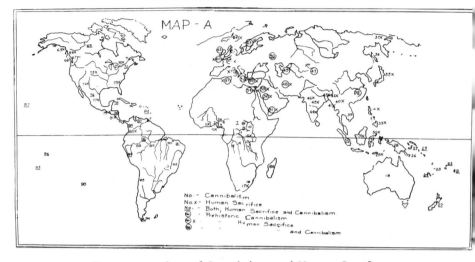

Figure 23–4. Sites of Cannibalism and Human Sacrifice
*man-eating . . . has been practiced at some time on every continent and may
well be in the heritage of every kindred living today*
(From Edwin Meyer Loeb, "The Blood Sacrifice Complex," *Memoirs of the American
Anthropological Association*, XXX [1923].)

time on every continent and may well be in the heritage of every kindred
living today.

Human sacrifice is another story. It may or may not be connected with
cannibalistic feasting, but if it is, that connection is incidental to the
sacrificial rite. The basic motivation of sacrifice is always placation and
entreaty, no matter how low the level of the religion it serves. It is always
directed toward a superhuman and supernatural power, a god or the
nearest to a god that the sacrificer knows; and it is this relation of men to
their godhead that has rarely been sifted for its real content of fear and
fantasy, working, in the main, below the level of explicit belief. The
professed beliefs of butcher-priests and their congregations as anthropologists and missionaries have received and reported them, such as "pleasing
their gods,"[52] are generally too simplistic to be anything but metaphorical

[52]So Peterson writes, in *Ancient Mexico:* "In Mexico, human sacrifice on a large scale
was instituted by the Aztecs, probably around 1450, when bad weather destroyed all the
crops and caused four years of national distress. . . . The Aztecs thought that
Huitzilopochtli [their chief god, the sun] was angry with them for not feeding him
sufficiently. . . . The most acceptable food for the sun was human hearts and blood—in
essence. . . . The drought and famine disappeared in due time; and the Aztecs thought
their god was pleased, and decided to continue mass sacrifice in order to keep
Huitzilopochtli happy." That is not the spirit in which religious rites are established.

conceits themselves. Their true motivation lies deeper. The priestly dogma that without such daily sacrifices the sun might turn away and not
rise, and might even go out altogether, is obviously a mythical conception of the possibility, if not yet the certainty, of dying,[53] unconsciously
(and therefore constantly) feared by the Inca for himself and by the
populace for itself, since the latter still felt largely as one body.[54] The
ritual offering was a substitution for the most precious life, like the ram
which Abraham found God-given to him in place of the intended victim,
Isaac. Every day the Inca bought the life of their society with the heart of
some virile young warrior taken for that purpose in battle or in a raid.
There is a phase in the evolution of mind, while the realization of
mortality is gradually asserting itself, overcoming rejection, denial, and
protest, but has not really won the day, when people try by every means,
from magical defense to offers of ransom, to stave off the never-admitted,
ineluctable end. In this phase of realization the most progressive natives
of South and Central America seem to have bogged down, instead of
transcending it by accepting and hallowing death. At the time of the
Spanish conquest they were still buying their emperors' lives and their
own, from day to day, with bloody sacrifice.

This interpretation is, of course, hypothetical, but there are other
phenomena that strongly corroborate it; one of these is the peculiar practice known as the emperor's *panaca*, said to have been introduced by Inca
Roca; it was a *post mortem* fictitious upkeep of each late Inca's court,
wherein ever-new, living persons played the roles of his former entou-
rage. According to B. C. Brundage, "The emperor was the *genius* of his

[53]I knew a child left motherless at the age of three, who four years later lost her father;
after that she was afflicted with a recurrent nightmare that the sun went out.
[54]Northcote W. Thomas, in his *Encyclopaedia Britannica* article "Sacrifice," distinguished several kinds of sacrifice: honorific—worshipping and bringing gifts; piacular—
restoring a broken bond with the deity; deificatory—identifying the victim with the god. In
this connection he makes the difficult statement, "Gods may be sacrificed (in
theriomorphic form) to themselves as a means of renewing the life of god," and later,
"Whereas the god receives a gift in the honorific sacrifice, he demands a life in the
piacular. This, according to Westermarck, is the central idea of human sacrifice: the
victim is substituted for the sacrificer, to deliver him from perils by disease, famine, or,
more indefinitely, from the wrath of the god in general." Similarly, René Girard has
written, in *La violence et le sacre* (1972), pp. 16–17: "Les observations faites sur le terrain
et la réflexion théorique obligent à revenir, dans l'explication du sacrifice, à l'hypothèse
de la substitution. Cette idée est partout presente dans la littérature ancienne sur le
sujet. . . . Le rapport entre la victime potentielle et la victime actuelle ne doit pas se
définir en termes de culpabilité et d'innocence. Il n'y a rien à 'expier.' La société cherche
à d'étourner vers une victime relativement indifférente, une victime 'sacrifiable,' une
violence qui risque de frapper ses propres membres, ceux qu'elle entend à tout prix
protéger."

panaca; his death was treated simply as a ceremonial incident, for the royal mummy held exactly the same position as had his animated person—his *coya* [queen], his wealth, his favorite women and servitors, all continued in his possession. In brief his estate was noninheritable and inalienable. The *panaca* was thus a special type of elective and ever-functioning family, the head of which never died, whose grip on his possessions never lapsed, and who was feted, entertained, and served *in perpetuum* in his palace."[55]

Finally, a fairly clear symptom of the Incas' recoil from thinking about death is the pathetic state of their eschatological ideas. Their pantheon contained no *Thanatos* and their cosmos no heaven or hell; their priesthood served its huacas to avert evil and influence the community's earthly luck, and especially its continuity. A sense of mystery and holiness surrounds every huaca, but it is all centered on the creative power of the fetish or of the god whom the fetish may ultimately come to represent. Their mythology is concerned almost entirely with origins—emergence of "first beings" from caves or a body of water, or from the hands of a divine potter.[56] The only end of such supernatural beings was to be

[55]*Empire of the Inca* (1963), p. 126. How completely the anxiety of these rulers was masked by the *panaca* is shown by a modern writer's innocent acceptance of the ruse. Carleton Beals says: "The Incas had no fear of death or the dead. Embalming was a perfected art, and the individual was considered not so much dead as merely dumb and deaf, and the bulk of his possessions accompanied him to the artfully decorated sepulcher in which he was placed in a sitting position. The mummies of kings and the Sinchis were especially decked out in their most gala costumes, for from time to time they had to pay courtesy visits to the sun; also, they were brought out to attend important fiestas. At the great Raymi fiesta they were seated in state on the great Aucaypatal Terrace, with major-domos and aides, and delivered imaginary speeches and held imaginary conversations, carried on by their spokesmen and interpreters" (*Nomads and Empire Builders*, p. 240).

[56]The commonest stated origin of men seems to have been caves, some "place of appearing." Brundage says, "Pacaritambo was a site some eighteen miles southeast of Cuzco. . . . Here in a hill was the Inca *pacarina*, the 'place of appearing,' three caves named respectively Tambotoco, Marastoco, and Sutictoco, where *toco* means 'hole'" (*Empire of the Inca*, p. 9). The Chancas, the same authority reports, are said to have claimed that "their *huaca* of origination was Choclococha (Fresh Corn Lake), a small body of water near the western border of the province of Vilcas" (p. 89). And Carleton Beals says that "A creator, Chimi-ni-guagua, began to shine in the eternal dark-nothing and made large black birds, then the Sun and Moon. The Graca version was about a sugamuxi cacique and his nephew who, when all was still dark, created men out of yellow earth and women out of a tall herb [instead of a rib], then his nephew became the sun and he the moon" (*Nomads and Empire Builders*, p. 203). Also, "In Tiahuanaco the creator had shaped the varied tribes of men as figurines in clay or stone and painted them in the colors, headgear, and garments which as nations they were ultimately to adopt. Then . . . he gave them life and a law . . . and sent them down into the earth from which, after the subsidence of the flood, they emerged at the selected place of origination. . . . These sites became *huacas* of supreme sanctity to each nation of the Peruvian world" (Brundage, *Empire of the Inca*, p. 68).

turned into sacred rocks, which remained active as powerful huacas. Human beings had a short time to make their spiritual exit from the world; the Mataco gave them only four years, during which they "became successively ghosts, birds, spiders, and bats before vanishing forever. But the souls of those stabbed in a drinking bout became mosquitoes or flies, then ants which turned into grass."[57] Such poverty of ideas points to the unwillingness of their theological thinkers to follow out any long thoughts on the subject of death, the ghost, and its final fate.[58]

Nothing is so directly opposed to cultural advance as fear to develop a line of thought or face one's own knowledge. The most dangerous effect of the South Americans' intellectual timidity, which held them for generations to a long-outgrown mythology, was the ever-widening gap between their military and political achievements and the low level of their religious conception, which evidently strained to the limit the unity and coherence of their minds. By the time the Spaniards came upon them, the Incas' administration of conquered lands and cities rivaled that of the Caesars in Rome, while their philosophical reflection was on a level with that of Andaman Islanders and Tasmanians except where it was invented with purely political motives to deify the emperor.[59]

The great Inca civilization, for all its wonderful achievements and constant religious rites, was spiritually hollow. As its domination spread it required more and more force to enlist and hold the Amerindian tribes who were not culturally ready for the officialdom and nationalism which their powerful rulers imposed on them. Like most despots, the Inca ruler became more and more removed from his people, and the aristocracy, which is normally staggered like the tiers of a step pyramid to fill the interval between the highest representative of a society and the lowliest class within it, gradually sank to a servile retainership itself. The simple-

[57]Beals, *Nomads and Empire Builders*, p. 142.

[58]Some of the Caingang tribes did have a notion of a "better land," but even there man's stay was short, limited to one more human lifetime, after which the soul became an insect, and died as insects do. See *ibid.*, p. 150.

[59]Brundage described at some length the "Council of Coricancha" (the sacred domicile of Inti) called by Pachacuti, at which he declared Inti the supreme huaca, an incarnation not of the sun but of a more complete and perfect power. "Pachacuti drew to the attention of the Council the certainty that there must exist a god greater in all respects than the Sun, and he left it to them to nominate that deity. All were aware of the answer implicit in the question, and together they acclaimed the Creator Ticci Viracocha Pachayachachic as the sole supreme god of the universe.

"The historian today can conceive of no credo by which both Inca and non-Inca could have been more securely harnessed to the exigent chariot of empire. . . . When Cobo makes the observation that the Incas changed their religious idea to conform to their ideas of empire he is, of course, referring to such events in Inca history" (*Empire of the Inca*, p. 164).

[187]

mindedness of folk beliefs made it possible for the priests of the firebird Inti, the personal huaca of Topa Inca finally elevated as a sun god, to shape an official theology entirely in support of the reigning monarch; no serious, sacred, arguable convictions stood in their way. All the religious governance that was required was to relate all huacas to Inti and kill anyone who still mentioned the shining cat or serpent they had stood for in the past.[60]

Actually, however, most of the South Americans were well past the mental state of denying the ineluctability of death even for their emperors. The rejected knowledge could no longer be quite successfully masked by pretense. The Incas' unadmitted realization grew more and more defiant and desperate, and that dreadful insecurity was reflected in their treatment of all their subjects, nobles and underlings alike, above all, of course, their newly conquered cities and most recently vanquished tribes. Their rule was increasingly based on terrorism, cruelty, threat and ferocity, and boundless self-elevation and alienation from the populace, so that just before the Spanish invasion took the Western world by utter surprise, their armies and subjugated peoples were already in revolt. All that the Spaniards had to do was to finish the collapse.

It was a strange situation; a nation had achieved a dominant civilization for which it was culturally not ready. While the mutineers were secretly gathered in the Montana of Peru laying their plan, Brundage writes, "In Tumibamba [where the emperor was putting down an insurrection] the imperial aplomb held as Huyana Capac, merely passing the comment that men were food for war, proceeded to take vigorous personal command. An Inca lord in such a situation is clearly at his most dangerous, as the event shows. Certainly few episodes in the annals of these people reveal as strikingly as this the skeletal stratum that lay just under the surface of the imperial office, that of the tribal *sinchi* [warleader], fierce, irresponsible, unconquerable, and relentless."[61]

---

[60]The story of this radical reinterpretation of the cult centering in the island of Titicaca, which bore the most holy huaca, The Rock of the Cat, so that Inti instead of the shining Cat made his periodic mystic appearances there, is told by Brundage, who says in conclusion: "The prestige and venerability of the site was transferred lock, stock and barrel to the Incas by this tale [invented by a Colla priest and told to Topa Inca to gain his protection], and its former deities were forever erased or recast in favor of Inca theology" (*ibid.*, p. 229).

[61]*Ibid.*, p. 256. How fierce and relentless these Indians could be was described by Brundage in an earlier passage on the Incas' defeat of the Chanca: "On the field of battle due vengeance was taken upon the captured Chanca magnates. They were mocked, insulted, tortured and finally destroyed, while their skulls were prepared to provide drinking bowls for the victor, in which he would toast both his own success and his enemy's

The Breaking

Much the same kind of ethnic distortion as in South America occurred in Mesoamerica, where several impressive civilizations have flourished only to break up on internal, deep-lying weaknesses at the first rude shock of a truly foreign contact, if not before, under their own inward strains. The Mayan tribes whose chief concentration was in Yucatan, and the widely influential Toltecs to the north and west of them laid many foundation stones for the brief but meteoric history of the last purely Indian power, the Aztec. In Mexico, in and around Lake Texcoco, these Aztecs—savage Indians from somewhere northwest of the saline lakes—managed to subdue the earlier settlers on the islands and promontories as well as the existing towns and farming communities of the great valley without destroying them, so that enough tribute could be extorted to let the Aztec usurpers live as a parasitic power in their midst. There these latest wild invaders developed a spectacular civilization in no more than a hundred years.

The secret of their rapid advance was an extraordinary receptivity for ideas, techniques, and opportune suggestions, however daring. They probably did not make as many true inventions as their Toltec and Mayan predecessors, but translated everything they found into tangible or usable realities. At the time of the Spanish invasion the Aztec capital, Tenochtitlan, built on an island in Lake Texcoco and connected with towns on the mainland by long causeways and busy canoe traffic, was one of the finest cities in the world (Fig. 23–5). Frederick Peterson has gleaned his description of it mainly from the earliest reports sent back to Europe and since then corroborated by archeological research. "The stepped pyramids," he says, "which rose out of the lake by the score, were covered with stucco and painted in bright colours. On huge plazas scattered throughout the city thousands of dancers participated in colourful ceremonies. Stone sculptures of idols and commemoration were found on every hand. Huge government granaries, treasuries, and arsenals occupied central locations. Bas-reliefs of warriors and serpents were placed on walls which enclosed the central courtyard. The houses were whitewashed and polished so that they seemed to be made of silver. . . . Nobles strolled in luxurious and brilliant costumes, with jade and feather

---

disgrace. The final humiliation to the corpses was to make them into *runatinyas* (mandrums). The skins were stripped off and stuffed with dried *ichu*-grass; flutes were tucked into their mouths; and their mummied hands, now empty of the scepters of rule, were so placed that, when pounded upon the distended drumheads of their bellies, they would hollowly sound forth the tattoo of their own ignomiy. These gruesome trophies were housed in a building erected on the site and were later seen by the Spaniards" (pp. 95–96).

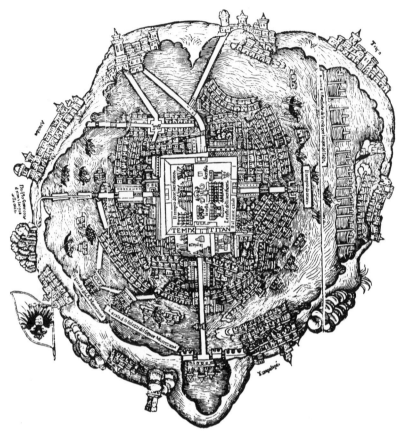

Figure 23–5. Map of Tenochtitlan
at the time of the Spanish invasion of the Aztec capital,
Tenochtitlan, . . . was one of the finest cities in the world
(From Lewis Spence, *The Civilization of Ancient Mexico* [Cambridge: At the University Press;
New York: G. P. Putnam's Sons, 1912].)

ornaments. Messengers of the emperor raced on various errands. Black-robed priests walked the streets with censers.[62]. . . The valley was dotted with villages of agriculturalists and their cornfields."[63]

[62]These priests were not Christian monks or missionaries, but priests of the many temples erected in honor of the gods, especially the great war god of the Aztecs, Huitzilopochtli. The similarities of their costumes and actions to those of Christian fathers is believed to be a case of pure convergence.
In many cases, however, the repetition of Old World customs as independent American inventions is too implausible for acceptance. Such actions as paternal couvade, which Marco Polo found in Asia, the suttee performed in India by royal widows as they leaped into the late rajah's funeral pyre, and the mummification of corpses almost exactly as in Egypt make some communication almost certain.
[63]Peterson, *Ancient Mexico*, p. 104.

[190]

The Breaking

In this unmistakeably civilized area of the Aztec realm there was a small royal clique of cultivated intellectuals often recognized by modern historians as "poet-kings" or "philosopher-kings." Most noteworthy was the emperor Topiltzin, who took the epithetical name "Quetzalcoatl." Topiltzin Quetzalcoatl, like Akhenaton in Egypt before him, made premature efforts to introduce a humane religion based on worship of the sun as a symbol of life and a ritual of equally symbolic, largely bloodless sacrifices of tamales, snakes, butterflies, and flowers. But if the Egyptians were not ready for such high thinking, much less so were the Amerindians. Their ethos always had a peculiar frangibility, so that with the destruction of a capital city their whole civilized life broke down again. Cities rose and fell in Europe and especially in Asia, too, but their scattered and often enslaved denizens did not generally turn back to nudism and cannibalism; affluence and starvation are the extremes of fortune on any level of cultured life, but even desperate hunger does not usually abolish all standards of human society in a population which, after all, manages to survive. And at the time of the Spanish invasion the Inca were certainly not a defeated people.

Neither were the Aztecs. By all material evidence they were triumphant in their wealth and power. No outside dangers were threatening them. It takes close looking to see the signs of weakness at the core of both civilizations. The signs were different in the two cultures, each of which extended over and beyond the political hegemony of the master tribe at its center, but both bespoke the same condition of unbalanced mentality, probably due to the immigrants' excessive freedom from both social stimulation and social restraint. In Peru the Inca capitalized for a while on the degeneracy which afflicted the oldest past societies first and worst and left them unresisting, while their conquerors fought and destroyed the still warlike braves around them. But along the coast the symptoms of decay were obvious. They showed up as a widespread tendency to drunkenness, drug addition and sexual aberrations of all sorts.[64] The varieties of psychedelic drugs these people without any systematic knowledge of chemistry managed to derive from plants and even animals around them indicates their interest in possible sources of alterations of consciousness:

---

[64]See Brundage, *Empire of the Incas*, p. 192: "Intricate forms of homosexualism and temple sodomy had long been entrenched in these coastal valleys. . . . Indeed sexual aberrations of all varieties flowered rankly in the hothouse atmosphere of these cultures. The coastal harems were served by creatures so grotesque as scarcely to be believable, men who had not only been emasculated but had had their lips and noses slit away so as to cause in those women whom they guarded revulsion and horror." Figures on vessels which record a broad span of abnormal sexual behavior are pictured by Victor von Hagen in *The Desert Kingdoms of Peru* (1964), p. 44 ff.

fermented palm juice and almost any fruit juice as intoxicants, but especially substances inducing visions, sensations of flying, vertigo, and dream states.[65] After generations and probably centuries of such enervating indulgence, South America harbored whole tribes of physically undermined human beings who, for all their ancient glories and all their warrior ideals, presented no real fighting force. Too many of them were self-defeated men.

In Mexico, as aforesaid, the visible effects of the Amerindians' long freedom from rival cultures were of a different sort, but they were equally pathological. The difference may have arisen from the fact that the Aztecs had a somewhat more sophisticated culture, and especially that they had reached the stage of worshipping gods with names and human ("all-too-human") characters. And again, their failing may have lain precisely where they excelled as masters of many tribes: in their tolerance of other faiths and their gods. Like the Inca, they sacrificed prisoners of war to their deities in the typical Amerindian way, by cutting out the victim's heart and holding it up as an offering while smearing their idols with the blood or pouring it on the ground for the oldest of all worshipped Beings, Mother Earth, known by any of her countless names. But all gods demanded sacrifice; and because of the Aztecs' tolerance and acceptance of all gods honored by friends or foes, their pantheon became enormous, and with it their ceremonial obligations passed all reasonable limits. Their sacrifices became mass slaughters.[66]

[65]A special delicacy was a serving of bamboo worms, which caused the eater to see visions in rich colors. Carleton Beals, in *Nomads and Empire Builders*, p. 146–47, says: "For some peoples, toads, lizards and bamboo worms, which caused visions, were considered great delicacies. . . . Yurema was drunk by the Cariri to induce ecstatic visions, the same effect as eating bamboo worms."

[66]Peterson, in *Ancient Mexico*, says that the beginning of human sacrifice in Mexico cannot be dated, but that the notorious practice of mass sacrifices seems to have begun in a national crisis when snow and ice ruined all crops and crushed many houses, around 1450 and again four years later (pp. 145, 96).

A similar account is given by Jacques Soustelle in his *Daily Life of the Aztecs* (1961), p. 101: "The sovereigns of Mexico, Texcoco and Tlacopan and the lords of Tlaxcala, Uexotzinco and Cholula mutually agreed that, there being no war, they would arrange combats, so that the captives might be sacrificed to the gods. . . . Fighting was primarily a means of taking prisoners; on the battlefield the warriors did their utmost to kill as few men as possible."

And further (p. 105): "While Tlazoltcotl came from the north-east, it was probably from the south, from the Pacific coast, that they imported the terrible cult of Xipe Totec, 'our lord the flayed one,' the god of the goldsmiths and also the deity of the spring rain, the renewal of nature and the fresh growth. His victims were . . . transfixed with arrows so that their blood should drop on the earth like rain: then they were flayed.

"The priests put on their skin, dyed yellow to look like gold leaf, and this magical act, which symbolized the way the earth 'makes a new skin' at the beginning of the rainy season, induced the vegetation to come again."

That bloody ritual, unfortunately, was shared by most of their fellow men in Mesoamerica; wars between tribes were carried on largely for the purpose of procuring prisoners. Relatively few warriors were killed in battle, but thousands on the altars.[67] The upper classes of the citizenry consumed the muscular parts of the victims (the common folk received no such magically strength-giving food, though there must have been more of it than the aristocracy could eat,[68] because it might have made the populace too strong for their masters' safety).

The practice of buying life from the gods thus became a religious obsession. In a brief course of time, inevitably, the strongest manhood—the Aztec army, not of naked savages but of clad, armed, and trained soldiers, and their similar opponents—was steadily culled by those constant wars, known as "wars of the flowers," fought to procure prisoners rather than for conquest. Whether several tribes sacrificed each other's young men or each its own made no difference in the effect on the inhabitants of a continent; either left the total native population overcharged with noncombatant age groups (i.e., children and elders), the sick and the crippled, while the ranks of virile youth were sorely depleted. Not drink and drugs (though these also played a part) but a psychotic compulsion to human sacrifice was the macabre symptom of the Mesoamerican's excessive freedom from foreign influences.

Sometimes the final failure of a progressive action will reveal what unsuspected conditions are really required to let it succeed. The Aztecs, like the Inca, suffered from their lack of intellectual conflict and competition. Though they were a bellicose people, their enmities were not based on conflicts of ideas[69] Their mental development could fall as far apart as it did because, in spite of an occasional "philosopher-king," there was no challenging source of radically new conceptions such as people met, especially in wanderings or migrations, in the Old World. If the Amerindian felt disinclined to think about death he could insist on offering blood in return for life until his whole religion became an emotional bulwark around the specter of death.

[67]Peterson, *Ancient Mexico*, p. 101, says: "Ahuizotl dedicated the huge temple of Huitzilopochtli begun by Tizoc, by sacrificing all the accumulated Matlatzinca, Huaxtec, and Zapotec prisoners. . . . At this dedication the prisoners to be sacrificed were lined up in four files, each over three miles long."

[68]This despite the fact that "they ate only the arms and legs," the obvious repositories of mobility and strength. They "burnt the rest or kept it for the sustenance of the beasts and birds of prey in the royal zoo" (Francisco J. Clavigero, quoted by Peterson in *ibid.*, p. 149).

[69]Both the Inca and the Mesoamericans, especially Maya and Toltecs, produced notable mathematical abstractions and computations; mathematics is safe from eschatological notions, and even today in our society is often the refuge of gifted minds unable to face the kaleidoscope of empirical reality.

It seems, indeed, that an evolving mind requires limitations of opportunity to achieve a unified phyletic career; it needs the pression of complex and crowding humanity to hold its form and balance in the ecological stream. Usually a biological function contains its own antagonist in a suppressed but still potential form striving for active expansion; the function of the brain in human beings to produce concepts which rule the flow of ever-changing actual expectations is normally hedged by the felt, even though unavowed, awareness of possible contrary assumptions. This remaining presence of the negative in every choice is what gives life and thought its dialectical form. But in a multi-millennial isolation such an essentially logical awareness is not enough to straiten the diffuse welter of otherwise unopposed ideas. The dialectic of thought alone, without a social need to evade or resolve inconsistencies arising from different basic concepts, does not generate enough "drive" to maintain a progressive mental life. And the lack which thus becomes apparent only with a relaxation instead of an increase of hardship reaches far down to the roots of human intellect.

In the speciation of the human race through its several crises of speech, fantasy, ritual, and the tribal feeling which finally has to break to make way for the cultural move to civilization, the phase of family organization has been so long extended that one may well wonder what has been going forward in all that enormous length of time during which the thousands of internally structured, blood-related units of society were naturally ordered by generations, each unit ruled by the eldest living generation within it. A tradition or even a tendency that has no function in the further development of the stock does not usually persist as the rule of elders has done in tribal groups from the beginning of human society to historic times.

Perhaps we owe it our longevity beyond the age of procreation, which has puzzled many evolutionists, especially those of a neo-Darwinian turn, who assume—rightly, I think—that a useless element such as the survival for decades of uncontributive members should be bred out of a species. The explanation that there is simply "no selection against it" is unconvincing, at best.[70] The aged survivors eat, require space and even

---

[70]Yet several evolutionists have offered arguments which—despite the differences their authors fight out along the way—converge on some such conclusion: See Alex Comfort, "Biological Aspects of Senescence" (1954); G. C. Williams, "Pleiotropy, Natural Selection, and the Evolution of Senescence" (1957); P. B. Medawar, *The Uniqueness of the Individual* [1961]; and George Wald, "Origin of Death" (1963), to cite only the leading thinkers on that evolutionary problem. They all establish the effects of "natural selection" by proper statistical methods, but the processes which supposedly lead to the statistical results are usually highly speculative and sometimes hard to follow.

charitable attention to live, and in only a few very primitive cultures are denied their necessities so they may "starve in the midst of plenty"[71] or be abandoned on the road.[72] As long as the clan or settlement is traditionally ruled by elders, these have a function; and a brain with a function provides its own stimulus to survive and enlist the services of the rest of the organism, as procreation used to do.[73]

But civilized countries are not organized by staggered generations, nor ruled by the most venerable of them. What happens, then, to the aged when they are no longer serving the community? That depends on how little or much that community honors the individual as an end in itself, not as a thing of relative value, however high, but as the ultimate measure of all value.[74] According to our present social feeling it is the duty of the community to serve them in return for their past discharges of their human responsibilities; and this duty toward the old and, perhaps, de-

[71]Dudley Kidd, in *Savage Childhood*, completes the passage quoted in Chapter 21 above (p. 105, n. 27) about the Kafir children's fear of old age with the explanation: "Old women are treated with scant attention, and are left to die extremely sad deaths in many cases, literally dying amid plenty, from starvation and neglect. But old men are treated with great respect" (p. 140). When, then, do boys share that fear? Is the attitude contagious, and the physical decline of old men made apparent to the boys by the girls' dread?

[72]Knut Rasmussen, in *The Netsilik Eskimos*, speaks of such abandonment with very different feeling, as in telling of the harsh necessity that drove people to such apparent cruelty: "Whereas the Netsilinguint only used stones for making meat caches, the Tunrit made use of them for graves and houses. . . . When they were driven from Sherman Inlet there was an old woman, Akusinguak, who was so feeble that she was unable to go with them. And, as she had to be left behind, they could not bear the thought that she might die among people who simply laid their dead out on the ground, so they buried her alive under great stones" (p. 114). To kill her first would have been too dangerous; her ghost would never have stood for it.

Franz Boas, in *The Central Eskimo*, written after his year in the Arctic almost a century ago and actually not published until 1888, tells a somewhat similar tale: "Another case was that of an old woman whose health had been failing for a number of years. She lived with her son, whose wife died late in the autumn of 1886. According to the religious ideas of the Eskimo, the young man had to throw away his clothing. When later on, his mother felt as though she could not live through the winter, she insisted upon being killed, as she did not want to compel her son to cast away a second set of clothing. At last her son complied with her request. She stripped off her outside jacket and breeches, and was conveyed on a sledge to a near island, where she was left alone to die from cold and hunger" (p. 207n).

There is the same difference of feeling and motivation between the Eskimos' cannibalism and the Mesoamericans'. Rasmussen says: "In years of very great distress it is not to be wondered at that cases of cannibalism are common. It is not practised as the outcome of any cannibalistic desire and is therefore excused by all as the last extremity in a starving people's fight for life" (*The Netsilik Eskimos*, p. 1350).

[73]Cf. Chapter 21, p. 92, n. 5.

[74]Immanuel Kant, in his *Grundlegung zur Metaphysik der Sitten*, makes a distinction explicitly between things of value and rational beings who have no value but a higher order of worth, "dignity": "Im Reiche der Zwecke hat alles entweder einen *Preis*, oder

crepit is directed to them as a class, though in most cases it falls upon individuals by virtue of a legal code or, in better and rare cases, of personal charity.

Charity, nobility, honor, and even pity are never in very generous supply among average people. Sometimes the inherent viciousness of human beings breaks out in "crime waves"; sometimes it appears more generally in long, slow periods of degeneration, when cynicism desecrates and corrupts even the most basic ethical commitments. Sometimes great individuals without fame live by their ideals from birth to death with purest candor in the "worst of possible worlds." As far back as we can trace or reconstruct the social history of man, such differences in personal worthiness and responsibility seem to have made the average distance between him and his avowed standards roughly the same at all ages in the long run. So what do we mean by the "moral advance" of society?

Perhaps, even though practice may never come much closer to its precepts than in any past ages, the advance has been on a different level of value; on the conceptual level of the moral structure itself. It is the standard that changes, and carries all idealistic effort, casual conformity, and ardent condemnation with it to a higher plane, usually without most people's conscious feeling of the change. And what holds true for the moral character of Mind does so as well for its intellectual quality. A new great age is long prepared, and finally is born with the rise and expansion of a new idea which automatically transforms the outlook and reach of human mentality, in our present evolving age, even to effect the evaluation and re-evaluation of the criteria of thought itself. That is the office of philosophy.

It is this progression by qualitative shifts—the current one some three thousand years old, if not more, in its preparation—that requires human culture as a whole to keep a certain balance between its highest and lowest degrees of change. A leading achievement can only lead by entraining the countless psychical activities that make up a mental life and an individual's or society's *Weltanschauung*. That seems to be why a culture capable of supporting a great civilization requires a single, complex yet balanced advancing front of many crowding evolutionary stocks and battling faiths to uphold the drive of incompatibilities.

In Europe, in our own passing era, a growing civilization has built itself up under intensely demanding pressions, from roots of inestimable

---

eine *Würde*. Was einen Preis hat, an dessen Stelle kann auch etwas anderes als *Äqui- valent* gesetzt werden; was dagegen über allen Preis erhaben ist, mithin kein Äquivalent verstattet, das hat eine Würde" (p. 66).

depth enmeshed with tributaries from every possible source—Asia, Africa, Oceania, perhaps lost continents with earlier prehuman primates than we have found. Egypt, Babylon, Greece, Rome, Phoenicia, and Jewry poured their cultural achievements into that little promontory of the vast Eurasian land mass Europe; in Europe the process has continued and is still increasing, being still supported by a many-sided mental development, religious, artistic, and, above all, intellectual. First one salient line of growth would lead, then another would overtake and all but strangle it, but the front was always moving, until Europe became the tiny heartland of the world's most powerful systematic thought, driven by success and steadied by its own reciprocal checks, spreading today over the whole small planet Earth.

Part VI

Mathematics and the Reign of Science

Foreword

THIS study of mind should culminate, of course, in a well-constructed epistemological and possibly even metaphysical theory, at least as firmly founded on other people's knowledge and hypotheses as any earlier parts of this essay which have been written in preparation for such a reflective conclusion. But the hindrances of age—especially increasing blindness—make it necessary to curtail the work at what should be its height, and contract the end into no more than a sketch of its presumptive final section. Further research is impossible when footnote print, photostat, or typewriting are unreadable, and normal fonts not much easier. So even the epistemological heading of the intended sixth part, with its promise of a theory of knowledge and truth, which was projected in the beginning of the book, has to give place to a more modest finale, dealing with the new intellectual standard, the concept of fact, and its impact on a human age which has but lately opened with the brilliant rise of mathematics—the age of mathematical physics, physico-chemistry, electro-physico-chemistry, electro-biochemistry, and whatever still may follow.

But even in its curtailed form, I hope my little concluding essay to end an Essay may serve what I consider the true purpose of the whole book: to suggest some ideas which other people may be able to use for their own work, anywhere and everywhere in the great domain of philosophical thought. Whatever may be wrong with it, all the dross that needs elimination notwithstanding, my fondest wish for it is that what is true or new in it may eventuate in a parade of projects for young thinkers with long ways to go.

24

The Open Ambient

I N WHAT today we deem the modern world, the evolution of man has come to be primarily the evolution of his brain, known by its incredible functional complex, the mind. Actually, his physical features are tending to reduction. His mouth and teeth have become small, especially in the most civilized populations, so the jaws of European people are very commonly too weak to support their thirty-two teeth, relatively small though they be, without unhealthy crowding: sometimes not the whole complement can erupt, and quite usually they are all pushed out of line for want of space and susceptible to early decay. His hands and feet are weak compared to those of primitive hunters and seafarers, not only from disuse in daily life but by hereditary regression. His stature is extremely variable; most mountaineers are tall, plains dwellers apparently more affected by diet than environment. Such purely physical functions as childbirth are less easily performed by highly civilized women than by most savages, especially nomads. Only one gain which might be considered physical (though I think it is not, having changed its motive source) is our longevity. One can still find anciently long-lived peoples in isolated deserts,[1] stocks whose heredity seems to endow them with as much as a couple of hundred years of life; where, however, that primitive asset is lost and not replaced by intellectual devices, individual lives (of those who survive infancy) may average less than thirty-five years.[2] That extreme

[1] Such tales come especially from the Levant and the Caucasus, where it is hard to get authentic figures; the alleged ages of Noah, Abraham, and other patriarchs fit the pattern, and may support the legend. For some modern reports see Norris McWhirter, "Longevity," in *Guinness Book of World Records*, 1981 ed., pp. 24–28, and the article by Lawrence Kaplan and Peter W. Frank under the entry "Life-Span" in the 1980 edition of the *New Encyclopaedia Britannica*.

[2] M. J. Meggitt, in *Desert People*, says of the Australian aborigines, the Walbiris, whom he studied in detail: "A man usually attains his highest social (as distinct from ritual) status between the ages of 40 and 55 years. . . . By the age of about 60, however, he is regarded as *bulga*, or *lailai*, 'grey-haired man,' a fate that no man I knew accepted with equanimity. . . . Very few attain 65 years, and a man who passes this age is in effect socially 'dead'—his physical death is not avenged and his corpse is not given the dignity of exposure on a tree-platform" (p. 235).

variability is characteristic of transitional phases in evolution.[3] But the transition henceforth is not so much to new somatic forms and functions as to new elaborations and powers of the brain.

These changes, physically unobservable as they have always been and still are, nevertheless have radical overt effects which produce stage after stage of our intellectual advance. The first step in the shift was almost certainly the rise and growth of speech, which I think has been sufficiently mooted, not only in this book but in a steady flow of writings since the first appearance of Ludwig Wittgenstein's *Tractatus Logico-philosophicus* in 1922. Of course there had been other philosophers, sometimes not professionally of that narrow stripe—mathematicians, grammarians, translators, and Bible scholars—who had been aware of the part which linguistic forms play in conceptualizing experience,[4] establishing memory, and recording the fictions of dream and free fantasy, expectation and fear; but the modern movement that found its philosophical spokesman in Wittgenstein had another broad intellectual base in what seems, at first sight, a distant, parallel advance of mental achievement. That great new phenomenon is physical science.

Civilization was well established in several parts of the world, and had even come and gone in some of them, yielding to new barbarian conquests and devastations, when a great, fresh, and immensely fertile concept emerged in the Greek cultural tradition: the concept of causality as a direct dyadic relation between two events, without any third term, such as an agent, to negotiate between the first event—the cause—and the second, the effect. The idea that anything could occur without an agent to will and start the movement was difficult for people everywhere who had always thought in terms of acts with immediate aims and covert intentional phases preceding their overt performances. Historically we meet the concept of causality scarcely before Aristotle, who lumped purposes, forms, materials, and motions together as so many kinds of "cause," and subscribed to the confusion of causality with agency to the extent of postulating a "prime mover" for every automatically continuous sequence of transmitted motion.

With the concept of causality as an impersonal relation between two events—Aristotle's "efficient cause"—came an equally innocent but all-important acceptance of such events as two simply given, knowable, impersonal "facts." It has taken learned, scientific thinkers extraor-

[3] Cf. above, Vol. II, p. 39 and n.
[4] The first philosopher of our day to take the whole problem of symbolism and its uses with due seriousness was Ernst Cassirer, whose three-volume *Philosophie der symbolischen Formen* appeared from 1923 to 1929.

dinarily long to realize that a fact of nature or of history is not a direct sensory datum, but a highly interesting cognitive construct. That Francis Bacon could adjure his contemporaries to "lay their notions by, and attend solely to the facts" is not surprising in view of the hard struggle in his days between the heresies of science and the glaringly anti-factual doctrines of the Church; but to find in our own day—that is, within the last fifty years—a similar superficiality in Henry Osborn Taylor's use of the term "fact" for any vague notion that may enter into human discourse and pass unquestioned[5] does suggest some obscure misgiving which prompted Taylor to treat that emerging idea as a product of fancy on a par with all other received assumptions instead of a harbinger of a new core of knowledge, setting up an explicit logical standard and stringent methodology, great with a radical change of attitude, intellectual ambition, and its own frustrating mistakes.

The concept of fact is the foundation of our natural science; and science is the wonder of our current evolutionary age. The meaning of "fact" is, therefore, a basic philosophical question, and as such has been mooted for the past half-century with varying results. That facts are conceived under the influence of language is generally recognized; that they determine the truth and falsity, respectively, of some kinds of proposition is also usually conceded. But when it comes to analyzing even quite ordinary and apparently clear statements to see what concepts have gone into their construction, what relations those concepts have to each other and to the facts which we see in their images, and especially what assumptions they imply or tacitly require, what conditions make a proposition as a whole true or false—there we are in the midst of the present-day labyrinth "logico-philosophicus."

Alfred Tarski has shown, I think, in "The Concept of Truth in Formalized Languages," that in any unformalized (i.e., "natural" or "ordinary") language no analysis is likely to reveal a set of unambiguous propositions which could be directly matched with a known set of facts constituting the actual world, so that the phrase "true proposition" could be defined as meaning an element in a logical, coherent system of verbal statements which could be correlated with a systematic array of facts composing the world or a determinable part of it. In concluding that thoughtful, authoritative essay, its author wrote: "In my opinion the considerations of § 1 prove emphatically that the concept of truth (as well

[5]In the preface to *Fact: The Romance of Mind* (1932), p. vii, Taylor writes: "Not meaning to be metaphysical, I hope to keep to the ordinary use of language. Current speech should be able to tell the tale of the sorts of things the human mind has accepted as facts and has fancied to be real or effective."

as other semantical concepts) when applied to colloquial language in conjunction with the normal laws of logic leads inevitably to confusions and contradictions. Whoever wishes, in spite of all difficulties, to pursue the semantics of colloquial language with the help of exact methods will be driven first to undertake the thankless task of a reform of this language. He will find it necessary to define its structure, to overcome the ambiguities of the terms which occur in it, and finally to split the language into a series of languages of greater and greater extent, each of which stands in the same relation to the next in which a formalized language stands to its metalanguage. It may, however, be doubted whether the language of everyday life, after being 'rationalized' in this way, would still preserve its naturalness and whether it would not rather take on the characteristic features of the formalized languages."[6]

Despite this discouraging prognosis, with its very real ring of truth, semanticists today are still hoping and trying to narrow down the principles of ordinary discourse to scientific precision and fixity. They are evidently convinced that conceptual clarity and especially permanence of word meanings are inherent in correctly used language and that the logic of empirical science must underlie such correct usage; that consequently it is possible to describe the actual world systematically in scientific terms culled from ordinary language. Yet all attempts to do so founder in the depths of more and more sophisticated linguistics. Whole books (largely, today, collections of articles) and the most serious philosophical journals are filled with theories that end in a despairing resort to behaviorism (as Wittgenstein himself did) or metaphysical questions which do not find metaphysical or scientific solutions but only more and more elaborate linguistic sidetracks.[7] The most ambitious of these word studies and perhaps the most consistently pursuant of its theme, is a heavy tome (made needlessly unreadable by an almost fantastic overuse of clusters of initials in place of phrases) entitled *Arc Pair Grammar* (1980), in which two authors, David E. Johnson and Paul M. Postal, offer apparently inexhaustible analyses and reformulations of sentences that purport to be "ordinary language," and to end with exact definitions of words as they occur in natural speech, even extending over several languages. One thing their system makes clear is that the words of our everyday social

[6]*Logic, Semantics, Metamathematics* (1956), p. 267.
[7]This holds, I think, for Noam Chomsky's *Aspects of Theory of Syntax* (1965) and *Essays on Form and Interpretation* (1972); for Norman Malcolm's *Thought and Knowledge* (1977); Saul A. Kripke's *Naming and Necessity* (1980); Donald Davidson's "True to the Facts" (1969); Keith Halbasch's "A Critical Examination of Russell's View of Facts" (1971); and a score, at least, of other fairly recent writings.

intercourse have no inherent tendency to pinpoint exact literal meanings, and to be afterwards applied metaphorically in other situations. On the contrary (as several scholars, notably Owen Barfield,[8] pointed out long ago), the original intentions of words seem to have been diffuse, following their informal, widening extensions wherever variants and even quite unintended metaphors were required to carry the key idea further afield. The 714 pages of text and diagrams (disregarding indexes and other adjuncts) in *Arc Pair Grammar* present some two hundred definitions, yet the reader is left with an uncertain feeling that not everything has been defined, that at any turn he might encounter new elusive assumptions which no available operation will automatically derive from a reasonably small number of "primitive ideas" and establish in the system. The authors deduce about a hundred theorems and claim that these, together with axioms occasionally introduced *sub rosa*, state the basic "laws of language"; yet it is hard to imagine that in the fields of intellectual activity where the precise meanings of words play their most important roles, e.g., in jurisprudence, the "science" proffered as "Arc Pair Grammar" might be resorted to as an instrument to check apparent ambiguities in juridical statements.

To formalize any observed relationship, especially in biology, one has to start from natural phenomena that show a distinct tendency to exhibit the hypothetical functional pattern and, upon more precise statement, to reveal further and further instances of that pattern in the empirical realm which yields their factual material. Growth, metabolism, procreation, in plants some highly special developments, as, for instance, for seed dispersal, in higher animals voluntary movement, are such phenomena. But upon closer acquaintance with language, which is a biological function, though peculiar to the single primate genus *Homo*, one finds no tendency of words in "ordinary" use to approach single, exact meanings; technical uses are consciously established and as soon as they are assimilated to colloquial speech they lose their precision and may even change their literal meaning, as non-technical words do. "Edify" no longer means to erect an edifice, nor does "lady" today mean "giver."

Yet words do organize our thinking around centered conceptual symbols, however vague those central images or other carriers of meaning may be, and define a context in which that core of meaning is embedded; it is the contexts which are not at all a logician's ideal. Each word, according to its grammatical form and syntactical position, immediately

---

[8]*Poetic Diction*, subtitled *A Study in Meaning* (1973; 1st ed., 1928). Cf. above, Vol. I, pp. 239 ff.

determines its own transitory context (this characteristic of language—possibly of all language—may be the allegedly universal trait on which the authors of *Arc Pair Grammar* rest their claim to have achieved an analysis of language *per se*). But the many implicitly assumed conditions that give sense to our conversational exchanges do not necessarily fit together to form a single and coherent background of verbal rules or verbally established facts, which might be expected to verify our true contingent propositions. They tend rather to make large and small islands of interrelated notions, each one a limited but logically organized context for a phrase or grammatical variant of a key word. Our thinking is adapted to this constant shift of ambient ideas. It is one of the essential powers of language to negotiate the turns of that mental kaleidoscope, though we are not aware of it. Language has so many functions in the shaping of mind out of the most intense, felt processes of lower animal brains that it goes no further in the perfection of any activity than the impulse reaches before most of its potential elaborations have been eclipsed, their energies entrained by other, overtaking impulses and distributed, perhaps to many parts of the brain, perhaps to restricted but complicated areas.

Where, then, do we get the abstract ideas on which we have modeled our standard of abstractness? There seems to be no particular cerebral locus for such thought-processing. But suppose areas, centers, regions, are not the whole or even most important seats of our concentrated mental activities; suppose some phenomena take shape between the stations where we have found them most ready to be elicited or, if they are in action, to be interrupted. It is possible (I would propose no more) that the abstraction of pure concepts occurs in the shifts from one island of orientation to another, from one mental focus to another, from the nimbus of one part of speech to another.[9] Such a transitional consummation is not altogether unknown in physiological acts; consider some of the observations cited above[10] on birds and beasts with eyes placed far apart and quite laterally on the head, so that even with a large field of vision in each eye they always have two views of their surroundings at once, which they seem to unite into one image by looking at an arresting object with alternately lifted and lowered, perhaps slightly rolled head, or with one eye after the other. Somewhat similarly, the play of conceptions instigated and kept going by words with rapid, shimmering changes of pe-

[9] Kurt Struntz, in an interesting article, "Zur Grundlegung der Psychologie des mathematischen Sinnverständnisses" (1940), remarks that in the use of a word in two different senses there is a phase in which the meaning jumps from one context to the other—"[wo] das Sinnerlebnis von der einen Bedeutung auf die andere überspringt" (p. 322).
[10] See Vol. II, pp. 221–23.

ripheral relations may precipitate a central concept common to all the grammatical variants of a verb or other highly inflected part of speech and make it stand more and more *in abstracto.*[11]

Yet "ordinary language" shows no steady tendency to impose a coherent pattern on the world of facts which it constantly creates for us. Even hundreds of definitions cannot satisfy a strict thinker if the definitions themselves bring him back to the ordinary language again. It takes something else than the transient agreements of our spontaneous discourse to work out ideas that are ready to be built into the great intellectual system of present-day physics, which has enabled men to fly in their machines to the moon, disembark on its lifeless, waterless, airless surface, and return to earth.

The spectacular success of the physical sciences has made them the models of exact thought. It is the most natural thing in the world that philosophers, seeking to think with the same exactitude about problems of mind and its functions as physicists about material processes, should first of all try to imitate their scientific colleagues; and in view of the role which language has played in our *Menschwerdung*, that words should be their first units. But the most searching linguistic studies give us no elements comparable to the things scientists talk about—atoms, molecules, or measures of energy in other forms. Words are incorrigible weasels; meanings of words cannot be held to paper with the ink. The abstraction of pure concepts may occur under stringent controls of technical terms, but the inveterate tendency of even such terms to become assimilated to common parlance and share the ways of "ordinary language" leads one to wonder whether the great frame of science can possibly be made of word-borne thought.

The formulation of "fact" may stem from language, but "science" in the modern sense does not. Its foundation is a younger achievement, though its beginnings may go back into the earliest ages of man—go back through eons of existence without realizing their potential. The instrument of scientific thought is mathematics, and the evolution of such thought had to wait for the development of concepts of number at least far enough to reach two essential functions: enumerating and calculating.

Enumerating—counting—probably came first, but even that has been very late compared to the humanizing work of language. Until quite

[11]Unhappily, for reasons mentioned in the Foreword to this part of the book, I cannot read all of the difficult, photostated typescript text of *Arc Pair Grammar*; but if I am expounding here some of its authors' ideas, priority of course belongs to them and my arriving at similar conclusions entirely independently should only assure them of their success.

recently, and perhaps to this day, there have been people who had not more specific numerals than "one," "two," and "many," the last of these meaning "more than two," but sometimes even including the dual case;[12] Greek, which was a high language in ancient times, has a special grammatical dual form which, still more anciently, may have been its only plural.

Mathematics, though generally treated as part of the gift of speech, on closer examination appears to have had a separate origin and prehistory; numbers and words have different primitive characteristics. In the first place, while words have always tended to broaden the use of language by their penchant for metaphorical extensions of meaning, numbers have no such tendency. They may have mystical associations—numerology, astrology, and all sorts of superstitious uses—but with exception of the prime mystery that One may be Three, numbers generally keep their literal meanings. Instances of "three," "four," "seven," and the fearful "thirteen" express the same numerosity in arithmetic as in tea-leaf reading, in counting as in magic-mongering.

Yet counting, which seems simple to us, has really been one of the difficult problems of abstraction and presentation, for it has required a shift from essentially physical consummations to symbolic ones in the human brain. Its elements—similar conceptual units following each other in a series—are almost certainly first presented by the visual and kinesthetic perception of our own bipedal steps, under control of old cerebral mechanisms. Their expression belongs to the legs and feet, whose functions are among the least intellectual of our voluntary behavioral acts.

Those same physical units, however, created bodily rhythms that entrained the whole musculature of a person's trunk and limbs, and broke up spontaneously into divisions within the steps even while, as wholes, they formed passages of movement often culminating in leaps or violent gestures. That created the Dance. The effect of this communal art was certainly enhanced by another motive, perhaps older (there is no telling),[13] that was emphasized by the formed bodily movement: the corresponding mobility of the visual ambient. The Dance, above all else, animated the dancer's world at the command of his own voluntary move-

---

[12]The Reverend P. Wilhelm Schmidt wrote, in the *Encyclopaedia Britannica*, 14th ed., under the entry "Numeral Systems": "There is no language without some numerals; the notion of unity and plurality is expressed at least in the formation of 'one' and 'two,' though 'two' is often equal to 'much,' thus concluding a numeration that has just only started."

[13]Cf. the theory of dance and its discussion in *Feeling and Form*, Chaps. 11 and 12.

ments, and must have been a magical activity from its beginning. All this seems, on the face of it, to have had nothing to do with mathematics, but it established the reality of the whole realm of distinct, self-identical units on which that recently emergent technique is based.[14]

The emotions of uncivilized people are stormier and harder to bear than those found in more sophisticated society. From earliest times they must have required the forceful imposition of formal expression which dancing provides in all situations of tribal excitement. The elaborations of steps went on to high degrees before anyone thought about the exactitude of their divisions; fractions were danced for thousands of years without awareness of their relations to single (or, more often, dual) steps. As pure dance elements they might never have led even to the art of counting. A fair example of the difficulty of counting without a convenient sequence of numerals, and especially without any plan for the formation of further segments of the number series, is strikingly illustrated in a report on some late-discovered tribes in the mountainous interior of New Guinea, where an awkward, limited method—used only in special need—allowed people to count up to 44;[15] but it did not implement or even suggest any operations. The method consisted in touching a succession of points on the body, which (as in most savage tongues) had names, for counters (Fig. 24–1). The number of men in a dancing group or of pigs for a feast might, accordingly, be "right shoulder."

More fertile ideas of relations among numbers seem to have arisen only where people counted on the fingers of both hands, the names of the fingers providing names which became names for the numbers themselves from 1 to 9, with the "empty" symbol o to mark the turn beginning a second, third, −nth round of counts.[16] The convenience of that meth-

[14]The recency of higher mathematics is attested by the actual dates of introduction of concepts and techniques which have developed that almost explosively opened field. There was a fairly long period of preparation, from the Ionian Greeks to the sixteenth century, and from then on a crowding succession of great mathematical thinkers—Copernicus, Galileo, Kepler, Newton, Leibniz, the Bernoullis, Laplace, Euler, Gauss, with some equally great names filling spaces between. A more complete list (from which this was extracted) may be found in H. W. Turnbull, "The Great Mathematicians," in James R. Newman, ed., *The World of Mathematics*, Vol. I (1956), p. 78.

[15] Hermann Strauss, *Die Mi-Kultur der Hagenberg-Stämme in Östlichen Zentral-Neuguinea*, fig. 1 and accompanying text.

[16]Philip E. B. Jourdain, in his little book *The Nature of Mathematics* (anthologized *in toto* by Newman in *The World of Mathematics*), wrote: "by means of the local value attached to nine symbols and a symbol for zero, any number in the decimal scale of notation can be expressed. It is important to realize that the long and strenuous work of the most gifted minds was necessary to provide us with simple and expressive notation which, in nearly all parts of mathematics, enables even the less gifted of us to reproduce theorems which needed the greatest genius to discover" (Vol. I, p. 13).

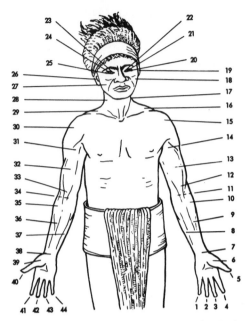

Figure 24–1. Counting-Points on the Body
*in the mountainous interior of New Guinea . . . an awkward, limited
method—used only in special need—allowed people to count up to 44. . . .
The method consisted of touching a succession of points on the body.*
(From Herman Strauss, *Die Mi-Kultur der Hagenberg-Stamme im Ostlichen Zentral-Neuguinea*
[Hamburg: Kommisionsverlag Cram, Degruyter and Co., 1962].)

1. *kali*
2. *labo*
3. *repo*
4. *mala*
5. *tshu*
6. *tshu menti* (saddle)
7. *kerepo* (pulse)
8. *palacki* (sinews)
9. *noe* (tendon)
10. *noe menti* (muscle)
11. *koma* (elbow)
12. *wineropa* (upper tendon)
13. *aliropa* (muscle)
14. *paea* (upper tendon)
15. *kuli*
16. *ma*

17. *noim* (neck)
18. *jacka* (cheek)
19. *pae* (ear)
20. *le packi* (outer corner of eye)
21. *le* (eye)
22. *le packi menti* (inner corner of eye)
23. *mendae le packi menti* (other side, inner corner of eye)
24. *mendane le* (other side, eye)
25. *mendane le packi*
26. *mendane pae*
27. *mendane jacka*
28. *mendane noim*

29. *mendane ma*
30. *mendane kuli*
31. *mendane aliropa*
32. *mendane aliropa*
33. *mendane wineropa*
34. *mendane koma*
35. *mendane noe menti*
36. *mendane noe*
37. *mendane palacki*
38. *mendane herepo*
39. *mendane tshu menti*
40. *mendane tshu*
41. *mendane mala*
42. *mendane repo*
43. *mendane labo*
44. *mendane kali*

od is obvious; a person always had his abacus with him. The basic duality was furnished by the fact that he combined the pentad patterns of two hands to make his decade, but employed new numerals for the second set instead of composites such as $5 + 2$, $10 - 1$, yet the patterns still were not too large to be seen at a glance; so a simple sort of addition and subtraction, and multiplication of rounds in repetition, were visibly suggested. [17]

Perhaps there was another natural advantage in finger-counting, which is not directly visible: namely, that it involved the most trainable and responsive appendages of the body, the hands; one might even say the most educated, for their skill is based on a highly developed sensitivity to feel their own positions and contacts and to judge, without words, of the extraneous surfaces they touch. Such articulate feeling bespeaks a high specialization of cerebral acts somewhere in hand-controlling "centers" or "areas," and makes those locations good candidates for an intellectual function, which might arise and grow to quite a high form without drawing in the other main source of intellect, the original humanizing apparatus of speech.

A really crucial advance in evolution is apt to be complex, and therefore long-prepared before several lines of successive changes meet at an apparently casual, incidental juncture and start a major development. Some traits of future value may have entered a gathering mainstream and been mingled with its swelling progression early in its formation, without showing themselves for biological eons. Gradually, in the differentiating brain, points of high activity find expression in specialized overt acts which influence the bodily parts employed in their performance, from large movements to smallest details of independent muscular reactions, involuntary or semi-voluntary reflexes like those of the eyelid, protective overgrowths like our fingernails.

This aspect of protoplasmic response to stimuli is a well-known source of articulation, to which D'Arcy Thompson called attention early in the present century; [18] but its influence on the forms of organisms goes further than even that great functionally oriented anatomist saw. It is probably the cause of the apparent tendency to duality in the vertebrate frame and

---

[17]Reverend Schmidt, still under the entry "Numeral Systems" in the *Encyclopaedia Britannica*, wrote: "The pure decimal system seems to have originated in the culture-cycle of the nomadic herders, who, in counting their large flocks of horses, cows, camels, sheep, etc., needed to employ high numbers with more facility. From the aristocracies of the nomadic herders it has spread everywhere, and it is now found in all nations of high culture on the whole globe, except those of Mexico and Central America, where the number 20 was used in astronomy, and thus was safe from competition."

[18]See above, Vol. I, Chapters 6 and 7, *passim*, for extensive references to his work *On Growth and Form* (1917).

of the various forms of symmetry in lower organisms. The relation of shape to the increase of vital functions is a matter of conditions offered for the upkeep of growth in a total being while the differentiating influences are acting on and in it. Its need of a constant stabilizing process is met first of all by the persistent metabolic changes carrying on its life; but the specialized forms of organs or appendages may need more than the self-propagating activity of the matrix *per se*.

This consideration throws some light on the obviously differential survival of organisms with and without bilateral symmetry, and on the evolutionary strength of the former to develop the most complex specializations. Paired anatomical forms immediately present a new potential source of energy, for they grow from their embryonic *Anlagen* under competitive conditions. Each cerebral hemisphere harbors its own neural mechanisms, usually for control of the contralateral side; this brings about a functional duality which tends to be unevenly developed,[19] so its own inherent potentialities drive each member to assert itself against its counterpart until their progressively heightened trophic responses lead to a more and more articulate structure, through their need of perpetually retrieving their formal balance.[20]

Obviously, the parts of a symmetrically structured creature which are most affected by such mutual stimulation are the limbs; and in a biped the hands and feet are developed from time immemorial under the influences of different functions. The brain centers closest to the ones which are directly involved in speech, and therewith in conceptual acts, are those activating and controlling the hands (the tendency of many people to gesticulate when they talk supports that widely held hypothesis); the feet, represented furthest away, seem to be less connected with the symbolic powers of mind.

Yet it is the step—that specialty of our two-footed stance and gait—that becomes all-important in some very elementary acts, walking and dancing. The equal pace of the human walk and its elaboration in festive dance provide some elements of pronounced bodily rhythm which have their own ways of breaking up internally, without losing their unity as whole elements. Only, because dance rhythms are too spontaneous, too quickly and fully consummated in action, they are not likely to enter into

[19]For an empirical study corroborating this general statement, see A. J. Berger's article, "Anatomical Variation and Avian Anatomy" (1956), on the great variability of structures even in two sides of one animal.

[20]Perhaps Aristotle's "formal cause" had a causal function after all.

[214]

non-physical complexes and support any intellectual functions. If such basic patterns as the step—walking or dancing—were to be entrained by higher cerebral processes, something would have to effect a shift from footwork to a more versatile neuromuscular system which could entrain the precise, elaborate rhythms of the dance in a new activity.

Now, there is just such a versatile system in our physiological makeup; it culminates in the expressive powers of the human hand, and the instrument which brought it into the center of communal life was the Drum.

I do not know whether there are any people who have not invented a drum or caught the idea from someone else and made it their own. Drumming, like dancing, is so ancient that drums of all shapes and sounds and uses are traditional in the deepest jungle and wildest mountains where some human beings have always lived. The drum abstracts the form of the dance and holds it when otherwise it might become frenzied; beats assert their character as a framework more forcefully than movements or voices. Above all, the early and apparently universal use of the drum drew the human hand into the techniques of its expression.

When a favored part such as the human hand reaches a high degree of competence for its normal employment its cybernetic system may acquire new potentialities,[21] which invite shifts of action from other brain centers to its refined and ready ones with their superior distribution of energy. This is likely to have happened wherever a dawning intellect felt the impulse to use the fingers as counters, and soon discovered the many ways they could be used to advantage over other means. In such progressive societies the fingers of men and women were skilled and sensitive (Fig. 24–2), so their innervation, clear back to its origin in the brain, must have been ahead of most of the physical organism and made the whole hand complex a dominant structure. The walking step may have furnished the first sense of equally spaced similar units, and the dance imposed its elaborations on them, but it was very probably the drum, activated by the hands, that clinched the evolutionary shift (Fig. 24–3), already prepared in several ways—the decimal systems born of finger-counting, which, despite their varying details (lifting or flexing the fingers, starting with thumb or little finger, left or right, etc.), embody the same algorithmic principle of naming ten numerals (i.e., o through 9)

---

[21]P. B. Medawar, in *The Uniqueness of the Individual* (1961), wrote: "The genetical mechanism is such that there are deep resources of hidden variation, of possible animals only awaiting the occasion to become real."

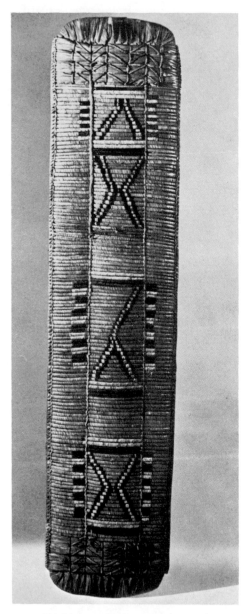

Figure 24–2. Shield from Karkar Island, North New Guinea
the fingers of men and women were skilled and sensitive
(From Tibor Bodrogi, *Oceanic Art* [Budapest: Athenaeum Printing House, 1959].)

Figure 24–3. Drummers
the walking step may have furnished the first sense of equally spaced similar units . . . but it was very probably the drum, activated by the hands, that clinched the evolutionary shift

(From Eudald Serra and Alberto Folch, *The Art of Papua and New Guinea* [New York: Rizzoli, 1977].)

and composing all higher numerosities out of these in a simple order of positions,[22] rendered in oral communication by a few verbal devices, e.g., suffixes like -teen, -ty, or prefixes made of large figures which had

[22]In a passage anthologized by Newman without exact reference, one writer says: "In the Muralog Islands, in the western part of Torres Strait, . . . Beginning with the little finger of the left hand, the natives counted up to 5 in the usual manner, and then, . . . they expressed the numbers from 6 to 10 by touching and naming successively the left wrist, the left elbow, left shoulder, left breast, left sternum. Then the numbers from 11 to 19 were indicated by the use, in inverse order, of the corresponding portions of the right side, . . . (*The World of Mathematics*, Vol. 1, p. 440, titled "Counting").

long acquired names—"one hundred," "two thousand"—with the simple connective "and": "four thousand, one hundred and twenty-three," for example.

The invention of a method of designating large and small numbers with equal ease marks the confluence of two great streams of mental evolution, language and number sense. It is hard to realize how long a non-linguistic talent which is really not at all rare can lie fallow in human beings, only to spring into meteoric career in a few centuries when the right forms of expression are found. The basic operations (excepting for a long time the most difficult, division[23]) emerged as of themselves from the practical uses of number concepts once they were drawn into the frame of a formal language. It has always remained a formal language, but of inestimable power for its purposes.

We feel that power today as an overwhelming force—physical science. It has risen on the foundation built up tier on tier by the outpourings of mathematical thought, like ever-recurrent lava flows from fires in the earth. The changes wrought in practical life have affected the average person remarkably little, because past conditions are quickly forgotten in struggles to estimate and exploit what is new; but the head-on clashes of old faiths and new scientific and (especially) pseudoscientific persuasions are more often fateful encounters. Some mathematicians themselves have tried to reject the knowledge that most physical observations present us with ineluctable facts, mundane and cosmic, and that these facts are expressible in equations from which other presumptive facts, with exact future dates and pinpointed locations, are calculable. They have based their objections on ideal grounds, such as that a material interpretation debased the noblest and purest product of human thought, which should have no application to practical aims;[24] but most of the great creative logico-mathematical thinkers today even try to justify their life work by claiming its scientific uses and empirical results.[25]

So great a stride in the evolution of man cannot fail to throw his whole ambient, social and physical, into convulsion and cause world-wide

---

[23]D. E. Smith and J. Ginsburg, in their essay in the same volume of Newman's anthology, say: "Division was rarely used in ancient times except where the divisor was very small. . . . On the abacus it was often done by subtraction" ("From Numbers to Numerals and from Numerals to Computation," p. 461).

[24]One of the strongest presentations, and surely the most romantic of this attitude is an early essay by Bertrand Russell, "The Study of Mathematics" (1907).

[25]John von Neumann has not only championed the view that mathematics began with empiric observation, but also expressed a belief that "as a mathematical discipline travels far from its empirical source, [it] is in danger of degeneration." (See Newman, Vol. IV, titled "The Mathematician.")

waves of emotional conflict to build up in every society, savage, barbaric or civilized. We live in a precipitous, heady transitional age, the Age of Science. Transitional—from a past whose image itself is changing under the influence of that very transformation which is triggering the new mentality, to a future (if our use of Science does not abrogate the further life of man on earth) as unpredictable today as were the towers and tunnels of New York when the first self-propelled organisms crawled out of the ocean for little sojourns on its brineless edges.

It will surely take long and different ages to retrieve the moral and mental balance mankind itself has blasted in the last three or four centuries (to start only with the time of terrifying acceleration), and there is no way of guessing whether or how we shall retrieve it, because that newest of natural phenomena—Mind—still faces the mystery of all things young, the secret of vital potentiality.

Bibliography

ADAM, LEONHARD. "Recht im Werden," in *Custom Is King*. Edited by L. H. D. Buxton. London: Hutchinson's Scientific and Technical Publications, 1936, pp. 217–36.

ADKINS, A. W. H. *Merit and Responsibility*. Oxford: Clarendon Press, 1960.

AGINSKY, B. W. "The Socio-Psychological Significance of Death among the Pomo Indians," *American Imago*, I (1940), 1–11.

ALI, AHMED. *Historical Aspects of Town Planning in Pakistan and India*. Karachi: Al-Ata Foundation, 1971.

ASCHOFF, JÜRGEN, ED. *Circadian Clocks*. Amsterdam: North-Holland, 1965.

BAKER, T. S., ED. *The Urbanization of Man: A Social Science Perspective*. Berkeley, Calif.: McCutchan Publishing Corporation, 1972.

BALIKCI, ASEN. "Shamanistic Behavior among the Netsilik Eskimos," in *Magic, Witchcraft, and Curing*. Edited by J. Middleton. Garden City, N.Y.: History Press, 1967, pp. 191–209. Reprinted from *Southwestern Journal of Anthropology*, XIX (1963), 380–96.

BARFIELD, OWEN. *Poetic Diction: A Study in Meaning*. Orig. pub., 1928. New York: Columbia University Press, 1973.

BEALS, CARLETON. *Nomads and Empire Builders: Native Peoples and Cultures of South America*. Philadelphia: Chilton Company, 1961.

BERGER, A. J. "Anatomical Variation and Avian Anatomy," *The Condor*, LVII (1956), 433–41.

BJERRE, JENS. *The Last Cannibals*. Translated by Estrid Bannister. New York: William Morrow and Company, 1957.

BOAS, FRANZ. *The Central Eskimo*. Lincoln: University of Nebraska Press, 1964. Orig. pub. in U.S., Bureau of American Ethnology, *Sixth Annual Report*, 1884–85. Washington, D.C.: Bureau of American Ethnology, 1888.

BOHANNAN, LAURA, AND BOHANNAN, PAUL. *The Tiv of Central Nigeria*. London: International African Institute, 1953.

BRAM, J. *An Analysis of Inca Militarism*. Monographs of the American Ethnological Society, IV. Seattle: University of Washington Press, 1966.

BRINTON, D. *The Myths of the New World, A Treatise on the Symbolism and Mythology of the Red Race of America*. Philadelphia: D. McKay, 1896.

BRØGGER, A. W., AND SHETELIG, HAAKON. *The Viking Ships: Their Ancestry and Evolution*. Los Angeles: Knud K. Mogensen, 1951.

BRUNDAGE, BURR CARTWRIGHT. *Empire of the Inca*. Norman: University of Oklahoma Press, 1963.

BUDDENBROCK, W. VON. *Vergleichende Physiologie*. Vol. I: *Sinnesphysiologie*. Basel: Verlag Birkhaüser, 1952.

CAILLIET, ÉMILE. *Symbolisme et âmes primitives*. Paris: Boivin, 1936.

CANNON, WALTER B. "'Voodoo' Death," *American Anthropologist*, XLIV (1942), 169–81.

CARPENTER, EDMUND, VARLEY, FREDERICK, AND FLAHERTY, ROBERT. *Eskimo*. Toronto: University of Toronto Press, 1959.

CASSIRER, ERNST. *Die Philosophie der symbolischen Formen*. 3 vols. Berlin: Bruno Cassirer, 1923–29.

CAZENEUVE, JEAN. *Sociologie du rite*. Paris: Presses Universitaires de France, 1971.

CHAGNON, NAPOLEON. *Yąnomamö: The Fierce People*. New York: Holt, Rinehart and Winston, 1968.

CHAI, C., AND CHAI, W., EDS. AND TRANS. *The Sacred Books of Confucius and Other Confucian Classics*. New Hyde Park, N.Y.: University Books, 1965.

CHANG, K. C. *Early Chinese Civilization: Anthropological Perspectives*. Cambridge, Mass.: Harvard University Press, 1976.

CHOMSKY, NOAM. *Aspects of the Theory of Syntax*. Cambridge, Mass.: M.I.T. Press, 1965.

———. *Essays on Form and Interpretation*. New York: North-Holland, 1977.

CHRISTENSON, J. A., JR. "Personality Dynamics in Hypnotic Induction," *Personality*, I (1951), 222–30.

COLERIDGE, SAMUEL TAYLOR. *Biographia Literaria*. Orig. pub., 1817. London: Leavitt, Lord, 1834.

Columbia Encyclopedia. "Circumcision." New York: Columbia University Press, 1947.

COMFORT, ALEX. "Biological Aspects of Senescence," *Biological Reviews of the Cambridge Philosophical Society*, XXIX (1954), 284–329.

CONANT, LEVI LEONARD. "Counting," in *The World of Mathematics*, Vol. I. Edited by James R. Newman. New York: Simon and Schuster, 1956.

CURTIS, NATALIE. *The Indians' Book*. New York: Harper and Brothers, 1907.

CUSINIER, JEANNE. *Sumangat: L'âme et son cult en Indochine et Indonésie*. Paris: Gallimard, 1951.

DART, RAYMOND. "Cultural Status of the South African Man-Apes," in *Smithsonian Institution Annual Report*, 1955. Washington, D.C.: Government Printing Office, 1956, pp. 317–38.

DAVID-NEEL, ALEXANDRA. *Magic and Mystery in Tibet*. New York: Crown, 1937.

DAVIDSON, DONALD. "True to the Facts," *Journal of Philosophy*, LXVI (1969), 748–64.

DAVIDSON, H. R. E. *The Viking Road to Byzantium*. London: George Allen and Unwin, 1976.

DAWKINS, R. M. "Greeks and Northmen," in *Custom Is King*. Edited by L. H. D. Buxton. London: Hutchinson's Scientific and Technical Publications, 1936, pp. 35–47.

DAWSON, W. R. "Mummification in Australia and in America," *Journal of the Royal Anthropological Institute*, LVII (1928), 115–37.

Bibliography

DE VAUX, ROLAND. *Studies in Old Testament Sacrifice*. Cardiff: University of Wales Press, 1964.

DEWEY, JOHN. *Experience and Nature*. Chicago: Open Court, 1925.

DIXON, ROLAND. *Oceanic Mythology*. In *The Mythology of All Races*, Vol. IX. Edited by L. H. Gray. Boston: Marshall Jones, 1916.

DOUGLAS, MARY. *Natural Symbols: Explorations in Cosmology*. New York: Pantheon Books, 1970.

DURKHEIM, ÉMILE, AND MAUSS, MARCEL. "De quelques formes primitives de classification," *L'Année sociologique*, VI (1901–2), 1–72.

EBERHARD, WOLFRAM. "Data on the Structure of the Chinese City in the Pre-Industrial Period," *Economic Development and Cultural Change*, IV (1956), 253–68.

ECKHARDT, C. D. "The Influence of the Church on Medieval Culture," in *The Urbanization of Man: A Social Science Perspective*. Edited by T. S. Baker. Berkeley, Calif.: McCutchan Publishing Corporation, 1972.

EDINGER, TILLY. "Paleoneurology versus Comparative Brain Anatomy," *Confinia Neurologia*, IV (1949), 5–24.

————. "The Pituitary Body in Giant Animals Fossil and Living: A Survey and a Suggestion," *Quarterly Review of Biology*, XVII (1942), 31–45.

EIBL-EIBESFELDT, IRENÄUS. "Angeborenes und Erworbenes im Verhalten einiger Säuger," *Zeitschrift für Tierpsychologie*, XX (1963), 705–54.

ELIADE, MIRCEA. "Remarques sur le 'Rope Trick,'" in *Culture in History*. Edited by S. Diamond. New York: Columbia University Press, 1960, pp. 541–51.

ELKIN, A. P. *Aboriginal Men of High Degree*. John Murtagh Macrossan Memorial Lecture. Sydney: Australian Publishing Company, n.d. [1945].

Encyclopaedia Britannica, 14th ed., "Fatalism."

ENDICOTT, K. M. *An Analysis of Malay Magic*. Oxford: Clarendon Press, 1970.

ENNEN, EDITH. *Frühgeschichte der europäischen Stadt*. Bonn: Ludwig Rohrscheid Verlag, 1953.

ESSERTIER, DANIEL. *Les formes inférieures de l'explication*. Paris: Alcan, 1927.

FAURÉ-FREMIET, PHILIPPE. *La re-création du réel et l'équivoque*. Paris: Alcan, 1940.

FIELDING, WILLIAM J. *Strange Superstitions and Magical Practices*. Philadelphia: Blakiston, 1945.

FISCHER, HANS. *Watut. Notizen zur Kultur eines Melanesier-Stammes in Nordost-Neuguinea*. Kulturgeschichtliche Forschungen, X. Brunswick: Albert Limbach Verlag, 1963.

FORSTER, F. M., BORKOWSKI, W. J., AND McCARTER, R. N. "Depression of the Cerebral Cortex Induced by Applications of Acetylcholine," *Federation Proceedings*, V (1946), 28–29.

FORTUNE, R. F. *Manus Religion*. Philadelphia: American Philosophical Society, 1935.

————. *Sorcerers of Dobu: The Social Anthropology of the Dobu Islanders of the Western Pacific*. New York: E. P. Dutton, 1932.

FREUD, SIGMUND. *The Interpretation of Dreams*. Orig. pub., 1900. Translated by A. A. Brill from *Die Traumdeutung*, 3d ed., 1928. London: G. Allen and Unwin, 1913.

_____. *The Psychopathology of Everyday Life.* Orig. pub., 1901. Translated by A. A. Brill from *Zur Psychopathologie des Alltagslebens.* London: E. Benn, 1935.

_____. *Totem and Taboo.* Orig. pub., 1912–13. Translated by A. A. Brill from "Über einige Übereinstimmungen im Seelenleben der Wilden und der Neurotiker." New York: New Republic, 1931.

FROBENIUS, L. *The Childhood of Man.* Orig. pub., 1901. Translated by A. H. Keane from *Aus den Flegeljahren der Menscheit.* London: Seeley and Company, 1909.

FÜHRER-HAIMENDORF, CHRISTOPH VON. "Zur Religion einiger hinterindischer Bergsvölker," in *Custom Is King.* Edited by L. H. D. Buxton. London: Hutchinson's Scientific and Technical Publications, 1936, pp. 273–87.

GARNOT, J. S. F. "Les fonctions, les pouvoirs et la nature du nom propre dans l'ancienne Egypte d'après les textes des pyramides," *Journal de psychologie normale et pathologique,* XLI (1948), 463–73.

GEHLEN, ARNOLD. "Uber die Verstehbarkeit der Magie," in *Studien zur Anthropologie und Soziologie, Soziologische Texte,* Vol. XVII. Berlin: Luchterhand, 1963, pp. 79–92.

GERSH, HARRY. *The Sacred Books of the Jews.* New York: Stein and Day, 1968.

GIBSON, J. J. *The Perception of the Visual World.* Boston: Houghton Mifflin, 1950.

GIRARD, RENÉ. *La violence et le sacre.* Paris: Bernard Grasset, 1972.

GLOTZ, GUSTAVE. *La solidarité de la famille dans le droit criminel de la Grèce.* Paris: A. Fontemoing, 1904.

GOTTSCHICK, J. "Entwicklung und Leistungsfähigkeit des Menschenhirns während der Menscheitsgeschichte," *Der Nervenarzt,* XXVI (1955), 271–75.

GREENE, W. C. *Moira: Fate, Good and Evil in Greek Thought.* Cambridge, Mass.: Harvard University Press, 1944.

HAEZRAHI, PEPITA. *The Price of Morality.* London: George Allen and Unwin, 1961.

HALBASCH, KEITH. "A Critical Examination of Russell's View of Facts," *Noûs,* V (1971), 395–409.

HAMMERSCHLAG, H. E. *Hypnose und Verbrechen: Ein Beitrag zur Phänomenologie der Suggestion und der Hypnose.* Munich: E. Reinhardt, 1954.

HANKS, JANE R. "Reflections on the Ontology of Rice," in *Culture in History.* Edited by S. Diamond. New York: Columbia University Press, 1960, pp. 298–301.

HASLUCK, F. W. "Depopulation in the Aegean Islands," in *The Emergence of Civilization: The Cyclades and the Aegean in the Third Millennium B.C.* Edited by Colin Renfrew. London: Methuen, 1972.

HENRY, ALEXANDER, AND THOMPSON, DAVID. "New Light on the Early History of the Greater Northwest," in *Primitive Heritage: An Anthropological Anthology.* Edited by Margaret Mead and Nicholas Calas. New York: Ran-

Bibliography

dom House, 1953. Originally published as *New Light on the Early History of the Greater Northwest*. New York: F. P. Harper, 1897.

HERRICK, C. J. "Mechanisms of Nervous Adjustment," in *L'Organisation des fonctions psychique*. Edited by Marcel Monnier. Neuchâtel: Editions du Griffon, 1951, pp. 79–83.

HICHAR, JOSEPH K. "Spontaneous Electrical Activity in the Crayfish Central Nervous System," *Journal of Cellular and Comparative Physiology*, LV (1960), 195–205.

HOFF, HANS. "Die zentrale Abstimmung der Sehsphäre," *Abhandlungen aus der Neurologie, Psychologie und ihren Grenzgebieten*, LIV (1930), 1–96.

HULL, CLARK. *Hypnosis and Suggestibility, an Experimental Approach*. New York: D. Appleton-Century Company, 1933.

ISAACS, N. "The Logic of Language," *Proceedings of the Aristotelian Society*, XXXIII (1932–33), 259–94.

JAMES, E. O. *Prehistoric Religion: A Study in Prehistoric Archeology*. New York: Frederick A. Praeger, 1957.

————. *Sacrifice and Sacrament*. London: Thames and Hudson, 1962.

JAMES, WILLIAM. *The Principles of Psychology*, Vol. II. New York: Henry Holt, 1899.

JEDREJ, M. C. "An Analytical Note on the Land and Spirits of the Sewa Mende," *Africa*, XLIV (1974), 38–45.

JENSEN, A. E. "Beziehungen zwischen dem alten Testament und der nilotischen Kultur in Africa," in *Culture in History*. Edited by S. Diamond. New York: Columbia University Press, 1960, p. 463.

JOHNSON, DAVID E., AND POSTAL, PAUL M. *Arc Pair Grammar*. Princeton: Princeton University Press, 1980.

JONES, FREDERICK WOOD. *The Principles of Anatomy, as Seen in the Hand*. Orig. pub., 1919. Baltimore: Williams and Wilkins, 1942.

JONES, GWYN. *A History of the Vikings*. New York: Oxford University Press, 1968.

JOURDAIN, PHILIP E. B. "The Nature of Mathematics," in *The World of Mathematics*, Vol. I. Edited by James R. Newman. New York: Simon and Schuster, 1956.

KANT, IMMANUEL. *Grundlegung zur Metaphysik der Sitten*. Edited by Wilhelm Ernst. Vol. V of *Sämtliche Werke*. Leipzig: Inselverlag, 1920.

KAPLAN, LAWRENCE, AND FRANK, PETER W. "Life-Span," in *New Encyclopaedia Britannica*, 1980 ed.

KARLGREN, BERNHARD. *Sound and Symbol in Chinese*. 2d ed.; 1st Eng. ed., 1923; orig. Swedish ed., 1918. London: Oxford University Press, 1946.

KELLOGG, W. N. *Porpoises and Sonar*. Chicago: University of Chicago Press, 1961.

KENYATTA, JOMO. *Facing Mount Kenya: The Tribal Life of the Gikuyu*. London: Seker and Warburg, 1956.

KHATAMI, DR. MANOOCHEHR. "Hypnosis as a Healing Art," in *The Human Influence in Medicine*. Philadelphia: Merck, Sharp and Dohme and the University of Pennsylvania Hospital, 1975.

KIDD, DUDLEY. *Savage Childhood*. London: Adam and Charles Black, 1906.

KLUCKHOHN, CLYDE. "Navaho Categories," in *Culture in History*. Edited by S. Diamond. New York: Columbia University Press, 1960, pp. 65–98.

KÖHLER, WOLFGANG. *The Mentality of Apes*. Orig. pub., 1917. Translated by Ella Winter from the 2d German ed. New York and London: Harcourt, Brace and Kegan Paul, Trench, Trubner, 1931.

KRIPKE, SAUL A. *Naming and Necessity*. Cambridge, Mass.: Harvard University Press, 1980.

KUBIE, LAWRENCE S., AND MARGOLIN, SYDNEY. "The Process of Hypnotism and the Nature of the Hypnotic State," *American Journal of Psychiatry*, C (1944), 611–22.

KÜHNE, WOLFDIETRICH. "Freilandstudien zur Soziologie des Hyänenhundes (*Lycaon pictus lupinus* Thomas 1902)," *Zeitschrift für Tierpsychologie*, XXII (1965), 495–541.

LAMPL, PAUL, ED. *Cities and Planning in the Ancient Near East*. New York: Braziller, 1968.

LANG, ANDREW. *Myth, Ritual and Religion*, Vol. I. 2 vols. London: Longmans, Green, 1887.

LANGER, SUSANNE K. *Feeling and Form*. New York: Charles Scribner's Sons, 1953.

_____. *Mind: An Essay on Human Feeling*, Vols. I–II. Baltimore: Johns Hopkins University Press, 1967, 1972.

_____. *Philosophy in a New Key: A Study in the Symbolism of Reason, Rite, and Art*. Cambridge, Mass.: Harvard University Press, 1942.

LEE, DOROTHEA DEMETRACOPOULOU. "Being and Value in a Primitive Culture," *Journal of Philosophy*, XLVI (1949), 501–15.

_____. "A Primitive System of Values," *Philosophy of Science*, VII (1940), 355–78.

LÉVI-STRAUSS, CLAUDE. "The Sorcerer and His Magic," in *Magic, Witchcraft and Curing*. Orig. pub., 1949. Edited by John Middleton. Garden City, N.Y.: Natural History Press, for American Museum of Natural History, 1967, pp. 23–41.

LIENHARDT, GODFREY. "The Western Dinka," in *Tribes without Rulers*. Edited by J. Middleton and D. Tait. London: Routledge and Kegan Paul, 1958, pp. 97–135.

LINDSLEY, D. B. "Psychophysiology and Motivation," in *Nebraska Symposium on Motivation*. Edited by Marshall R. Jones. Current Theory and Research in Motivation, V. Lincoln: University of Nebraska Press, 1957.

LOEB, EDWIN MEYER. "The Blood Sacrifice Complex," New York: Kraus Reprint Corporation, 1964. Orig. pub. in *Memoirs of the American Anthropological Association*, XXX (1923).

LOISY, ALFRED F. *Essai historique sur le sacrifice*. Paris: Emile Nourry, 1920.

LUCKENBILL, D. D. "Ancient Records II, 6," in *Cities and Planning in the Ancient Near East*. Edited by Paul Lampl. New York: Braziller, 1968.

MALCOLM, NORMAN. *Thought and Knowledge*. Ithaca, N.Y.: Cornell University Press, 1977.

MALGAUD, W. *De l'action à la pensée*. Paris: Alcan, 1935.

MALINOWSKI, BRONISLAW. "Baloma: The Spirits of the Dead in the Trobriand

Bibliography

Islands," in *Magic, Science and Religion and Other Essays*. Orig. pub., 1926. Garden City, N.Y.: Doubleday Anchor Books, 1948, p. 150.

_____. "Magic, Science and Religion," in *Magic, Science and Religion and Other Essays*. Orig. pub., 1926. Garden City, N.Y.: Doubleday Anchor Books, 1948, p. 17.

_____. *Sex and Repression in Savage Society*. New York: Harcourt Brace and Company, 1927.

MARSHALL, W. H., AND TALBOT, S. A. "Recent Evidence for Neural Mechanisms in Vision Leading to a General Theory of Sensory Acuity," in *Visual Mechanisms*. Edited by Heinrich Klüver. Lancaster, Pa.: J. Cattell, 1942, pp. 117–64.

MARTIN, M. K. "South American Foragers: A Case Study in Social Devolution," *American Anthropologist*, LXXI (1969), 243–60.

McWHIRTER, NORRIS. "Longevity," in *Guinness Book of World Records*. New York: Sterling Publishing Co., 1981, pp. 24–28.

MEDAWAR, PETER B. *The Uniqueness of the Individual*. New York: Basic Books, 1961.

MEGGITT, M. J. *Desert People: A Study of the Walbiri Aborigines of Central .Australia*. Sydney: Angus and Robertson, 1962.

MEYERSON, IGNACE. "Discontinuités et cheminements autonomes dans l'histoire de l'esprit," *Journal de psychologie normale et pathologique*, XLI (1948), 273–89.

MIDDLETON, JOHN. "The Concept of 'Bewitching' in Lugbara," *Magic, Witchcraft and Curing*. Garden City, N.Y.: Natural History Press, 1967, pp. 55–67. Originally published in *Africa*, XXV (1955), 252–60.

_____. *Lugbara Religion*. London: Oxford University Press and International African Institute, 1960.

MILLER, WALTER B. "Two Concepts of Authority," *American Anthropologist*, n.s., LVII (1955), 271–89.

MONOD-BRUHL, ODETTE, AND LÉVI, SYLVAIN. *Indian Temples*. 2d ed.; orig. English ed., 1937. Translated by Roy Hawkins. London: Oxford University Press, 1952.

MOOREHEAD, ALAN. *The Fatal Impact: An Account of the Invasion of the South Pacific 1767–1849*. London: Hamish Hamilton, 1966.

MUMFORD, LEWIS. *The City in History: Its Origins, Its Transformations, and Its Prospects*. New York: Harcourt, Brace, and World, 1961.

MURPHY, JOHN. *Lamps of Anthropology*. Manchester: Manchester University Press, 1943.

OHNUKI-TIERNEY, EMIKO. *Sakhalin Ainu Folklore*. Anthropological Studies, II. Washington, D.C.: American Anthropological Association, 1969.

OPLER, M. E. "The Concept of Supernatural Power among the Chiricahua and Mescalero Apaches," *American Anthropologist*, XXXVII (1935), 65–70.

OSWALD, IAN. *Sleeping and Waking. Physiology and Psychology*. New York: Elsevier, 1962.

PARKER, SEYMOUR. "Ethnic Identity and Acculturation in Two Eskimo Villages," *American Anthropologist*, n.s., LXVI (1964), 329–43.

PENFIELD, WILDER. "Mechanisms of Voluntary Movement," *Brain*, LXXVII (1954), 1–17.

PENTIKAINEN, JUHA. *The Nordic Dead-Child Tradition.* Translated by Anthony
Landon. Helsinki: Helsingin Liikekirjapaino Oy, 1968.
PETERSON, FREDERICK. *Ancient Mexico: An Introduction to the Pre-Hispanic
Cultures.* New York: Capricorn Books, 1962.
PHILLPOTTS, BERTHA. *Kindred and Clan in the Middle Ages and After: A Study
of the Teutonic Races.* Cambridge, Mass.: Harvard University Press, 1913.
PIRENNE, HENRI. *Mediaeval Cities: Their Origins and the Revival of Trade.*
Princeton: Princeton University Press, 1925.
PRECHTL, H. F. R. "Problems of Behavioral Studies in the Newborn Infant," in
Advances in the Study of Behavior. Edited by D. S. Lehrman, R. A. Hinde,
and E. S. Shaw. New York: Academic Press, 1965, pp. 75–98.
PREUSS, K. T. "Die religiöse Bedeutung der Paradiesmythen," in *Custom Is
King.* Edited by L. H. D. Buxton. London: Hutchinson's Scientific and
Technical Publications, 1936, pp. 119–39.
RACHEWILTZ, BORIS DE. *An Introduction to Egyptian Art.* Orig. pub., 1960.
London: Spring Books, 1966.
RADCLIFFE-BROWN, A. R. *The Andaman Islanders.* Glencoe, Ill.: The Free
Press, 1948.
RASMUSSEN, KNUT. *The Netsilik Eskimos, Social Life and Spiritual Culture.*
Copenhagen: Gyldendal, 1931.
RATLIFF, FLOYD. "Inhibitory Interaction and the Detection and Enhancement
of Contours," in *Sensory Communication.* Edited by W. A. Rosenblith.
Cambridge, Mass., and New York: M.I.T. Press and John Wiley & Sons,
1961.
RE, ARUNDELL DEL. *Creation Myths of the Formosan Natives.* 2 vols. Tokyo:
Hokusseido Press, 1951.
REICHARD, GLADYS A. *Navaho Religion: A Study in Symbolism.* Bollingen
Series, XVIII. Princeton: Princeton University Press, 1950.
RENFREW, COLIN, ED. *The Emergence of Civilization: The Cyclades and the
Aegean in the Third Millennium B.C.* London: Methuen, 1972.
REYNOLDS, BARRIE. *Magic, Divination and Witchcraft among the Barotse of
Northern Rhodesia.* Berkeley and Los Angeles: University of California
Press, 1963.
ROHDEN, PETER RICHARD. "Das schauspielerische Erlebnis," in *Der
Schauspieler.* Edited by E. Geissler. Berlin: Bühnenvolksbundverlag, 1926,
pp. 36–40.
ROSE, H. J. "Fate," in *Encyclopaedia Britannica,* 14th ed.
––––––. "Greek Religion," in *Encyclopaedia Britannica,* 14th ed.
––––––. *A Handbook of Greek Mythology.* Orig. pub., 1928. New York: Dutton,
1959.
––––––. "The Wiro Sky-God," in *Custom Is King.* Edited by L. H. D. Buxton.
London: Hutchinson's Scientific and Technical Publications, 1936, pp.
51–60.
ROSE, RONALD. *Living Magic.* London: Chatto and Windus, 1957.
ROSTOVTZEFF, M. I. *Caravan Cities.* Translated by David and Tamara Talbot
Rice. Oxford: Clarendon Press, 1932.
––––––. "Social and Economic Development of the Empire in the First Two

Bibliography

Centuries," in *The Urbanization of Man: A Social Science Perspective.* Edited by T. S. Baker. Berkeley, Calif.: McCutchan Publishing Corporation, 1972, pp. 187–97.

RUSSELL, BERTRAND. "Le principe d'individuation," *Revue de métaphysique et de morale,* LV (1950), 1–15.

_____. "The Study of Mathematics," *Philosophical Essays.* London: Longmans, Green, 1910, pp. 71–86.

SALE, GEORGE, TRANS. *The Koran.* London: Frederick Warne, n.d.

SANTAYANA, GEORGE. *Skepticism and Animal Faith.* New York: Scribner, 1923.

SARGANT, WILLIAM, AND FRASER, RUSSELL. "Inducing Light Hypnosis by Hyperventilation," *Lancet,* 1938, p. 778.

SCHALLER, GEORGE B. *The Year of the Gorilla.* Chicago: University of Chicago Press, 1964.

SCHARER, HANS. *Ngaju Religion: The Conception of God among a South Borneo People.* The Hague: Martinus Nijhoff, 1963.

SCHELER, MAX. *Der Formalismus in der Ethik und die materiale Wertethik.* Halle: M. Niemeyer, 1921.

SCHMIDT, P. WILHELM. "Numeral Systems," in *Encyclopaedia Britannica,* 14th ed.

SCHNEIDER, D. M., AND SHARP, LAURISTON. *The Dream Life of a Primitive People.* Anthropological Studies, I. Washington, D.C.: American Anthropological Association, 1969.

SCHNEIDER, KURT. "Die Schichtung des emotionalen Lebens und der Aufbau der Depressionszustände," *Zeitschrift für die gesamte Neurologie und Psychiatrie,* LIX (1920), 281–86.

SELIGMAN, C. G. "Anthropological Perspective and Psychological Theory," *Journal of the Royal Anthropological Institute,* LXII (1932), 193–228.

SHARMA, I. C. *Ethical Philosophies of India.* Edited by Stanley M. Daugert. Lincoln, Nebraska: Johnson Publishing Company, 1965.

SHORTLAND, E. *Maori Religion and Mythology.* London: Longmans, Green, 1882.

SIMMONS, LEO. *The Role of the Aged in Primitive Society.* New Haven, Conn.: Yale University Press, 1945.

SINGH, S. PIARA. "Shri Guru Nanak and Shaik Farad Shagar Ganj," *The Sikh Review,* XIX, no. 215 (1971), 4–9.

SKEAT, W. W. *Malay Magic.* 1st ed., 1900. New York: Barnes and Noble, 1966.

SMITH, D. E., AND GINSBURG, J. "From Numbers to Numerals and from Numerals to Computation," in *The World of Mathematics,* Vol. I. Edited by James R. Newman.

SOMMERFELT, ALF. *La langue et la société; caractères sociaux d'une langue de type archaïque.* Oslo: Aschenhoug (W. Nygaard), 1938.

SOUSTELLE, JACQUES. *Daily Life of the Aztecs.* London: Weidenfeld and Nicolson, 1961.

SPINOZA, BENEDICTUS DE. *Ethics.* Translated by A. Boyle. New York and London: E. P. Dutton and J. M. Dent and Sons, 1934, pt. iv, prop. 54, p. 17a.

STRASSER, STEPHAN. "Zur Gefühlssteuerung des menschlichen Aktes," *Zeitschrift für philosophische Forschung*, VII (1953), 171–90.

STRAUSS, HERMANN. *Die Mi-Kultur der Hagenberg-Stämme in Östlichen Zentral-Neuguinea.* Hamburg: Kommisionsverlag Cram, De Gruyter, 1962.

STRUNTZ, KURT. "Zur Grundlegung der Psychologie des mathematischen Sinnverständnisses," *Archiv für die gesamte Psychologie*, CVI (1940), 261–374.

TARSKI, ALFRED. "The Concept of Truth in Formalized Languages," *Logic, Semantics, Metamathematics.* Oxford: Clarendon Press, 1956.

TAYLOR, HENRY OSBORN. *Fact: The Romance of Mind.* New York: Macmillan, 1932.

THOMAS, NORTHCOTE W. "Sacrifice," in *Encyclopaedia Britannica*, 11th ed.

THOMPSON, D'ARCY. *On Growth and Form*, Vol. I. Orig. pub., 1917. Cambridge: The University Press, 1951.

TITCHENER, EDWARD BRADFORD. *A Textbook of Psychology.* New York: Macmillan, 1911.

TURNBULL, HERBERT WESTREN. "The Great Mathematicians," in *The World of Mathematics*, Vol. I. Edited by James R. Newman. New York: Simon and Schuster, 1956, p. 78.

TURNER, VICTOR W. *The Drums of Affliction: A Study of Religious Processes among the Ndembu of Zambia.* Oxford and London: Clarendon Press and International African Institute, 1968.

UCHENDU, V. C. *The Igbo of Southeast Nigeria.* New York: Holt, Rinehart and Winston, 1965.

VON HAGEN, VICTOR W. *The Ancient Sun Kingdoms of the Americas: Aztec, Maya, Inca.* Cleveland: World Publishing Company, 1961.

_____. *The Desert Kingdoms of Peru.* Greenwich, Conn.: New York Graphic Society, 1964.

VON HOLST, ERICH. "Relations between the Central Nervous System and the Peripheral Organs," *British Journal of Animal Behavior*, II (1954), 89–94.

VON NEUMANN, JOHN. "The Mathematician," in *The World of Mathematics*, Vol. IV. Edited by James R. Newman. New York: Simon and Schuster, 1956, pp. 2053–63.

WAITE, ARTHUR E. *The Book of Ceremonial Magic: The Secret Tradition in Goetia.* New Hyde Park, N.Y.: University Books, 1961.

WALD, GEORGE. "Origin of Death." Lecture, April 9, 1963, Connecticut College, New London.

WALTER, W. GREY. "The Functions of Electrical Rhythms in the Brain," *Journal of Mental Science*, XCVI (1950), 1–31.

WEISS, PAUL A. "The Compounding of Complex Macromolecular and Cellular Units into Tissue Fabrics," *Proceedings of the National Academy of Sciences*, XLII (1956), 789–830.

WERNER, HEINZ. "Motion and Motion Perception: A Study in Vicarious Functioning," *Journal of Psychology*, XIX (1945), 317–27.

WHITE, C. M. N. "The Supreme Being in the Beliefs of the Balovale Tribes," *African Studies*, VII (1948), 29–35.

Bibliography

WHITEHEAD, ALFRED NORTH. *Symbolism, Its Meaning and Effect.* New York: Macmillan, 1927.

WIENER, NORBERT. *Cybernetics: Control and Communication in the Animal and the Machine.* New York: John Wiley & Sons, 1948.

WILLIAMS, G. C. "Pleiotropy, Natural Selection, and the Evolution of Senescence," *Evolution*, XL (1957), 398–411.

WITTGENSTEIN, LUDWIG. *Tractatus Logico-philosophicus.* London and New York: Kegan Paul, Trench, Trubner and Harcourt, Brace and Company, 1922.

Indexes

Index of Names

Index of Subjects

Index of Subjects

Seasonal impulses, 139
Self-affirmation, and assertion as primary act of mind, 21, 24–25
Self-assertion, and punishment, 122–23
Selfhood concept: and death, 107–8; development of 101–3
Self-torture, 70n. *See also* Torture
"Sense of life." See *Lebensgefühl*
Sensory organs, 49; intellectuality of, 49–50; and perceptual interpretation of visual experience, 52–56; and species-specific features, 93
Sexual aberrations of the Inca, 191
Sexual intercourse: abstinence from, 127n; evolution of man and instinct concerning, 139–40; ritual ignorance of, 58–59
Shaman, 34; as actor in sacred drama, 69–70; claims of, 40n; and healing as drama, 65–69; "helpers" of Eskimo, 83; and illusory performances, 72–76; magical powers of, 78–79; power of Australian, 44n; spirits of a Netsilik Eskimo, 16; training of, 65n, 85; Eskimo transfer of power to inanimate objects, 83, 84
Ships, 159, 177
Sierra Leone, and Sewa Mande village ancestors, 114n
Sin, 146; atoned for by sacrifice in Yahweh worship, 134–35; living as, 133n
Skin, 49n
Social organization: of Chinese cities, 172–73; and group action, 120; and punishment, 125; and seafaring, 160; and tribal "we" and individual "I," 99–103; and verbal abstractions, 130; and warfare, 174–75
Soldiers, 174
Sorcery, 77–78
Soul: and the Inca, 187; in Manus religion, 57n; purification of, 147–48
Species-specific features, 93
Speech: development and importance of, 3–4; and early human mental evolution, 21; and imagination, 137; and intellectual advance, 204; and symbolism, 30, 82
Spells, 78; verbal (as prized possessions), 82
Spirit world: and ancestor worship, 35–37; and assertion as affirmation of mind, 20–25; beings in, 45; and colonial Europeans, 18–19; and death, 103–4; and ghosts, 12–16; and magic power, 83; and myth of human origin, 16–18; and origin of myth, 25–26, 29; and primitive imagination, 10–11; and primitive man's attitude, 5–10; and primitive man's nature, 3–4; and ritu-

al, 5, 8–9, 32–35, 38–39; and stories as real to primitive mind, 30–32; and structure of past and future, 26–29; worlds in, 11–12
Standards, 196
"Standing alive" (resurrection), 106
Story-telling: as real reports to primitive people, 30–32; and the Yanomamö tribe, 23
Stupa, 151–53
Submission: to Allah, 145; and sacrifice, 133
Suffering, 133n
Suggestion, 21, 33; and magic, 70–71, 72–76
"Sung into": objects into people, 68, 73n, 78; power into inanimate objects, 83
Supernatural beliefs, 10, 11
Supernatural helpers, 16–17
Supernaturals: and delegation of power, 110–14; nonbiologic events as acts of, 124; power of, 84
Symbolism, 204n; and conceptual talents, 124; and fetishism, 131–32, 133n; and life-supporting function saved by symbolic activity, 124–25; magic and theory of, 43–44; and origin of myth, 25; and ritual, 32–33, 38; speech as essence of, 82
Symbols: food as, 149; and intuition, 49–50; and magical thinking, 51; and magic power, 83; natural, 29–30, 32; presentational, 66; and primitive imagination, 10; and primitive man, 4
Sympathy, 180, 183; and cannibalism, 141–42; loss of empathy with development of, 140–41; and magic, 60–63, 64

T

Taboos, 78, 84; and names, 80n; punishment and breaking of, 122n, 123
Tadmor. See Palmyra
Technology, 51n
Tension, and different rates of mental development, 182
Thought: Adam's on savage, 18n; contemplative (in the West), 39; and early human mental evolution, 21; ethical (in Asia), 38–39; primitive modes of, 5; symbolic, 49; and thinking process, 9; of Trobrianders, 6
Tibet: and abstinence from sexual indulgence, 127n; Dalai Lama's analysis of white race visiting, 18n; trance of *nal-jorpas* in, 71n
Time, as known to man, 27n
Tiv concept of *Akombo*, 133n, 136